Reel Power

REEL POWER

Hollywood Cinema and American Supremacy

Matthew Alford

Foreword by Michael Parenti

First published 2010 by Pluto Press
345 Archway Road, London N6 5AA and
175 Fifth Avenue, New York, NY 10010

www.plutobooks.com

Distributed in the United States of America exclusively by
Palgrave Macmillan, a division of St. Martin's Press LLC,
175 Fifth Avenue, New York, NY 10010

British Library Cataloguing in Publication Data
A catalogue record for this book is available from the British Library

ISBN 978 0 7453 2983 3 Hardback
ISBN 978 0 7453 2982 6 Paperback

Library of Congress Cataloging in Publication Data applied for

This book is printed on paper suitable for recycling and made from fully managed and sustained forest sources. Logging, pulping and manufacturing processes are expected to conform to the environmental standards of the country of origin.

10 9 8 7 6 5 4 3 2 1

Designed and produced for Pluto Press by
Chase Publishing Services Ltd, 33 Livonia Road, Sidmouth, EX10 9JB, England
Typeset from disk by Stanford DTP Services, Northampton, England
Printed and bound in the European Union by
CPI Antony Rowe, Chippenham and Eastbourne

Contents

Acknowledgements

Thank you to the friends and colleagues who took the time to offer me help and advice at various key stages, specifically Eric Bienefeld, David Castle, David Clarke, Nathan Blunt, Alison Edgley, Matthew Edwards, Tiago Faia, David Gillespie, Robbie Graham, Brett Morton, Brian Neve, Mark Rodgers, Carole Saunders and Ian Scott.

Special thanks, as ever, to all my family.

The author can be contacted through the publisher or on reelpoweralford@gmail.com

Foreword

Michael Parenti

Every year on Oscar night, Hollywood invites the world to join in the illusion that a great industry is serving humankind by creating superb entertainment, bringing us joy and emotional enrichment, romance, sorrow, dazzling action and hopeful yearnings. Lost in this self-adulatory celebration is the fact that 'the world of cinema' is a rather tightly centralised, profit-driven industry – like all big corporate industries – less interested in creating an art that nurtures our dreams and more interested in dipping into our pockets.

Also easily overlooked is the fact that Hollywood operates within fixed ideological parameters. Along with its endless pursuit of money and fame, the film industry is also a culture industry. The commodities it markets consist of personalities, images, narratives, experiences and ideas (of sorts), things that impact directly on public consciousness. So while the prime goal is big profits for the major studios, another goal, whether explicitly acknowledged or not, is ideological control. This latter function is exercised by staying within the boundaries of the dominant belief system while presenting that belief system as a truthful and natural representation of life. Perhaps then it is more accurate to describe the movie industry as engaged not only in ideological control but in ideological *self*-control.

Film industry leaders would deny such assertions. They would argue that our society is a cultural democracy whose end product is not ideologically determined but birthed by the many free choices of a free market. For them, it's Adam Smith's invisible hand reaching from Hollywood and Vine down to Main Street. To make money for its owners, the industry must reach the largest possible markets; that is, it must give the people what they want.

Popular culture therefore is a product of popular demand, the movie moguls insist. If the cinematic world offers up trashy films, they say, it does so because that is what the public likes; that's what sells. People prefer to be entertained and distracted rather than informed and uplifted. So it is argued, and certainly so it is often true.

But is it just a matter of public taste, or is it the power of marketing and distribution that determines the respective audience sizes of various films? Millions of people saw the *Rambo* sequels, extravagant productions glorifying murderous militaristic heroics. Each of the *Rambo* films upon release opened in over two thousand theatres in the United States in the wake of multi-million dollar publicity campaigns. To give another example: in August 2001, despite appropriately lamentable reviews, Disney unexpectedly decided to extend *Pearl Harbor*'s nationwide release window from the standard two to four months to a staggering seven months, meaning that this 'summer' blockbuster would now be screening until December. Enjoying such a massive and saturating distribution, *Pearl Harbor* could not help but reach large numbers of people. In contrast, only a few thousand people ever saw *Salt of the Earth* (1954), a low-budget dramatisation of the struggles faced by Mexican-American union workers. This gripping and stirring film, preserved decades later by the Library of Congress and New York's Museum of Modern Art, was subjected to all sorts of coercion in its production and distribution, and managed but a brief run with only eleven small exhibitors.

If dissident films like *Salt of the Earth* fail to reach a mass audience, could it not be because they are kept from mass audiences by the minimal distribution and limited publicity they receive? Lacking huge sums, they must rely on word of mouth and on reviews that are often politically hostile. This is in sharp contrast to the multimillion-dollar publicity campaigns that help *create* the mass markets for the supposedly more popular movies. If a *Rambo* film or a film like *Pearl Harbor* has a 'natural' mass-market and is craved by millions of viewers, why is it necessary to spend scores of millions of dollars on publicity hype whose sole purpose is to muster a mass audience?

In short, it is not simply a matter of demand creating supply. Often it is the other way around: supply creates demand. A first and necessary condition for all consumption is availability of the product. Be it movies, television shows, or soft drinks, consumption will depend in large part on distribution and product visibility. A movie that opens in every shopping mall in America wins large audiences not because there is a spontaneous wave of popular demand surging from the base of the social order, but because it is being heavily marketed from the apex.

In time, people become conditioned to accepting slick, shallow, mediocre and politically truncated cinematic presentations. The standardised images and formulaic scenarios become the readily digestible ones. With enough conditioning, consumers will consume even that which does not evoke their great enthusiasm. Hardly ever exposed to anything else, they are all the more inclined to seek diversion in whatever is offered.

This argument should not be overstated. The public is not infinitely malleable. Supply does not always create demand. Some Hollywood offerings are dismal flops, despite lavish publicity and energetic distribution. Irrespective of all the talk about giving the public what it wants, industry heads often get it wrong. Audience preferences can be difficult to divine, especially if one's perception of public preferences is itself shaded by one's own socio-political proclivities.

Thus for a period of over two decades, spanning the entire 1970s and 1980s, mainstream media pundits and news commentators repeatedly and tirelessly announced that the US public was moving into a 'conservative mood', the very direction they hoped the public was headed. Network television bosses and the heads of major studios readily took up the cry in what became one of the longest standing attempts at a self-fulfilling prophecy. Having so decided that the nation was drifting into a conservative mood, they set to work helping to create that drift and that mood. Network brass produced a number of law-and-order television series like *Walking Tall*, *Strike Force*, and *Today's FBI* (1981–82). All such offerings were laced with conservative subtexts, and all suffered dismal ratings and died early deaths. Something similar happened in the 2000s with series like *Threat Matrix* (2003–04), *She Spies* (2002) and the CIA-sponsored *The Agency* (2001).

Likewise with the film industry. *The Right Stuff* (1983), a film that glorified America's space ventures, was a box-office flop. Action films like *Cobra* (1986), *Rambo III* (1988), and *The Dead Pool* (1988) did poorly. Given their multimillion-dollar publicity campaigns, these motion pictures had fairly strong opening weekends but then swiftly flopped after that. Another right-wing war movie, *Inchon* (1982), costing $48 million plus another estimated $10–20 million for publicity, had everything the public supposedly craves: a star-studded cast, a spectacular production, a love angle, blood-filled battle scenes, super-patriotism, a simplistic rewrite of political history, and an empty-headed plot about murderous communist aggressors who are wiped out by a right-wing war hero. Yet *Inchon* was a box-office disaster. This suggests that even a viewing public conditioned to consuming junk sometimes gets tired of consuming the same old junk.

In sum, 'giving people what they want' is too simple an explanation of what the film industry does. The major studios foist upon us what *they* think we want, often promoting films that we never asked for and do not particularly enjoy. But with enough publicity and distribution, even these flops are destined to reach many more people than the financially starved dissident films that are accorded no distribution or mass-market publicity to speak of.

* * *

The image of Hollywood as a den of leftist shills is tirelessly propagated by conservative commentators and publicists. We are told by various right-wing propagandists that the 'cultural elites' of Hollywood (and other places like New York, San Francisco and Washington, DC) propagate values that are dedicated to undermining patriotism and other such 'American virtues'.

Such incantations about an elitist leftist agenda are put to rest by the commanding critique offered by author Matthew Alford in the pages ahead. Alford's dissection of Hollywood war films offers an implicit revelation of the misrepresentations of US imperial policy itself and the dominant political myths that sustain it.

This book shows in revealing detail how the agencies of the US empire play an active role in the very scripting and production of films about US politico-military ventures abroad. The muted debate about the hidden and not-so-hidden politics of empire are played out in movie productions themselves, in what gets downplayed, what gets celebrated, and what ends up on the cutting-room floor.

After an exploration of just about all the significant films of recent years, Alford concludes that while certainly 'there are prominent liberals in Hollywood', there is no 'left-wing establishment' pursuing an agenda. He also reminds us that there are 'numerous right-wing stars, censors and industry professionals' actively operating in the film industry. There are national security agencies and Pentagon representatives breathing down the necks of screenwriters, editors and producers. And most importantly, there are the industry's wealthy and conservative business leaders and bankers who operate 'within a rigid corporate system'.

Through an extensive examination of the actual plots, dialogues and characters of scores of mainstream films, Alford not only *tells* us but *shows* us that mainstream cinema offers no critique of 'the fundamental assumptions of US benevolence on the world stage'. To the extent that critical remarks are allowed in one film or another, they rest only upon very narrow grounds. Heroes confine themselves to rectifying operational blunders, unfortunate mishaps, and individual failings. Instances of excessive military power might be criticised but not US military power *per se*, it being assumed that US forces have every right to operate militarily in any chosen 'trouble spot' on the planet. Alford describes films that propagate the notion that war is a 'regrettable tragedy, which resulted from the US blundering idealistically into a situation it did not fully understand and was unable to control'.

In the world of cinema, US military engagements are always well-intentioned undertakings that sometimes go wrong. Nothing is said about the transnational global interests behind such ventures, about who pays and who benefits from what is transpiring. Such questions would bring us right to the heart of how politico-economic power is wielded in the United States and much of the world.

In short, film-makers (with some notable exceptions) go only so far in their criticisms, knowing in the back of their minds, if nowhere else, that they cannot make a truly radical film; they cannot get to the root, exposing the exploitative interests of global empire or the dangerous and undemocratic nature of the national security state. To attempt as much would invite trouble for the film one is trying to produce and distribute. There would come a loss of funding, a scarcity of viewing outlets, and an endless savaging by mainstream movie reviewers who know for whom they work. About this we have only to ask Oliver Stone, who endured a relentless pummelling for his attempt in *JFK* (1991) to venture into forbidden territory regarding the Kennedy assassination.

So it can be said that we are being more than entertained. Mainstream film-makers have a built-in capacity to handle burning issues in ways that mute their impact and reduce their meaning. Oppositional realities are incorporated into the script, but in a pre-digested form. Official injustice and corruption become the doings of a few bad apples or rogue elements. War becomes little more than a tough, bitter experience for the American soldiers involved. As Alford puts it: 'It is standard practice in Hollywood, as it is amongst US elites [in the real-life political realm], to assume that foreigners don't matter, US enemies are implacably villainous, and US power is by definition selfless and good.'

In the celluloid world, political leaders face hard choices about integrity and fair play, but rarely take a stand on real economic issues. Resistance to injustice is expressed through gutsy individual defiance ('One man and one man alone stood up to the threat of ... ').

Through its cinematic alchemy, Hollywood produces films that might appear topical and socially relevant, without having to deal with the actual dimensions of social conflict, 'fighting terrorism' without getting too close to reality.

* * *

If all this is true, if movies are implicitly conservative in their supportive representation of the US national security state and of America's imperial reach and presumed moral superiority, then why do conservatives complain about a 'leftist liberal bias' in Hollywood? It is the same complaint they make of the ever-compromising, ever-timid, right-leaning US news media, and for much the same reasons.

Movies repeatedly confine their critical attention to a narrow and superficial sphere and rarely proffer a truly radical critique. But even this limited application is seen as a liberal denigration of the US politico-economic system and its global imperium. Showing a US soldier ruthlessly killing one innocent civilian, in what is otherwise presented as a noble military venture against terrorism, is more than the right-wing ideologues can countenance. *Anything* critical – however diluted, incidental and innocuously decontextualised – will still be found offensive by the uncompromising reactionaries.

Furthermore, in certain cultural ways, Hollywood actually has been 'subversive', with its sexually explicit scenes, verbal profanity, tolerance of deviant lifestyles (including homosexuality), and its supposed disregard for family values. For reactionaries, such seemingly decadent proclivities are seized upon as proof that the film industry rests in the hands of America's enemies.

Depicting Hollywood as ridden with leftists also is a way of continually exerting the kind of pressure that helps shift the centre of political gravity rightward, keeping the industry off-balance, obliging it to demonstrate its patriotic bona fides. So the film industry constantly dresses up for the Right while never daring to move too decisively to the Left on any fundamental issue.

Much of the process of ideological control is carried out implicitly. Alford reminds us that people working within power systems are not always fully able 'to recognise the ideological boundaries set by state and corporate forces within which they work'. And if they did raise troublesome views about the dangers of undemocratic and plutocratic power, he adds, this would seriously jeopardise their careers.

We might remember that the most repressive forms of social control are not always those we consciously rail against, but those that so insinuate themselves into the fabric of our consciousness as to remain unchallenged, having been embraced as part of the nature of things. There no doubt are liberals and progressives in Hollywood who themselves remain unaware of how their efforts serve the powers that be.

Alford ends this book with a plea that we all should heed, a call for a freer, less concentrated, system of ownership and production in which film-makers would create imaginative and compelling narratives and 'be less afraid to interrogate the corporate roots of US power'. In short, to make better films and therefore Oscar nights that serve democracy, instead of plutocracy.

Part I

Controlling the Dream Factory

Reporter [to Emilio Estevez]: 'Emilio, how historically accurate … '

Orange representative: 'Hey, sister, the Discovery Channel is down the block. We just want to blow things up and sell some phones, don't we Emilio?'

Orange mobile phone advert, 2009

1
Hollywood Screened

Conventional wisdom holds that Hollywood has long opposed and undermined US power. From its inception in the early twentieth century, the LA-based movie industry was viewed with suspicion by European and American elites who saw it as a degraded, Jewish influence undermining traditional values with minority views. In the 1950s, conservative concerns about Communists in Hollywood became so severe that the US embarked on a purge, blacklisting film-makers who were considered 'un-American'. Setting the tone of public debate for the 1990s and beyond, Michael Medved's bestseller *Hollywood vs America* argued that since at least the 1960s Hollywood had presented America, including its military, as 'the enemy'.[1]

In fact, as *Reel Power* demonstrates by analysing scores of high-budget contemporary movies that depict the application of US power, such as *True Lies* (1994), *Independence Day* (1996) and *Iron Man* (2008), the film industry routinely promotes the dubious notion that the United States is a benevolent force in world affairs and that unleashing its military strength overseas has positive results for humanity. US intervention, furthermore, is rendered not pre-emptive but rather the only reasonable response to 'bad guys' and the best way in which the US can gain closure.

Absent from these films is much, if any, sense that US authorities serve private interests (although there may be 'bad apples' who are weeded out by the system itself), that US action is irrational or nationalistic, or that there might be more satisfying and effective peaceful solutions worth pursuing. The most critical position Hollywood adopts on screen is to say that well-meaning forays into other countries may backfire, with Americans – particularly those representatives of powerful institutions – being the significant victims of such innocent lapses, as in *Black Hawk Down* (2002), *Munich* (2005) and *The Siege* (1998).

These films are not usually made or rejected through 'conspiracies', censorship, or other heavy-handed government activity, but rather, as George Orwell put it in regard to literary censorship: 'Unpopular ideas can be silenced, and inconvenient facts kept dark, without the need for any official ban not because of direct government intervention but rather because of a general tacit agreement that "it wouldn't do" to mention that particular fact.'[2]

It is the case that there is some public demand for simplistic, unchallenging narratives and also that it is not always easy within traditional genre constraints to present more interrogative political perspectives. However, there are several less obvious but decisive industrial factors that ensure Hollywood generates considerable sympathy for the status quo and, indeed, frequently glorifies US institutions and their use of political violence. The cumulative effect of these factors, which are discussed below in detail, is that it is extremely difficult for a film to emerge through the Hollywood system that criticises US power at a systematic level, while it is relatively easy for an explicitly pro-establishment or status-quo film to be made, particularly one which is America-centric and at ease with the spectacle of US high-tech violence against villainous foreigners.

Of course, most of the time, any issues of US power politics are simply ignored altogether in favour of other narratives, with a particular emphasis on formulaic, commercially friendly films and franchises that dominate the highest box-office lists.

So what are these factors and how do they affect the content of Hollywood studio productions?

CONCENTRATED CORPORATE OWNERSHIP

Just six theatrical film studios, known collectively as 'the majors', control the vast majority of the world's movie business from production to distribution: Disney, Columbia/Sony Pictures Entertainment, Paramount Pictures, 20th Century Fox, Warner Brothers and Universal. The majors are owned by multinational 'parent' corporations, respectively the Walt Disney Company, Sony, Viacom Inc., News Corp, Time Warner Inc. and (until 2009) General Electric/Vivendi.[3] Smaller but still significant companies include MGM, United Artists, Lionsgate, as well as Dreamworks SKG, which is named after its billionaire founders Steven Spielberg, Jeff Katzenberg and David Geffen. 'The studios are basically distributors, banks, and owners of intellectual copyrights,' summarises Richard Fox, vice-president of Warner Brothers.[4]

Claiming that its cultural heritage must not be 'surrendered to another nation',[5] the US government has jealously protected the

US film market, as well as supporting the majors with numerous tax incentives,[6] representation at an international level and very relaxed media consolidation rules. Some of the majors have overseas owners – News Corp (Australian), Vivendi (French), Sony (Japanese) – but Washington limits foreign ownership to 25 per cent and control of studio output remains in California and New York.[7] The magazine *Canadian Business* even dubbed the studios 'Hollywood's welfare bums'.[8]

What impact does concentrated corporate ownership have on film content? First of all, it has squeezed out competition from foreign films, which accounted for nearly 10 per cent of the North American market in the 1960s, 7 per cent by the mid-1980s, but just 0.5 per cent by the late 1990s.[9] For the 2006 Oscars, a record 91 countries submitted entries to the foreign language category but only seven had American distributors.[10] *Variety* magazine had already summed up the situation with the pithy headline, 'Earth to Hollywood: You Win'.[11] Thus, while of course Hollywood is aware of its international markets, it is liable to make films about and for America and Americans, marginalising the importance of foreigners and foreign perspectives.

Secondly, the majors use their main tool – capital – to set the industry standards for bankable stars and high-tech special effects, thereby marginalising lower-budget productions. But with the average cost of producing and marketing a movie sky-rocketing to $106.6 million in 2007[12] – the last year for which data was released – studio executives are under pressure not to squander any opportunity to maximise profits. Films will consequently tend to avoid political narratives that are unfamiliar to American audiences. Producer Robert Evans explains that film-makers 'don't do the unexpected, they're too scared – the prices are too high'. Evans believes it would no longer be possible to make a movie like *The Godfather* (1972) – the biting metaphor for capitalism in America that he helped make in the 1970s – because studios would consider it too risky for the price tag.[13]

Former president of Paramount David Kirkpatrick agrees: the result is that 'You need a homogenized piece of entertainment ... something that is not particularly edgy, particularly sophisticated.'[14] That much is accurate, although Kirkpatrick's characterisation of the resultant output as 'fluffy' is not so appropriate for the scores of distinctly non-fluffy national security-themed films discussed in this book, such as *The Kingdom* (2007), *Body of Lies* (2008) and *Vantage Point* (2008).

COMMERCIALISATION

Product placement and merchandising deals for toys, clothing, novelisations and soundtracks are attractive to movie-makers because, even if the movie fails, the manufacturer incurs the loss. This is only fair, since the movie is the advertisement. Product placement in motion pictures is valued at $1.2 billion annually and, since the average movie costs $30 million just to market,[15] such deals can be very useful in adding millions to turnover.[16] Indeed, the James Bond movie *Die Another Day* (2002) made between $120 and $160 million from associated brands for the twenty or so product placements.[17]

Nowadays, and particularly since the 1990s, the majority of Fortune 500 companies are involved in product placement[18] and specialist companies exist to place products as efficiently and comprehensively as possible.[19] 'We choose projects where we have maximum control,' explained one plugster as early as 1990. 'We break a film down and tell the producers exactly where we want to see our clients' brands.'[20]

The most obvious impact on Hollywood productions is that the value placed on artistic quality is further diminished. 'Studios are run by MBAs whose entire training and experience is to avoid risk,' explained Mark Litwak in an article that pointed to the importance of networking, rather than creative talent, in Hollywood. 'Ironically it's movies that are most original that become blockbusters. People want variety even if the studios don't.'[21]

Peter Bart (2001), editor-in-chief of industry magazine *Variety*, recalls his experiences of making the decision to move a film project to the pre-production phase (known as 'green-lighting'):

> The green-light meeting, when I first started at Paramount, would consist of maybe three or four of us in a room. Perhaps two or three of us would have read the script under discussion. And people said stupid things like, 'I kind of like this movie.' Or, 'I look forward to seeing this movie.' Inane things like that. The green-light decision process today consists of maybe 30 or 40 people. There's one group there to discuss the marketing tie-ins. How much will McDonald's or Burger King put up? There's somebody else there to discuss merchandising toy companies and so forth. Someone else is there to discuss what the foreign co-financiers might be willing to put up. So everyone is discussing the business aspects of this film. And it's sometimes unusual for

> someone actually to circle back and talk about the script, the cast, the package – whether the whole damn thing makes any sense to begin with.[22]

Bart goes on to explains that the movies now being made are those which 'appeal to the marketing and distribution team most of all. [They] have the heavy votes.' In some cases, large chunks of script are generated with the primary aim of selling products, as with James Bond's BMW scene in *GoldenEye* (1995), the extensive Bugs Bunny/Michael Jordan brand associations in *Space Jam* (1998) and the alien in *Mac and Me* (1988), who lives on a diet of Coke and Skittles. Just as insidious though, explains David Lancaster, 'a fog of fudge and compromise hangs over almost everything';[23] the order of the day is happy endings, light entertainment and an absence of disturbing political narratives.

The economic penalties for not buying into this system can be serious. In 1997, Reebok sued Tristar Pictures, claiming it had reneged on its promise to feature its placement prominently in the 'happy ending' scene of *Jerry Maguire*.[24] The parties settled out of court, purportedly for millions, and the Reebok advert was reinstated for the DVD.[25] In a similar case in 1990, Black & Decker settled a $150,000 lawsuit out of court over a promotion it had developed for a drill that Bruce Willis ended up not using in *Die Hard 2*.[26]

There was also the case of the kids' cartoon movie *Iron Giant* (1999), an unusually sensitive Cold War allegory, which was a box-office flop despite receiving a spectacular 97 per cent rating on rottentomatoes.com (a website which processes all available movie reviews from established critics). A major reason was that the film had been poorly marketed by Warner Bros.[27] Writer Tim McCanlies explained:

> We had toy people and all of that kind of material ready to go, but all of that takes a year! Burger King and the like wanted to be involved. In April we showed them [Warner Bros] the movie, and we were on time. They said, 'You'll never be ready on time.' No, we were ready on time. We showed it to them in April and they said, 'We'll put it out in a couple of months.' That's a major studio, they have 30 movies a year, and they just throw them off the dock and see if they either sink or swim, because they've got the next one in right behind it. After they saw the reviews they [Warner Bros] were a little shamefaced.[28]

Others took away a more reductive lesson from *Iron Giant*. 'People always say to me, "why don't you make smarter movies?"', said Lorenzo di Bonaventura, Warner Bros' president of production at the time. 'The lesson is: every time you do, you get slaughtered.'[29]

Jay May, president of a Los Angeles-based product placement agency, sees the logical outcome of Hollywood's commercialisation emerging on DVDs, where 'All of a sudden, a bar code is going to pop up letting you know something in that scene is for sale, and you'll be able to buy it right off the screen.'[30] Perhaps such a sales device could include the cigarette brands smoked onscreen by the likes of Sylvester Stallone and Timothy '007' Dalton – for which they each pocketed hundreds of thousands of dollars.[31] Maybe Desert Eagle guns used extensively by Arnold Schwarzenegger in pictures like *Commando* (1985), *Last Action Hero* (1993) and *Eraser* (1996) will be available at the press of a button.[32] Or could it be that we will soon simply be able to touch our screens and buy a stake in the aerospace/arms giant Boeing that is credited in the *Iron Man* franchise? Hardly fertile ground for dissenting voices.

Hollywood also must sell the film itself, of course. To do so, instant brand recognition has become key. Hollywood output is now highly derivative, characterised by sequels, prequels, adaptations and remakes, especially amongst the highest grossing products.[33] 'It used to be sequels, on average, earned about 65% of the gross of the original,' explains Geoffrey Anwar, Columbia's president of marketing. 'Now, if you make a good one, you can earn more than the original, sometimes much more.'[34]

This contributes, again, to the frequently lamented result that studios are set on 'fiscally predictable fare' rather than on making Oscar-calibre material.[35] To illustrate, Jeremy Pikser, the screenwriter of Warren Beatty's satire on US domestic politics *Bulworth* (1998), said that Universal producer Tom Craig told him his pitch for *Bulworth* was 'a really good story and it could be really good movie' but that Craig's studio would never buy it. Craig explained that 'we don't want to buy things that have to be well made to be successful' and added 'but if you say "Tom Hanks and a bulldog are partners in a police thing" [in reference to Disney/Touchstone's *Turner and Hooch* (1989)] it could be the worst movie ever made and we won't lose a dime'.[36] *Turner and Hooch* certainly didn't lose a dime.

The significant overseas markets mean that film-makers are liable to internationalise their messages where possible, but this is not necessarily part of an opening for dissenting viewpoints. Indeed, Hollywood's attempts to appeal to foreigners (and children) can easily lead to ever more simplified stories and dialogue. For example, conservatives were horrified that the 2009 action film *GI Joe* changed the old 'GI' acronym to mean Global Integrated Joint Operating Entity, rather than 'Government Issued'.[37] This was indeed a sop to the international market but the *GI Joe* team was still largely comprised of Americans, fighting for the West and the film was labelled by the *Atlantic Monthly* as 'the Green Berets of the Iraq war', after the 1968 John Wayne Vietnam War propaganda film.[38] Foreign markets, though growing, are not necessarily going to reverse the trends I discuss here.

Modern film-makers also now routinely make use of test screenings, where sample audiences of 300–500 people provide feedback. While these can of course be useful in determining quality, their political impact is likely overall to encourage conformity. 'People fill in test cards according to social norms, so they don't necessarily reflect a true reaction to the film,' explains Australian director Bruce Berestew.[39] Psychology studies such as the Asch Conformity experiments, which showed the effects of peer pressure, support Berestew's observation;[40] this might explain why cinematic villains often score badly no matter how well they are depicted by the actor.[41] Mike Medavoy, chair of Phoenix Pictures, says that 'there is a kind of homogenization built into the film testing system' and that 'no one at the studios is willing to take chances anymore – anticipating how they will test'.[42]

Specifically in terms of foreign policy films, if it weren't for test audiences, who baulked at John Rambo's suicide depicted at the end of *First Blood* (1982), we might never have had one of cinema's most enduring symbols of interventionist foreign policy.[43] Similarly, test audiences' desires for happy endings to *Rules of Engagement* (2000) and *Basic* (2003) apparently led to studio decisions to heroise state-sanctioned murder by the main characters, despite the original intentions of the film-makers.

STATE SUPPORT AND INFILTRATION

Government and corporate bureaucracies such as the Pentagon (Department of Defense, or DOD) have public relations divisions, which ensures special access to the media. Film-makers have made use of military advice and material to save costs and create authentic-looking films since the early twentieth century – including the Ku Klux Klan-recruitment classic *Birth of a Nation* (1915) and the Oscar-winning *Wings* (1927) – typically in exchange for scripts that are highly favourable to recruitment and public relations drives.[44] This can involve extensive rewrites and screenings for the brass before public release.[45] Major David Georgi, one of the Army's on-set technical advisers says poetically 'If they don't do what I say, I take my toys and go away.'[46]

Some films, such as *Top Gun* (1986), *Pearl Harbor* (2001) and *Behind Enemy Lines* (2001) are so dependent on the Department of Defense that it seems unlikely they could have been made without DOD assistance. Ridley Scott said that he could have made *Black Hawk Down* (2002) without the Pentagon but 'I'd have had to call it "Huey Down"', in a reference to the much smaller brand of helicopter.[47] He was joking of course – the film was completely reliant on the Black Hawks because he was recreating the Battle of Mogadishu in Somalia where these helicopters were famously shot down.

The Pentagon's muscle was similarly demonstrated over the controversial 'big money' script, *Countermeasures*. In 1994, *Daily Variety* reported that Disney subsidiary Touchstone had 'revived its zeal' for the film, following Sigourney Weaver's decision to 'come aboard'. Although producer Gail Ann Hurd had not yet nailed down a director, Peter Osterlund and Amy Brooke Baker had written the script with rewrites by Darrell Ponicsan.[48] Weaver was to play a Navy psychiatrist who uncovers a murderous crime ring on board a nuclear aircraft carrier during the Persian Gulf War. She also finds out that her patient was part of a White House cover-up to ship jet parts to Iran, in a plot that echoes the real-world 1980s Iran-Contra scandal, whereby the Reagan administration secretly sold weapons to its ostensible enemy Iran in order to create a slush fund for the Contra army in Nicaragua. Investigative reporter David Robb found that when the Pentagon read the *Countermeasures* script it refused to cooperate, commenting 'There's no reason for us to denigrate the White House or remind the public of the Iran-Contra affair.' On hearing that the Department of Defense had turned it down, the Spanish Navy followed suit. The film-makers needed an aircraft carrier, so the Department of Defense's decision effectively terminated the production.[49]

The majors were so keen on Pentagon support that when the DOD Hollywood liaison Phil Strub found his job under threat as part of an 'overall downsizing' of Department of Defense spending, production executives were up in arms and Jack Valenti wrote to Defense Secretary William Cohen to campaign, successfully, for Strub to remain in post.[50] Similarly, the Writers Guild of America, which claims to fight for the creative rights of its members, has never complained about Pentagon interference and David Robb found that one of its presidents, Charles Holland, was a former Army officer and writer for *JAG* who wholeheartedly endorsed Pentagon involvement.[51]

Other government agencies such as NASA, Homeland Security and the Secret Service have also been able to exert some influence over scripts by offering assistance on products, though none of them have the Pentagon's leverage. Historically, the FBI wielded influence, working on projects like *G-Men* (1935), *The Untouchables* (1959–63), *The FBI Story* (1959) and the highly deferential ABC TV series *The FBI* (1965–74), which thanked J. Edgar Hoover for his cooperation on the credits of every episode.[52] Not anymore, though efforts have been made between Fox and the FBI to develop a series centring on an Iraq war veteran who is appointed as the Fed's new anti-terrorism head.[53]

The CIA's role in Hollywood, though, remains relatively significant, judging by what little information is made public. The historical context is instructive. Letters discovered in the Eisenhower Presidential Library from the secret agent Luigi G. Luraschi, the Paramount executive who worked for the CIA's Psychological Strategy Board (PSB), reveal just how far the CIA was able to reach into the film industry in the early days of the Cold War. For instance, Luraschi reported that he had secured the agreement of several casting directors to subtly plant 'well dressed negroes' into films, including 'a dignified negro butler' who has lines 'indicating he is a free man' in *Sangaree* (1953) and another in a fancy golf-club scene for the Dean Martin/Jerry Lewis vehicle *The Caddy* (1953). Elsewhere, the CIA arranged the removal of key scenes from the film *Arrowhead* (1953), which questioned the US's treatment of Apache Indians, including a sequence where a tribe is forcibly shipped and tagged by the US Army. Such changes were specifically enacted to hamper the USSR's ability to exploit its enemy's poor record in race relations.[54]

The CIA made other efforts specifically on foreign policy issues. The PSB tried – unsuccessfully – to commission Frank Capra to direct *Why We Fight the Cold War* and to provide details to film-makers about conditions in the USSR in the hope that they would use them in their movies. More successfully, in 1950, the CIA, the Office of Policy Coordination (OPC) and the PSB cooperated to buy the rights and invest in the cartoon of George Orwell's *Animal Farm* (1954), which was given an anti-Soviet spin to satisfy its covert investors. The Michael Redgrave feature *Nineteen-Eighty Four* (1956), overseen by the CIA-supervised American Committee for Cultural Freedom, was altered to associate Big Brother more with Communism.[55]

Graham Greene's novel *The Quiet American* (1955) depicted the killing of a CIA protagonist because he is discovered manufacturing plastic explosives for an anti-Communist terror campaign in Indochina. For the 1958 film version, the plastic explosives became plastic toys – meant to be doled out to Vietnamese children – but the agent is brutally murdered by Communists anyway. The change was suggested by CIA operative Edward Lansdale – the man behind the sabotage and assassination operations in Cuba and the inspiration for Marlon Brando's *Ugly American* (1963) – when he met producer/director Joseph L. Mankiewicz scouting for locations in Vietnam. Executive vice-president of Figaro Productions Robert Lantz met with CIA director Alan Dulles, who liked the direction the film was taking and offered government assistance.[56] After watching the movie, Greene remarked, 'One could almost believe that the film was made deliberately to attack the book and the author.'[57] It was.

Trying to get information from the CIA about their involvement in the entertainment industry is not easy. Daniel Leab, author of *Orwell Subverted* (2007), commented 'The information I requested ... [about *Animal Farm*] might just as well have gone down Orwell's "memory hole"';[58] my own Freedom of Information Act request prompted no new material.[59] It seems likely that the CIA's influence occurs less formally than that of the Department of Defense. If there is a paper trail, they're not willing to show it, which is hardly surprising since they still haven't even volunteered more than the most scant information about their media subversion activities from generations past.

In 1995, the CIA began pursuing an ostensibly more open policy, setting up its own Hollywood liaison office and 'advising' on several movies (either as a formal organisation or by individual case officers), such as *Enemy of the State* (1998), *Bad Company* (2002), *The Rogue* (forthcoming), *Fard Ayn* (forthcoming) and – most significantly for this book's focus on US foreign policy – *Charlie Wilson's War* (2007) and *The Good Shepherd* (2006). The CIA advised on the television series *24*, *Alias* and *JAG*, and was even more intimately involved in *The Agency* and the 1997 TV movie *In the Company of Spies*, starring Tom Berenger (both were filmed at the CIA's Langley headquarters with technical advice teams).[60]

In 2007, former associate general counsel to the CIA Paul Kelbaugh delivered a lecture on the CIA's relationship with Hollywood, at which a local journalist was present. The journalist (who wishes to remain anonymous) wrote a review of the lecture which related Kelbaugh's discussion of the 2003 thriller *The Recruit* (2003), starring Al Pacino. The review noted that, according to Kelbaugh, a CIA agent was on set for the duration of the shoot under the guise of a consultant, but that his real job was to misdirect the film-makers: 'We didn't want Hollywood getting too close to the truth,' the journalist quoted Kelbaugh as saying. Peculiarly, in a strongly worded email to me, Kelbaugh emphatically denied having made the public statement and claimed that he remembered 'very specific discussions with senior [CIA] management that no one was ever to misrepresent to affect [film] content – EVER'.[61] The journalist considers Kelbaugh's denial 'weird', and told my colleague Robbie Graham that 'after the story came out, he [Kelbaugh] emailed me and loved it ... I think maybe it's just that because [the lecture] was "just in Lynchburg" he was okay with it – you know, like, no one in Lynchburg is really going to pay much attention to it.'[62]

In 1997, the CIA's first entertainment liaison officer, Charles 'Chase' Brandon was advising on Gary Devore's 'The Big Steal',[63] an unusually critical feature-film script set during the 1989 US invasion of Panama. A draft contains lines like 'Shit, we're really kicking the crap outta this itty bitty country to get one man [General Noriega]. It's embarrassing,' with the reply 'Starting a war you can't lose is good for morale.' The story presents a country ravaged by the US military, in which the Pentagon takes advantage of the chaos to steal Noriega's laundered drug money.[64] However, just as the script was completed and the production deal finalised,[65] Gary Devore disappeared while driving home through California's 'Aerospace Valley'. A year later, his car was found in a shallow aqueduct, with a decomposed corpse dressed in Devore's clothing sitting in the front seat; three things were strangely absent: Devore's gun, his script and both his hands.[66] The LA County Sheriff's Department decided not to mount a criminal investigation and the Devore case was laboriously described as a bizarre accident,[67] although at least one law-enforcement professional held private doubts,[68] and some friends and family have raised muted cries of 'murder'.[69] Only the first 51 pages of an early draft of 'The Big Steal' remain – unread by virtually anyone.

Whatever the precise truth about these tales, the CIA admits to having an impact on scripts during pre-production. When interviewed by Tricia Jenkins, the CIA's 2007–08 Hollywood liaison Paul Barry said 'The added value we provide is at a story's inception. We can be a tremendous asset to writers developing characters and storylines.' This sentiment was seconded in Jenkins' interview with the CIA's Tony Mendez, who advised on *The Agency* and testified that Brandon was 'very adept at wielding his influence', especially during a film's early stages.[70] In a recent interview with *Spy Game* and *The Agency* writer Michael Frost Beckner, he reveals that Brandon often suggested plotlines in order to intimidate terrorists ('Terrorists watch TV too ... scare them') and to think through assissination scenarios.[71]

One wouldn't have thought that the elected White House itself could be so brazen as the CIA. However, in 2000 it was revealed that its drug war officers had spent tens of millions of dollars paying the major US networks to inject 'war on drugs' plots into the scripts of prime-time series such as *ER*, *The Practice*, *Sabrina the Teenage Witch* and *Chicago Hope*.[72]

Then, on 11 November 2001, the Bush administration spread its post-9/11 message on foreign policy to the entertainment media, when at least forty top Hollywood executives met with Karl Rove, Bush's chief political adviser. Almost all the major studios, TV networks and unions were represented, as well as Hollywood's overarching trade association, the Motion Picture Association of America (MPAA) – which has since its early days referred to itself as 'a little state department'.[73] Rove outlined several themes he wanted Hollywood to publicise: the US campaign in Afghanistan is a war against terrorism, not Islam; people can 'serve in the war effort ... in their communities'; US troops and families should be supported; 9/11 requires a global response; this is a 'fight against evil', and government and Hollywood are responsible for reassuring children of their safety. Employing exemplary double-think, Rove made his requests whilst insisting that 'content [of films] was off the table.' There was supposedly to be 'no propaganda'.[74]

One of those attending, the producer Lionel Chetwynd, commented 'There was a feeling around the table that something is wrong if half the world thinks we're the Great Satan, and we want to make that right.'[75] Paramount Picture's chief Sherry Lansing said that about 150 people from the creative community, who she declined to identify, had volunteered their talents.[76]

It's hard to say to what extent actual Hollywood products and activities were directly prompted by this meeting and subsequent closed meetings. There was certainly a initial flurry of celebrity activity as USO tours and public service announcements utilised the likes of Jennifer Lopez, Brad Pitt, Robin Williams, George Clooney, Matt Damon, Julia Roberts and Mariah Carey.[77] Chetwynd went on to make dramas like the White House-supported *DC 9/11: Time of Crisis* (2003)[78] and the anti-Michael Moore documentary *Celcius 41.11* (2004). A five-minute short film, *Enduring Freedom* (2002), also emerged, made by Hollywood for the Marines and Navy and distributed by Regal Entertainment Group, the nation's largest theatre chain. The film used the 9/11 Twin Towers attacks to encourage recruitment, in which a Navy man says 'Nobody's going to come over and tell my kids how to run their life or take their freedoms away.' Elsewhere, unprecedented short adverts were screened to recruit CIA agents.[79]

As with merchandising, what the internal record outlined above does not show is the inevitable self-censorship which goes on when any film-maker anticipates involvement from the national security apparatus. Indeed, the consequences can be severe – all CIA agents sign a lifelong disclosure form, meaning that anything they write must be submitted to a review board to be edited before publication. According to my sources, the penalty for non-adherence is that the CIA can seize their assets, which is one reason why it hardly ever happens (the book of *Syriana* being an exception, as the CIA thought it was more prudent to ignore it). Similarly, if the DOD decides that a film-maker isn't playing ball, it is able to prevent screenings of the movie on all of its properties around the world – a significant market – as happened with *Thirteen Days* (2000).[80]

RETRIBUTION BY THE POWERFUL

The ability to punish films and film-makers is invariably related to power. Grassroots pressure groups have had some successes too but not on the same scale as government, military and corporate forces. Such entities are not always successful in their suppressive efforts, but they are at the least a dis-incentive to anyone aspiring to question the foreign policy system in Hollywood.

The most famous case is that of Jane Fonda, who campaigned against the Vietnam War. She was most reviled for being photographed behind Communist weaponry in 1972, a mistake that she regretted but which left her open to the charge that she opposed US troops. Fonda had in fact worked with Vietnam Veterans Against the War, an organisation that believed individual soldiers should not be made scapegoats for policies designed at the highest levels of government.[81] Also, rather less well known, the FBI used false pretences to arrest her and acquire her personal records.[82] Politicians variously said 'I think we should cut her tongue off', and called for her to be 'tried for treason and executed';[83] the Nixon White House seriously compared their surveillance and overall treatment of 'Hanoi Jane' with that of Soviet Premiere Brezhnev.[84]

Fonda has remained politically active throughout her life but has never shaken off the associations constructed by the government in the early 1970s. She was publicly silent about the Persian Gulf War[85] and according to the tabloids at least, this is because pro-war cable television magnate and husband-to-be Ted Turner insisted 'If you love me, you'll shut up', lest she be dubbed 'Baghdad Jane'.[86]

Airport (1970) star Jean Seberg caved in under similar pressure. In 1970, as part of its Counter Intelligence Program (COINTELPRO), the FBI decided to 'neutralise' the married and pregnant Seberg because of her financial support for the Black Panthers. Declassified documents show that the *Los Angeles Times* printed a lie that had been leaked by the FBI, namely that the father of Seberg's unborn child was a prominent Black Panther. Shocked by the story, Seberg immediately collapsed and went into labour. Her baby daughter (revealed to be white, after all) died three days later. Seberg then attempted to commit suicide on the anniversary of the child's death every year until 1979, when she finally succeeded. Just over a year later, her husband Gary also killed himself.[87] FBI head J. Edgar Hoover had been directly involved in the operation to ruin Seberg's life, just as he had tried (unsuccessfully) to spread through a gossip columnist the lie that Jane Fonda exhorted a crowd of Black Panthers to chant 'We will kill Richard Nixon and any other motherfucker who stands in our way.'[88]

There are many other cases of powerful people and organisations causing problems for films and film-makers. As such, any deviation from standard ideological lines can receive considerable opprobrium and the Right has a particularly well-organised attack machine in operation.

On the eve of the Iraq War, the Rupert Murdoch-owned *New York Post* called for a boycott of products by the likes of Susan Sarandon, Sean Penn, Janeanne Garofalo, Martin Sheen and Danny Glover, all of whom opposed the war.[89] The following month, Tim Robbins' invitation to attend the 15th-anniversary screening of his movie *Bill Durham* (1988) at the National Baseball Hall of Fame was revoked because the Hall of Fame's president, a former Reagan administration press secretary, felt Robbins' presence might harm US efforts in Iraq.[90]

Disney made the release of Michael Moore's *Fahrenheit 911* (2004) difficult by telling its subsidiary Miramax not to distribute the film because it feared the political fallout. Disney denied claims that it ditched the film because Moore was challenging the interests of its parent company, which had links with the Bush and Saudi Royal families.[91] Subsequently, CBS, NBC and ABC all refused to advertise the DVD in between their news programming, which stunned the distributor Sony, according to an investigation by the *LA Weekly*.[92]

Fox News anchor Bill O'Reilly gave a series of vitriolic straight-to-camera pieces about the 'vile' Brian de Palma film *Redacted* (2007), accusing the film of putting US troops 'in even more danger'.[93] At the same time, a Republican ranking member of the House Armed Services Committee, Duncan Hunter, also complained to the chairman of the MPAA that the film 'portrays American service personnel in Iraq as uncontrollable misfits and criminals'.[94] The film was screened in just 15 theatres throughout the US.

Anyone intimating that Jewish organisations, lobbyists, or Israel itself might not be striving for all things holy is equally liable to receive a particularly swift lashing. For instance, the Zionist Organization of America (ZOA) called for a boycott against Steven Spielberg's *Munich* (2005), which had dared to raise the concern that by adopting a necessarily brutal secret assassination programme we might make ourselves emotionally upset.

There are other historical precedents too. The US Justice Department can prohibit unwelcome film imports by invoking the 1938 Foreign Agents Registration Act. It did so successfully in the 1980s leading to a ban on Canadian documentaries about nuclear war and acid rain, which it labelled 'political propaganda'.[95]

Gulf and Western, then the parent company of Paramount, quietly tried to thwart the release of Haskell Wexler's classic anti-war documentary *Medium Cool* (1969), apparently due to its economic ties to the Democratic Party, which was criticised in the film. Wexler explains: 'Paramount called me and said I needed releases from all the [protesters] in the park, which was impossible to provide.' Although Paramount was obliged to release the film, they successfully pushed for an X rating, advertised it feebly, and forbade Wexler from taking it to film festivals.[96]

In summary, then, 'all publicity' is not necessarily 'good publicity' when film-makers come up against the strict limits of dissent in the US political system.

In this context, it is worth noting that the motion picture industry itself is not exactly renowned for its day-to-day human decency. Producer Jon Avnet opined that 'working hard, doing good work, being loyal and paying your dues count for nothing in Hollywood ... you find people willing to compromise their souls to work in Hollywood. It breeds a kind of person who is invested completely in power and money, and human considerations and concerns are secondary.'[97]

In an extensive series of anonymised interviews with industry figures, the magazine *Fade In* documented the inner business workings of the studios, including widespread allegations of brutish behaviour by numerous executives – often naming names. One screenwriter claims 'Paramount is a mess. I've worked on a number of movies at Paramount, and I believe it comes from the top. [Parent company Viacom Chief Executive Officer Sumner] Redstone likes instability in his executive branch. He doesn't want anyone to feel too secure in their position.'[98] A producer claims that Fox 'hate filmmakers, they hate producers, and they hate directors after the movie is shot ... It's common knowledge that [Chief Executive Officer] Tom Rothman *hates* producers. He's very vocal about it. But they're unbelievable marketers.'[99] A director claims 'Everyone there is operating out of fear. Everyone is scared of the iron fist, whether it's Rupert Murdoch or Peter Chernin or Tom Rothman. So the atmosphere is a negative atmosphere.'[100]

Fade In's revelations include eye-watering claims of racism and sexism, indicating that the 'open-minded liberalism' of Obama's America does not 'hold true when it comes to hiring minorities and women to write, direct and produce projects'.[101]

Similarly, the National Association for the Advancement of Colored People (NAACP) claimed that racial/ethnic minorities still face 'employment and promotion opportunities [which are] directly tied to highly subjective practices', resulting in a 'serious shortage' of minorities, particularly in television.[102] Neil Gabler, author of *An Empire of Their Own: How the Jews Invented Hollywood*, prefers to call this the result of 'a set of traditions, misconceptions, fears and prevarications' which 'have the unfortunate effect of racism without its motive'.[103] The entertainment industry has been especially resistant to Muslim or Arab presences, partly because they have little in terms of an organised pressure group. There are numerous instances reported where Arabs, having been typecast as terrorists, have anglicised their names and even changed their ethnic appearance in attempts to further their careers.[104]

OTHER EXPLANATIONS

What about the apparently benign explanations for the lack of critical content in Hollywood cinema? One common assumption is that generic conventions, particularly in Action Adventure films, are not conducive to generating oppositional narratives. It is true that the easiest film to write would be a US soldier going behind enemy lines and killing a stereotypical enemy, but films throughout Hollywood history have 'broken the mould' and all films can find ways – even if just by making small and simple cuts and adaptations – to reduce their slavishness to or glorification of established power systems.

Another argument is that audiences actually demand simplistic escapism, and so cinema will always produce stereotypical fodder. Yet if simplicity is all that is required, films would be able to promote slogans expressing solidarity against government/corporate repression, like 'Freedom to the Workers' and 'No Blood for Oil', but this is not the case, so political factors appear to be decisive.

Nor should film-makers – in a truly free political system – feel bound by what they think audiences expect. The renowned creative-writing instructor Robert McKee draws the distinction between a stereotype and an archetype – the former is narrow, stale and culture-specific, while the latter is 'so true to humankind that it journeys from culture to culture'.[105] Good stories, McKee informs us, should be archetypal. He explains that we watch movies to 'live in a fictional reality that illuminates our daily reality. We do not wish to escape life but to find life, to use our minds in fresh, experimental ways, to flex our emotions, to enjoy, to learn, to add depth to our days.'[106] In other words, audiences enjoy being challenged – rather than patronised. McKee is presumably not a fan of *Not Without My Daughter* (1991) (repressive Iranian families), *In the Army Now* (1994) (filthy Arabs), or *Collateral Damage* (2002) (murderous Colombians).

But any tendencies toward social responsibility and political free thought are feeble at best in Hollywood and, in such an atmosphere, the movie industry is liable to fall into reinforcing ideologies that are promoted by official and unofficial mouthpieces of the state. Most notably, influential commentators frequently promote foreign policy narratives that polarise 'good' and 'evil', with the West as the good guy, or at least 'the lesser evil'. This has translated well into cinema, hence Communists have provided convenient enemies in countless moving pictures, from *The Red Menace* (1949) and *Invasion USA* (1952) to *Rambo III* (1988) and *The Hunt for Red October* (1990). The Nazis have been similarly long-standing villains, from *Confessions of a Nazi Spy* (1939) to *Saving Private Ryan* (1998) and *Inglourious Basterds* (2009).

This does not mean that the films will necessarily present simplistic villains or heroes. For instance, in *The Siege* (1998), a film about countering international Islamic terrorism on US soil, the villains are Muslims from all strata of American life, but the movie also questions the well-meaning but heavy-handed military tactics of Bruce Willis's military, which imposes martial law. Therefore, as Canadian-based broadcaster Jian Ghomeshi puts it, *The Siege* 'cloaks its offensive typecasting and hawkish ideas in the veneer of a well-meaning liberal sensibility'.[107] He adds that 'making a jingoistic action film that has the US military triumphing over a well-known enemy comprised of racist caricatures is not as easy as it once was. Not when you want credulity, not when you want to be taken seriously' and not in a 'racially and sexually "correct"' era.[108] Quite right, and this is a key stylistic factor behind films like *Spy Game* (2001), *Crimson Tide* (1995) and *GI Jane* (1997), which use touchy-feely characters (the guilt-ridden assassin, the conscientious black serviceman, the female struggling in a male workplace) to promote stories that are otherwise thoroughly at ease with nationalistic violence.

The notion that 'we' are good is in fact widely assumed and propagated by policy-makers and commentators on both liberal and conservative sides of the debate. Senior Fellow and Director of Europe Studies at the Council on Foreign Relations Charles A. Kupchan endorsed Clinton's notion that the US is the 'indispensable nation', arguing that the US 'serves as a critical extra-regional balancer in Europe and East Asia, is the catalyst behind multilateral efforts to combat aggression and peacefully resolve longstanding disputes, and is the engine behind the liberalization of the world economy'.[109]

Similarly, Robert Kagan, a founding member of the neoconservative Project for the New American Century that spearheads the campaign to maintain and extend US hegemony through military strength, explained that 'the benevolent hegemony exercised by the United States is good for a vast portion of the world's population.'[110] The United States and its people are 'guided by the kind of enlightened self-interest that, in practice, comes dangerously close to resembling generosity'.[111] Likewise, Eaton Professor of the Science of Government and Director of the Olin Institute of Strategic Studies at Harvard Samuel Huntington, said that the US is the 'only major power whose national identity is defined by a set of universal political and economic values', namely 'liberty, democracy, equality, private property, and markets'.[112]

Even former Defense Secretary Robert McNamara, who vehemently criticised his own decisions and US war policy in Vietnam (and also more broadly), never asserted that it was driven by dominant US economic, political and military interests to the detriment of the people of South East Asia. Rather, McNamara's *mea culpa* was predicated on the statement that 'we made an error not of values and intentions, but of judgment and capabilities' and puts emphasis on America's suffering while marginalising the Vietnamese.[113]

The concept of a benevolent US foreign policy emerges from the widespread historical belief in 'American exceptionalism', which describes the belief that the US is an extraordinary nation with a special role to play in human history; that is, America is not only unique but also superior among nations. The French political thinker and historian Alexis de Tocqueville was the first major figure to use the term 'exceptional' in the mid nineteenth century to describe the US and the American people in his classic work *Democracy in America*,[114] but the idea of America as an exceptional entity can be traced back to the earliest colonial times.[115]

Two main strands of exceptionalist thought have been commonly used to describe US foreign policy. One is that of the US as an exemplar nation, as reflected in ideas such as the 'city upon the hill', 'non-entangling alliances', 'anti-imperialism', 'isolationism' and 'fortress America'. The other, often more dominant, strand is that of the missionary nation, as represented by the ideas of 'Manifest Destiny', 'internationalism', 'leader of the free world' and the 'new world order'.[116] While both strands have been important and distinct aspects of US history and self-image, they are both similar in that they tend to assume that the US acts upon its decent values over and above the interests of its constituent domestic concentrations of power.

As former President George W. Bush – who was himself on the board of Silver Screen Management from 1983–93 – put it in response to the 9/11 attacks: 'I'm amazed that ... people would hate us ... because I know how good we are.'[117] Hollywood liberals disliked Bush, just as they disliked his movie-star predecessor Ronald Reagan, but the Reagan-Bush mentality has long underpinned Hollywood output on foreign affairs. If you believe Reagan and Bush, *Reel Power* will no doubt mystify you. If you have doubts about the professed benevolence of our leaders, I hope the book will help you make sense of how films are key components of this deceptive myth.

2
Hollywood Deactivated

Regardless of all the high-level structural influences discussed in Chapter 1, what about the effect of the stars and directors themselves who are actually hands-on in the studios? Aren't we now in a fresh era of celebrity power, far removed from the cliché of the scheming, cigar-chomping moguls that dominated the mid twentieth century?

Tell that to Tom Cruise – 'the world's most powerful celebrity' at the time, according to *Forbes* magazine[1] – who lost his contract with Paramount in 2006 following a spate of manic public activity, including declaring his love for Katie Holmes whilst bouncing up and down on *Oprah* (the chat show, not the woman). The man who delivered the knock-out blow was none other than Viacom's notoriously irascible CEO Sumner Redstone, who remarked to the *Wall Street Journal*, 'We don't think that someone who effectuates creative suicide and costs the company revenue should be on the lot. His [Cruise's] recent conduct has not been acceptable to Paramount.'[2]

'Power lists' drawn up by leading publications like *Forbes* magazine, the *Hollywood Reporter* and *Vanity Fair* over the past decade or so have consistently placed the likes of Redstone, News Corp's Rupert Murdoch, and a few other CEOs jockeying for the top spots.[3] 'These people are the supreme rulers, the way there were in the old days [when studio bosses virtually owned stars],' explained Hollywood marketer Tony Angelotti. 'Yes they have partners, and they have to divide up their fiefdoms, but they have unbelievable power.'[4] Director Don Simpson pointed out that 'The people who are at the very top [of the conglomerates], by those I mean the chairmen of the boards ... Unfortunately, sometimes, oftentimes, if not all the time, they also say yes and no to what movies get made.'[5]

At the other end of the spectrum is the average screenwriter, who is 'basically a very well-paid typist', according to dramatist Terry George.[6] 'They all get treated like shit and they are raped right and left,' noted agent Bobbi Thompson.[7] One screenwriter picks out Fox for comment, saying Fox is

> … the quintessential example of what Tim Robbins is talking about in *The Player* (1992): 'If we can just get rid of these pesky writers and directors, we'd really have something.' They feel that they are making the movie, and you're there to copy down their ideas and maybe provide some snappy dialogue … I refuse to work for them because I'm not interested in being hired to be the world's most expensive typist. It's a Tom Rothman thing, it's a [News Corp President and Chief Operating Officer] Peter Chernin thing, it's a Rupert Murdoch thing. It's the corporate culture at Fox. The whole company is run with this incredibly arrogant attitude of 'everything we say goes.'[8]

Are these corporate leaders politically disinterested? Do they support the leftist agenda supposedly followed by the stars we know and love? Some are Democrats, to be sure, although lifelong Democrat Redstone, for instance, voted for Bush in 2004 because he thought it was a 'better deal' for Viacom.[9] Most importantly, virtually no one could be labelled a radical – with the odd exception, such as the billionaire eBay founder Jeff Skoll, who set up Participant Media in 2004 with a socially emancipatory platform and made relatively challenging films like *Syriana*.

On the other hand, many high-profile business leaders comprise what we might call a rogues' gallery.

Jack Welch, CEO from 1981–2001 of Universal's parent company General Electric is a major Republican contributor,[10] openly declares disdain for 'protocol, diplomacy, regulators';[11] he employed Republican Bob Wright as the long-term boss of NBC and 'used to boast openly about helping turn former liberals [NBC News anchor] Chris Matthews and [former NBC Senior Vice President] Tim Russert into neocons'.[12] Welch wore his epithet 'Neutron Jack' as a badge of honour around the Reagan White House, though he received the name because he was known for destroying people whilst leaving his businesses intact.[13] He was even accused by California Congressman Henry Waxman (at the request of Al Gore) of pressuring his NBC network to declare Bush the winner prematurely in the 2000 'stolen election', when he turned up unannounced in the newsroom during the poll count.[14] NBC refused a Congressional request to turn over the surveillance tapes to prove it one way or another.[15] Welch's successor at General Electric is the Republican Jeff Immelt,[16] who identifies Fox as the leading news outlet and is reportedly 'as right wing as they come'.[17]

Similarly, Jack Valenti had Washington credentials by the dozen, having been 'special assistant' to President Lyndon Johnson before becoming head of the MPAA in 1966. Valenti was so loyal to Johnson, while the President ramped up the war in Vietnam, that a common phrase emerged: 'If LBJ dropped the H-bomb, Valenti would call it an urban renewal project.'[18] He called Oliver Stone's conspiracy classic *JFK* a 'smear', a 'monstrous charade', and compared it to Leni Riefenstahl's Nazi documentary *Triumph of the Will* (1935), which he said was 'equally a propaganda masterpiece, and equally a hoax'.[19] In contrast, he praised *Forrest Gump* (1994) as one of his favourite films.[20]

Following the Hollywood-Rove 9/11 meetings, Valenti said that Hollywood should tell Muslims that America has 'clothed and fed and sheltered millions and millions around the world without asking anything in return. We have educated hundreds of thousands of people from all over the world in our universities.'[21] This message from Hollywood's leading official could have sounded like a presidential speech had his rhetoric not then become quite so graphic: 'Americans are going to have to screw their courage to the sticking place. It's going to get brutal. Anybody captured will surely be tortured, their arms and legs torn off, by these malignant zealots.'[22] Valenti apparently saw no need to caution the US about overstepping its rights domestically and/or internationally and instead explained the need to 'avenge' the 9/11 deaths, adding that 'benevolence is a word that must be struck from our vocabulary in this war.'[23] In 2007, he expressed tactical opposition to the Iraq War (reluctantly, since he was aware of President Bush's 'personal agony' in committing troops) because 'no matter how benign the occupiers' motives' and no matter that US troops only kill civilians by accident – the price was too high because natives tend to resist invasions.[24]

Consider Rupert Murdoch – named several times as Hollywood's most powerful living figure[25] – who is 'extraordinarily aware of the power of movies',[26] even though he doesn't like them or the people who make them.[27] According to Andrew Neil's *Full Disclosure*, Murdoch claims to be a man of the 'common people'[28] but is 'much more right-wing than is generally thought', because he adapts his views for commercial gain.[29] Neil, who worked closely with Murdoch as editor of the *Sunday Times*, revealed that his former boss's favourite presidential candidate in 1988 was the 'far right religious fanatic' Pat Robertson; that Murdoch wanted the hard-right Norman Tebbit to be British Prime Minister Margaret

Thatcher's successor,[30] and that he thought Oliver North – the National Security Council member who illegally sold arms to Iran – deserved the Congressional Medal of Honor.[31] Apparently, during negotiations with China over the future of Hong Kong in the 1980s, Murdoch expressed his view that the British should 'make no concessions and [should] tell the Chinese that there's a Trident submarine off their coast: if the Red Army moves into Hong Kong they should be left in no doubt that we'll nuke Beijing.' Neil says Murdoch then thought about this for a moment before adding 'though I suppose we could fire a warning nuke into a desert first.'[32] I have never found these comments duplicated online or in print and Murdoch, who now has vast economic interests in China, presumably wants it to stay that way.

In 2003, Murdoch described British Prime Minister Tony Blair as 'extraordinarily courageous' over Iraq and predicted that the 'greatest thing' once the war was completed was that 'the whole world will benefit from cheaper oil' – hopefully $20 a barrel – 'which will be a bigger stimulus than anything else'.[33] Oil prices did indeed drop precipitously – after five years of war and prompted by the worst recession since the 1930s. Congratulations, Rupert.

Some Hollywood figures and companies even have a clear financial interest in actively promoting the image of a hostile world and a heroic America. For instance, John E. Bryson simultaneously sits on the boards for the Walt Disney Company and the Boeing Company. Each board consists of only a dozen people, which makes this a particularly jarring link between the world's leading family entertainment brand and one of the world's largest arms contractors.[34] The same is true of Lewis Coleman, who is simultaneously president and chief financial officer of Steven Spielberg's DreamWorks Animation while also working as non-executive chairman of the scandal-ridden arms company Northrop Grumman.

General Electric is one of the wealthiest corporations in the world and invests heavily in manufacturing crucial components for high-tech war planes, advanced surveillance technology and essential hardware for the global oil and gas industries. Three of GE's biggest clients are Israel, the Department of Defense and post-Saddam Iraq.[35] GE has been involved in numerous scandals, including admitting to bribery and fraud involving the Pentagon and Israeli Air Force, dumping pollution in the Hudson River and testing radioactive materials on the genitals of volunteers in the 1960s.[36] Through its ownership of 80 per cent of Universal Studios, GE also became one of the world's major storytellers. In 2009,

Comcast began the process of acquiring a controlling stake in NBC/Universal while GE's share declined to 49 per cent, but hopes for a better corporate culture should be tempered by various stains on Comcast's reputation, including reports that it 'has repeatedly given work to prominent public officials, their relatives or their friends'.[37]

Even without the presence of such 'crazies' and external interests, Hollywood would still produce similar material as a rule. Hollywood is controlled by a corporate mentality and the upper echelons are more liable to discourage critical, investigative, or responsible films rather than directly encourage the opposite.

Still, while the image of Hollywood being run by bean-counters is relatively comforting, as we can see, this is not always the case and, indeed, there are some suspicious cases of apparent direct interference in studio products from higher up the corporate food chain. For instance, producers of GE/NBC's mini-series *Asteroid* (1997) altered the script to show off the USAF's jet-mounted Airborne Laser, a controversial and then obscure weapons technology that was being developed by a consortium which included GE.[38]

Jack Welch was certainly conscious of the importance of film – he had been infuriated by the Oscar-winning guerrilla documentary *Deadly Deception: General Electric, Nuclear Weapons and Our Environment* (1991), which, with a budget of just $65,000, exposed GE's disastrous involvement in nuclear weaponry.[39] The film, which also won more than a dozen other awards and recognitions, was rejected for broadcast by the Public Broadcasting Service (PBS) supposedly because it breached network guidelines by being funded by a small activist organisation.[40] Despite calls by Oliver Stone and Robin Williams to end the censorship, PBS refused to budge, leading to suspicions of GE's nefarious influence, but it nevertheless ultimately contributed to Welch's decision to sell off GE's arms manufacturing division in 1993.[41]

Similarly, former Reagan-era official General Alexander M. Haig Jr worked with Frank Yablans, CEO of MGM/United Artists to transform a script about 'the brutalisation of the innocent' and the 'futility of war' to being a 'flagwaving, jingoistic movie' with a backstory about 'America's political bankruptcy and the permissiveness of its enemies', according to Peter Bart. The film was *Red Dawn* (1984), about a Soviet invasion of the United States and the subsequent uncompromising rebellion by a gang of teenagers. Bart said Haig was 'a stiff, unapproachable man with a total disinterest in showbusiness', who recognised the propaganda value of the piece. Haig sat on the board of MGM for three decades until his death in 2010, as well as being former president of and then high-level adviser to the arms manufacturer United Technologies.[42]

The ultimate arbiter of who can watch what is the MPAA classification board. Head of the board since 1988 is registered Republican Joan Graves. The identities of the rest of the members are kept secret, apparently to prevent them being subject to lobbying. The result is an unaccountable organisation making arbitrary decisions that can seriously restrict audiences for films. It is known that two permanent members of the appeals board are clergymen, further adding to the sense that the MPAA is a bastion of traditional morality.[43] Violent images are apparently less likely to attract the attention of the censors than are scenes of a sexual (particularly homosexual) nature,[44] again helping immunise from censure depictions of violence, including the variety that is bloodless and cartoonish. Such 'happy violence', as one study archly dubbed it,[45] is a common facet of state representations of US-led shoot 'em/beat 'em ups in 'family' products like *True Lies* (1994), *Air Force One* (1997), *The Peacemaker* (1997) and the *GI Joe* (2009–) franchise.

In *Apocalypse Now* (1979), Marlon Brando's Colonel Kurtz famously remarked, 'We train young men to drop fire on people [in Vietnam]. But their commanders won't allow them to write "fuck" on their airplanes because it's obscene.' Kurtz's comment seems appropriate in the light of the MPAA's attempt to give an R rating to *Gunner Palace* (2004) because it portrayed bad language and drug use – hardly avoidable, since it was a fly-on-the-wall documentary about front-line US troops in Iraq. The director Michael Tucker appealed the decision, a petition was started and surprisingly, the MPAA's ruling was overturned. Tucker later drew a stark lesson from history: 'When the Americans liberated [the Nazi concentration camp] Buchenwald and they saw these images of people, is that PG? Is that PG13? Is that R?' He concluded, 'You can't rate reality.'[46] The MPAA nevertheless continues to try, thereby providing yet another obstacle to critical political cinema.

POLITICS AT THE GRASSROOTS

What about at the level of celebrity power, though? Surely there exists what is widely described as a 'progressive Hollywood',[47] characterised by figures in Hollywood that have embarked upon what Ben Dickenson calls a 'tumultuous path' to 'social justice'?[48] Such trends have been highly exaggerated.

Indeed, the creative talent that has made the 'power lists' over the past two decades has usually been placed a long way from poll position and tends to be the same tiny group of familiar names – almost exclusively the actor Tom Cruise and the film-makers Steven Spielberg (*Saving Private Ryan*, *Munich*) and Jerry Bruckheimer (*Armageddon*, *Black Hawk Down*). Other figures like Will Smith (*Independence Day*), Arnold Schwarzenegger (*True Lies*, *Collateral Damage*), Brad Pitt (*Mr and Mrs Smith* (2005)) and George Clooney (*The Peacemaker*) have made some appearances.

Strikingly, Spielberg has been keenly glad-handed by the powers-that-be with awards like the Defense Department's Medal for Distinguished Public Service.[49] In the build-up to the Iraq War, Spielberg said 'If Bush, as I believe, has reliable information on the fact that Saddam Hussein is making weapons of mass destruction, I cannot not support [Bush's] policies',[50] which he later insisted – in his triple negative – was not an endorsement of the war policy.[51]

At the same press conference, Tom Cruise told reporters that Bush's policies are 'solid' and 'rooted in reality'.[52] Sketchy newspaper reports indicated that a year later, Cruise met Dick Cheney's chief of staff and soon-to-be convicted perjurer, Scooter Libby for unspecified reasons[53] and that Cruise had met CIA officials to discuss ways to present the agency 'in as positive a light as possible' for *Mission Impossible III*.[54]

Meanwhile, Bruckheimer contributed financially to both George W. Bush and John McCain, and has maintained a close relationship with the Pentagon ever since *Top Gun* (1986). After 9/11, Bruckheimer made a documentary television series with the Department of Defense called *Profiles From the Front Line* (2003), about US troops in Afghanistan. When Bruckheimer was asked if he would screen a 'mammoth military cock up' or 'human rights violation' if he came across it, he actually replied, 'as long as it's not something they [the Pentagon] would consider sensitive'.[55]

In fact, even the lower stratum of celebrities in Hollywood have generally been unconcerned by American actions beyond its borders. For example, on the eve of the Persian Gulf War in 1991, one hundred Hollywood celebrities – including Tommy Lee Jones, James Woods, Jean-Claude Van Damme, Meryl Streep, Richard Gere, William Shatner, Michelle Pfeiffer, Whoopie Goldberg, Bette Midler, Kurt Russell and Kevin Costner – recorded a charity record 'Voices That Care', which assiduously avoided commenting on the legitimacy of Operation Desert Shield/Storm while endorsing whatever it was the American troops were doing out there.[56] The song was intended to be the more overtly flag-waving 'Voices for Freedom', but the nationalist associations were toned down to ensure the support of such principled activists as Mike Tyson.[57] Lyrics for the final version included the following: 'Right or wrong, we're all praying you'll remain strong, that's why we're all here and singing along' – surely more toxic than anything Saddam Hussein dared to produce, since the early 1990s at least.

When US troops returned home in April 1991, Hollywood's 'Welcome Home Desert Storm' parade deliberately excluded peace messages collated by a body of social activists.[58] Then, as the US again dropped bombs on Iraq in 1998, following a Congressional vote for 'regime change' in that country, mega-stars Jack Nicholson, Barbra Streisand and Alec Baldwin showed up at a rally of a thousand people in LA not to protest the attacks but to oppose Clinton's impeachment over the Monica Lewinsky sex scandal.[59]

A few month's later, in the midst of NATO's bombing campaign against Serbia in the Kosovo crisis of April 1999, an extensive interview with leading dissenting Hollywood stars appeared on the pages of *The Nation*; none of them even mentioned foreign policy, except for a brief and pertinent comment from actor Tim Robbins who alluded to Iraq: 'You talk about the Hollywood Left, where the hell are they? The same people who will be absolutely crazy about animals being sacrificed in the name of medical research will not raise a voice about human beings who are killed in the name of oil.'[60] Meanwhile, leading liberal activist and *M*A*S*H* star Mike Farrell actually did speak up about Kosovo – declaring he was 'in favor' of the war.[61]

Even with regard to the exceptionally controversial 2003 Iraq War, Hollywood celebrities were unwilling to do anything more than make the odd anti-Bush quip; many more stayed tight-lipped. Many others, like Ben Stein (*Amerika*), Robert Duvall (*Deep Impact*) and Ron Silver (*In the Company of Spies*, *FahrenHYPE 9/11*) were sympathetic to Bush's actions. James Woods declared to Jay Leno 'I love George Bush – and I always have!',[62] and became a leading voice against the 'fraud' Michael Moore, who had used his Oscar acceptance speech to criticise the President.[63] In 2008, *Naked Gun* producer David Zucker enlisted the support of stars like James Woods, Jon Voight (*Mission Impossible*, *Pearl Harbor*, *Transformers*, *24*), Leslie Nielson (*Spy Hard*) and Kelsey Grammer (*Swing Vote*) to make *An American Carol* aka *Big Fat Important Movie*, lambasting leftist documentary-maker Michael Moore and promoting a conservative view in which American liberalism results in Islamic fundamentalists taking over ... you've guessed it: Hollywood. Zucker had already made a series of outrageous adverts for the Republican Party which depicted Clinton's Secretary of State Madeleine Albright giving North Korean dictator Kim Jong Il a basketball, painting the walls of Bin Laden's cave and changing a tyre for a Middle Eastern dictator's limousine.[64] The GOP declined the ads.

Soon-to-be Republican Governor of California Arnold Schwarzenegger repeatedly dodged questions about the legitimacy of the Iraq War, once reportedly 'when he experienced a shockingly sudden movement at one Oscar party, forcing him into the toilet and away from journalists probing his opinion on the conflict in Iraq'.[65] However, he seemed to be broadly in favour of the use of US force, as he allied himself closely with George W. Bush and had already flown to Saddam Hussein's former summer holiday palace to tell US troops on 4 July 2003 'Congratulations for saying "Hasta la vista, baby," to Saddam Hussein.'[66] When visiting Ramstein air base in Germany the following year, to accompanying whoops and hollers Schwarzenegger asked 'Do you know how they translate "Ramstein" in the English language? It means "we're gonna kick some ass!"'[67] He long ago expressed the view that 'My relationship to power and authority is that I'm all for it. People need somebody to watch over them ... Ninety-five percent of the people in the world need to be told what to do and how to behave.'[68]

Jack Valenti argued, 'This is not an easy one [the Iraq War]. That's why you don't see people clamoring on the rooftops with a megaphone.'[69] If anything, this was an understatement. In late 2002, the *New York Times* reported that while 104 Hollywood figures had signed a message from 'Artists United to Win Without War', which urged the continuance of UN weapons inspections, there was little other activity.[70] 'If there is a nascent antiwar movement in America, it is not being led, at least not yet, by Hollywood', commented the *New York Times*,[71] massively understating the case. By this measure, more MPs in the British House of Commons registered their disapproval of the war than all the celebrities in Hollywood combined.

Lara Bergthold, former executive director of the Hollywood Women's Political Committee, which had been the town's most active opponent of the Reagan administration's covert military intervention in South America during the 1980s, said that there was a 'conversation' about the 'antiwar response', but that this 'should begin and take place in Washington',[72] echoing the organisation's lack of a public stance over Iraq in 1991.[73]

As surreal as it sounds, Bill Maher – whose *Politically Incorrect* show was cancelled after he made some politically incorrect remarks about US foreign policy – even called for a pause in the criticism of the Iraq War, just after it had started, although he added that this shouldn't mean we 'shut up indefinitely'.[74]

Warren Beatty, the 1960s radical, used his words so carefully he was in danger of saying nothing at all. 'The rush to pass such a far reaching resolution before the election will be deemed by many to be opportunistic and will benefit neither the administration nor its opponents,' pontificated Beatty in a widely quoted speech about Congress's vote to authorise force against Iraq: 'I don't like to speak out about public matters until I'm aware enough of what I'm saying to avail myself of the attention that comes to me because I'm a movie actor. I have found I need to be much more careful of what I say because when those opinions go against the grain, then one is subjected to all kinds of ad hominem attacks.'[75] Go, Warren!

Even up to the brink of war, the media was hyping the imminent Hollywood rebellion. In an article for the BBC, Tom Brooke claimed that 'celebrities are proving to be the most powerful voice against a possible US attack on Iraq, surpassing the efforts of the Democrat Party to be President Bush's most vocal opposition', but this was little more than a puff piece that highlighted comments from a handful of the usual suspects – Sean Penn, Danny Glover and George Clooney.[76] By 3 March 2003, on the eve of war, the number of Artists United to Win Without War had limped to 130 supporters.[77] The 'Artists' element of Win Without War's website never even had a weblink.[78]

Hollywood's political activism was more concerted in 2006, when during Israel's otherwise unpopular assault on Lebanon, 85 Hollywood figures signed a letter effectively condoning its actions. The letter, coordinated and publicised by the US/UK-approved Israeli government in a full-page advert in the *LA Times*, *Variety* and *Hollywood Reporter*, blamed 'terrorist organisations such as Hizbollah and Hamas' for having 'initiated' the 'terrorist actions', and added that 'we need to support democratic societies and stop terrorism at all costs', apparently ignoring the fact that Hamas had been elected into power in the Palestinian Territories.[79]

Signatories included film-makers Joel Surnow (*24*), William Friedkin (*Rules of Engagement*), Ivan Reitman (*Dave*), Michael Douglas (*The American President*) and William Hurt (*Vantage Point*), all lined up behind the hard-right billionaire leaders of Tinseltown: Rupert Murdoch (CEO of News Corp), Sumner Redstone (CEO of Viacom) and Haim Saban (founder of Fox Family Worldwide). One might think the participants in the anti-Lebanon campaign letter had all been influenced by Disney's exhibit at its theme park in Orlando – made with $1.8 million of Israeli government assistance – that naturalised Jerusalem as Israel's capital.[80]

Still, those who assign a 'Jewish conspiracy' to Hollywood might be asked to explain the presence of gentile signatories on the letter, including Ridley Scott (*GI Jane*, *Black Hawk Down*, *Body of Lies*), Tony Scott (*Crimson Tide*, *Spy Game*, *Man on Fire*, *Top Gun*), Nicole Kidman (*The Peacemaker*) and Bruce Willis (*Tears of the Sun*) – the latter in the process of back-pedalling over his apparently 'metaphorical' public offer at a concert for US troops in Iraq to give a million dollars to whoever captured Saddam Hussein and allowed him 'four seconds' with the former dictator.[81] Willis had already 'called President Bush and asked what I could do', but was told he was too old to join the Armed Forces.[82]

In sum, Hollywood's opposition to US foreign policy in the contemporary era is all too easily exaggerated. In fact, there has been widespread apathy about US power in a political environment driven by money and narrow self-interests. *The Nation* explained that 'corporate Hollywood does expect and receives legislative favors from the political forces it finances' and that Disney, Time Warner and News Corp all conducted successful lobbying efforts on targeted legislation.[83]

Liberal fundraiser Stanley K. Sheinbaum, who befriended Bill Clinton in the 1980s, explained that for Hollywood funders, 'their interest isn't ideological. They just want to be invited to Camp David. They want to sleep in the White House. Just like I did.'[84] Even the conservative organiser David Horowitz, who despises what he sees as a liberal agenda in Hollywood, concurs, saying that '98% of people in Hollywood have no politics to speak of, or their politics are an inch deep. People do what they have to do to get ahead in this town.'[85].' Director John Milius put it with characteristic bluntness, saying that if you are successful all the time 'you can be a member of the [Nazi] SS and nobody will care.'[86]

Grassroots apathy towards, and complicity with, the general stance of state and private power sets the context for understanding how entertainment conglomerates produce movies that support the idea that the US is a benevolent power in world affairs and frequently endorse the application of US force.

A NOTE ABOUT THIS BOOK

Reel Power cannot examine every film in detail but it does cover a great many relevant pictures and places a particular emphasis on those films that have some claim to being critical of US power, through their own publicity or reception in the media. As such, I hope readers will recognise my coverage of the body of movies – from the end of the Cold War (*circa* 1990) to the present day – as being fair.

As this is a study of corporate output, the films discussed were produced and/or distributed by the major studios. I have set a budget of above approximately $30 million. Generally, where budgets are lower than this, a subsidiary or independent studio has taken more of a lead in the film's production. The final chapter of the book, 'The Low Budget Battlefield' examines the films which have been championed as Hollywood's most subversive work, and have come in at under the $30 million budget mark.

The films *Reel Power* discusses are overtly political in that they show some element of the US civilian and/or military authorities implementing foreign policy. *Reel Power* does not provide detailed examination of films unless the films refer to the US role in the world to a significant degree. Nor does it read films as metaphors for US foreign policy. This may seem like an obvious decision but the practice of reading films in this way is common amongst film analysts, from *Aladdin* (1992) to *Toy Story* (1995) to *In the Bedroom* (2001).

When analysing the films, the book examines the representations of US government, foreigners and the effectiveness of US power in creating positive resolutions to fictional and non-fictional world events. Without examining these three aspects together we can only attain a partial understanding. Hence, right-wing critics complain that films like *Rambo: First Blood, Part II* (1985) and *A Few Good Men* (1992) are 'anti-American' because they depict unstable characters in the US military. Such an approach ignores the broader narratives in the films that perpetuate the myth that the US military was stabbed in the back during its noble destruction of Indochina (in the case of *Rambo*), and that the military authorities are self-correcting (in *A Few Good Men*). In the same sense, just because we sympathise with the character of National Socialist

Oscar Schindler in *Schindler's List* (1993) does not make it a Nazi propaganda film.

One of the recurrent themes of the body of films in *Reel Power* is that even many of the most politically sophisticated of them assume the essential benevolence of US foreign policy, even where they express tactical concerns over using force. To suggest that US foreign policy is the result of deeper, more unseemly economic and political interests is virtually unsayable. Negative consequences of warfare are not the result of government policy but rather of 'bad apples' or 'rogue elements' in the mix. The most reprehensible crimes, such as the US assaults on Indochina and the Middle East, at worst create trauma for the US itself.

One of the strengths of such an approach to reading these films is that it closely resembles the Pentagon's own view of how movies need to be constructed for its own ends. So, for instance, the Pentagon's Hollywood liaison Phil Strub has even been able to ruminate on the possibility of supporting a film about the infamous 1968 My Lai massacre, where US troops wiped out hundreds of civilians:

> If it is handled in such a way that the viewer understands how something horrible like that can take place in some kind of awful catastrophic extremes of events, how people may or may not feel guilt, how wrongdoers are punished, how steps are taken to prevent that from happening again, you know, all these are factors that would mitigate our apprehension over the subject matter.[87]

In other words, the Pentagon would consider supporting a whitewash of one atrocity that occurred a few decades ago, if such a script were to emerge. The idea of representing military campaigns in Indochina that made the death toll of My Lai 'look trifling by comparison', as *Newsweek* reported in 1972, are presumably unthinkable.[88]

To clarify, just because a film might be a conscious or unconscious endorsement of US power does not mean it is *only* that. So, for instance, *Independence Day* (1996) is still about aliens from outer space; *United 93* (2003) and *World Trade Center* (2006) are still about real heroism; *Team America: World Police* (2004) is still a parody of *Thunderbirds*. But just because these might be their most salient, memorable, or enjoyable characteristics does not mean we should ignore it when the same films endorse the actions of the superpower.

The way that occasional films frame political events is less important than the general trends. Does it really matter that, say, *GI Joe* is consistent with government mythology about the Armed Forces? Not particularly, in isolation. But we should see Hollywood's *de facto* purging of critical content right across the board as a result of a range of very disturbing factors. It is up to us to decide whether and to what extent these should be resisted.

Part II

Power Projected

'If everything isn't black and white, I say "why the hell not?"'
John Wayne

'Art is not a mirror held up to reality, but a hammer with which to shape it.'
Bertolt Brecht

3
WAR

The typical War Film draws in the audience by following the journey of a small group of soldiers; it therefore has an built-in tendency to sympathise with the troops and, by extension, the status quo, hence the likes of the Pentagon-backed products *Black Hawk Down* (2001) and *Behind Enemy Lines* (2001). However, the genre still leaves open the possibility for narratives that challenge US benevolence: *Apocalypse Now* (1979) established the insanity and brutality of US involvement in Vietnam, for example, famously juxtaposing an American helicopter assault on a poorly defended Vietnamese rural village to Wagnerian musical accompaniment; *Full Metal Jacket* (1987) showed how ordinary men were dehumanised by the US military training system and then let loose in Vietnam, while *Casualties of War* (1989) showed in detail and with some consideration the suffering of a Vietnamese victim at the hands of US soldiers.

Remarkably, since the late 1970s and 1980s, when some space had opened up in Hollywood to criticise the Vietnam War, the debate over the conflict has shut down again. The Pentagon-backed *We Were Soldiers* (2002) re-enacted the US's first major engagement in Vietnam, in 1965, which makes great play of Mel Gibson's Lt.-Col. Hal Moore's honourable insistence that his feet – not those of the men he leads – will be the last off the battlefield. In *Rescue Dawn* (2006), Christian Bale's US pilot crashes in Laos and escapes from a prison camp. Strikingly, the film assumes the US is doing the right thing in bombing Laos, while only tacitly acknowledging that this was a secret war, and paying no heed to the fact that this was a serious, illegal escalation with a deadly legacy.[1] Decades on, the catastrophic war in Indochina is still being thoughtlessly utilised as a convenient backdrop for Hollywood dramatisations.

Over the past twenty years, however, it has been films about the Second World War that have dominated the genre and have provided particularly self-congratulatory endorsements of the benevolence of US power. Pentagon-backed films like *Pearl Harbor* (2001) (made with the connivance of Secretary of Defense William Cohen),[2] *Hart's*

War (2002) and *The Great Raid* (2005) emphasise the merits of the 'good war', which is typically characterised as entirely the product of the US's legitimate desire to end the genocidal doctrine of fascism. Hollywood even rubbed out real-world British successes – leaving Americans to crack the Nazi's Enigma Code without assistance (*U-571* (2000)), land alone at Normandy (*Saving Private Ryan* (1993)) and – in an earlier era – organise a celebrated escape from Stalag Luft III POW camp (*The Great Escape* (1963)).

Few would disagree that in reality the Allied campaign in the Second World War was overall the right thing to do. Nevertheless, we should not hide from the morally ambiguous motives and tactics of our governments (targeting civilians, the use of nuclear weapons, the cynical approach to the Soviet Union, and so on); even the notoriously calculating former Defense Secretary Robert McNamara was able to shed a tear about his part in firebombing Tokyo. However, while some have learned lessons from the past about the nature of state behaviour, these are assiduously ignored by Hollywood.

WINDTALKERS

The Nicolas Cage vehicle, *Windtalkers* (2002), is set in 1943 and centres on the real-life story of the US Marine Corps' relationship with a group of Navajo Indian recruits in the battle of Saipan against imperial Japan. In the movie, Sgt. Joe Enders (Nicolas Cage) is a decorated Marine haunted by his decision to hold ground in a gunfight, leading to the deaths of his entire company. The Marine Corps assign him and Sgt. Pete 'Ox' Anderson (Christian Slater) the task of protecting a crucial code, which is based on the little-known language of the Navajo Indians. Enders is responsible for Private Ben Yahzee (Adam Beach) and, in the heat of battle, must decide whether he should follow orders and execute Ben to prevent his capture by the Japanese.

Initially, *Windtalkers* suggests that the US military may not be blandly heroic: Enders' first appearance shows him as a hapless leader – a tool of the US government, who insists that his men continue to hold suicidal positions. He then appears as Ben's emotionally stunted protector, unwilling to engage in the mission and more keen just to 'kill Japs'. Private Chick (Noah Emmerich) expresses racist hostility to Ben. Major Mellitz (Jason Isaacs) clearly values the protection of the code over and above the well-being of the Navajo personnel.

And yet all of these aspects of US power are redeemed and their controversial actions ameliorated. We are invited to gain an increased respect for Enders as he comes to realise the moral importance of his engagement and we learn to understand that his angst comes from his taking on a glut of responsibility for the deaths of his men. Because he emerges from an America that is becoming increasingly enlightened through its experiences in the Second World War, Enders is too sensitive and decent to use the Nazi's famous excuse – trotted out simplistically by Ben but rejected by Enders – that he was 'only following orders'.

Enders' brave use of force, even when reckless, is effective in producing positive outcomes. By the finale, Enders is heroically unafraid to die and enters some kind of transcendental mindset, which raises him morally over all others and gives him quasi-messianic powers. Although Ben asks to be executed to protect the code, Enders refuses and – through sheer willpower ('no one else is gonna die') – he sacrifices himself to save the Navajo, giving US warplanes enough time to annihilate the Japanese positions and for him to regain his Catholic faith. The film concludes with Ben further sanctifying Joe Enders in a glorified tale of heroism to his son, named George Washington, completing his canonisation even amongst the Navajo.

The rough edges of Chick's character are also softened: his aggression towards Ben is limited and his racism is the exception rather than the rule in the military, in stark contrast to historical accounts.[3] Chick soon comes to the realisation that the Navajo are a key part of the war effort and he even begins to fulfil a comic function towards the end of the film. His spiritual salvation seems assured and, as such, he represents the fight for a more equitable world that the US's efforts in the Second World War were supposedly all about.

The film protects the reputation of the Marine Corps leadership even more jealously. In fact, the Pentagon – which the credits thank for its 'crucial assistance' – negotiated for weeks with the producers to ensure that the film did not explicitly say that the Marine command ordered its men to kill the Navajo if captured, even though this is an historical fact established by Congress.[4] The result is that Mellitz appears as a hard-nosed leader making tough and morally appropriate decisions and yet is simultaneously so sensitive that he cannot bring himself to say 'If it comes to it, Enders, you're going to have to take your guy out', as the original script had stated before the Pentagon put a pen through it.[5]

Two further sequences were removed from the original script following Department of Defense pressure; in the first, a Marine stabs a dead Japanese soldier in the mouth to retrieve a gold filling. 'The activity is unMarine,' said the Department of Defense, insisting on its removal and trying to pin the blame for such activities on conscripts, even though the National Archive has footage of a Marine yanking teeth from the jaw of a dead Japanese soldier.[6] Secondly, the original script has Enders kill an injured Japanese soldier who is attempting to surrender by blasting him with a flame-thrower. The Department of Defense complained; the scene was eliminated.[7] Another scene, where a Marine is brutally shot in the back by Japanese while he is handing out chocolates to children, is left in for our viewing pleasure.

Windtalkers has a certain novelty value because the Navajo as well as the white Americans are sympathetic characters. Even so, the film still focuses almost exclusively on the suffering of the military white contingent, especially Enders, whose angst-ridden journey dominates the film. Enders must relive his worst nightmare when Private Charlie Whitehorse (Roger Willie) is captured and Enders is obliged to kill him to protect the code. At other points a soldier runs onto the battlefield to save his friend who has just had his legs blown off ('I got you Mac!'); white Marines discuss in clichéd terms what should happen to their wedding rings if they die; Christian Slater's character is graphically beheaded while defending his Navajo charge. And so, although the Navajo are supposedly the subject of the film (even the title suggesting this is the case), much more time is spent on the suffering and heroism of the Marine Corps.

Racist terms are casually applied to the Japanese without comment or redress and these are sometimes linked with expressions of violence (as in the phrase 'touchdown' against the 'Nipponese'). Far from being what the *Financial Times* described as a 'coruscating vision of why wars are fought and perhaps why and how they should be fought',[8] *Windtalkers* in fact suggests that US force is morally justified because contemporary America and its military are informed by deeply entrenched values of democracy and multiculturalism.

Ultimately, it is the Navajo who comes to love and respect the white man, specifically the Marine Corps (with its consciously moronic slogan, expressed within the film, 'ours is not to question why, ours is but to do or die'), even though Enders' supposed benevolence consisted of little more than a brief burst of protective behaviour in amongst his more typically casual contempt for Navajo practices, which he twice calls 'horseshit'. In turn, the white man gains respect from the Navajo not through challenging the legitimacy of the Marine Corps, but rather by enforcing its will through violence.

THE THIN RED LINE

An exception to the straightforward endorsement of US power was Terence Malick's *The Thin Red Line* (1998), which was denied cooperation from the Pentagon due to its depictions of cowardly soldiers, callous leaders and alcohol abuse on the battlefield.[9]

The Thin Red Line is set in 1943, where the first major US offensive of the Second World War is drawing to a close on the South Pacific island of Guadalcanal; the film is a remake of *The Thin Red Line* (1964), which was in turn based on the 1962 book by James Jones. The exploits of a division are seen from several soldiers' perspectives: the war-weary First Sgt. Edward Welsh (Sean Penn); the power-hungry Lt.-Col. Gordon Tall (Nick Nolte), and the fatherly Captain James Staros (Elias Koteas). As in the book, the film shows that all individuals, including those in power, fight separate wars, dependent on their own idiosyncratic neuroses. A particular focus of the film is on Lt.-Col. Tall who, having been passed over for promotion and never having had the opportunity to fight a war until late middle age, tries to assert his authority in morally ambiguous ways. Faced with opposition from Staros, Tall temporarily relents but ensures Staros is shipped home to Washington with a fake case of malaria, leaving a hapless new colonel in charge.

The Thin Red Line creates ambiguity about the legitimacy of the struggle, though without actually interrogating it. At one point, under fire, Welsh screams in rage that the war is about 'property', but neither he nor the film expands upon this allusion to the importance of great power interests. Even Marxist critics of US policy in the Second World War do not usually refer to property itself as a motivation for the US's actions and Welsh's remark is therefore rendered as an isolated cry from a cynical character rather than a more profound insight into the workings of power systems. The civilian government is not depicted at all and the highest authority is a group of generals shown at the outset of the film, explaining the key strategic importance of Guadalcanal Island to the war effort. With the struggle against fascism virtually morally unassailable, particularly in contemporary movies, it is easy to read the scene as a justification for the US attack.

In *American History and Contemporary Hollywood Film* (2005) – one of just a few books that analyse in detail modern representations of US power on film – Trevor McCrisken and Andrew Pepper point to other elements which they see as important in disrupting the official narrative of *The Thin Red Line*. They argue that the film shows that 'no one seems immune' from the random, unforgiving nature of warfare,[10] essentially endorsing the bleak viewpoint that one man cannot make any difference in such a huge war.[11] They observe that the film admits in conclusion (through a character, Captain Bosche, played by George Clooney) that 'the war's not going to be over for a long time', implying that a propensity for war is central to US foreign policy.[12]

In truth, though, McCrisken and Pepper's points are rather tangential and have little bearing on the film's approach to US power. The random nature of victimhood is limited to the American soldiers only, therefore emphasising the tragedy of their involvement in the conflict. McCrisken and Pepper's analysis of Clooney's comment would be more persuasive if the film made any further reference to US foreign policy beyond 1943. As it stands, the more obvious reading is that Clooney is making the banal observation that this particular struggle against fascism will continue – as of course it did until 1945. McCrisken and Pepper point out that such elements open up space for audiences to consider philosophically the random nature of combat from a range of American viewpoints, but if it is true that the film encourages broader musings on the nature of US foreign policy than the other Second World War films in recent years, it is not providing much useful information for that debate.[13]

Virtually the entirety of *The Thin Red Line* depicts the tragic, graphic suffering of American troops, while they kill Japanese people from a distance, barely able to see their faces. One extended scene shows American soldiers being killed from the perspective of a Japanese machine-gun. The US military are prepared to kill as well, but the film does not depict the US creating any unnecessary or civilian deaths. When the US takes the hill, we see the Japanese close up for the first time, but they are unsympathetic victims who continue their insane efforts to fight their American captors.

Ultimately, *The Thin Red Line* does not emphasise the importance of American values in the generation of policy, as other War Films typically do, nor does it actively challenge and interrogate the key assumption of US benevolence. McCrisken and Pepper end up fluently articulating the film's ideological bent, saying that it 'never develops a coherent critique of the economic imperative underscoring American dominance … [and] for all its ruminations on the meaning and effects of war [it] does little to directly challenge or undermine the myth of the Good War.'[14]

In many ways, then, *The Thin Red Line* does not depart from the premises of the archetypal War Film. Like *Saving Private Ryan* (1998) and many others, war is shown to be a great burden on the souls of men, but action is seen purely through American eyes and the enemies are the usual disposable brutes. US forces in *Saving Private Ryan* are sent into battle for an ambiguous cause – that of rescuing a missing soldier to spare the feelings of his mother who has lost her other sons. *Saving Private Ryan* answers the ambiguity of the mission by having present-day Ryan in tears by the graves of the fallen, asking his family if he has led a good life, as Tom Hanks's Captain Miller implored him to 'earn it [his rescue]'. Such a scene would not fit so well in Malick's darker aesthetic, but the sentiment is still there: the Second World War was a terrible experience for the greatest generation of Americans and so it is up to its beneficiaries to ensure that their sacrifice perpetuates the noble ideals for which they ultimately fought.

FLAGS OF OUR FATHERS

Two other films, Clint Eastwood's *Letters From Iwo Jima* (2006) and the Marine-assisted *Flags of Our Fathers* (2006), made similar steps towards generating a different, sombre perspective on the conflict.[15] *Flags of Our Fathers* observed that the US actually used troop successes for propaganda, even if these successes were fabricated and the men involved did not feel like heroes. *Letters from Iwo Jima* remarkably came from the perspective of ordinary Japanese soldiers on the ground in the same battle in the Pacific. The iconic moment from the first film, where the flag is raised, is rendered in *Letters from Iwo Jima* as merely a speck on the horizon.

Taken together, this series is at least respectful of foreigners and shows some appreciation of the state's tendency to distort reality through the media. Again, however, there is no mention of America's own atrocities in the war.

BLACK HAWK DOWN

In movie representations of the modern battlefield, we see the same pattern, sometimes with even less mitigation. *Black Hawk Down* (2001) acts as a warning about the perils of US military intervention in a new security environment by recreating the 3–4 October 1993 US raid on Mogadishu ('the Mog') in Somalia, which resulted in the deaths of 19 US troops and nearly a hundred injuries, as well as perhaps around a thousand Somali casualties. The film was promoted as a faithful recreation of the battle, with director Ridley Scott emphasising that he thinks 'every war movie is an antiwar movie'.[16] It was based on a book by journalist Mark Bowden, who was – prior to working on the film, at least – quite critical of the behaviour of the US military in Operation Restore Hope. Despite these apparently radical indications, *Black Hawk Down* received considerable Pentagon assistance, including eight helicopters and a hundred soldiers.[17]

Amongst the Pentagon brass at the film's Washington premiere were such luminaries as Oliver North, Donald Rumsfeld, Paul Wolfowitz and Dick Cheney.[18] As a quid pro quo, the producers made various amendments, including changing the name of one of the characters, Ranger Specialist John Stebbins, because in real life he had been sentenced to 30 years in jail for raping and sodomising his six-year-old daughter.[19]

In the film, US Special Forces capture a suspected Somali arms dealer Osman Ali Atto, a close associate of the powerful warlord General Muhammad Farrah Aidid. Under pressure from Washington to achieve clearly identifiable results, the military then decides to make an audacious attempt to capture two other close associates of Atto at the Olympic Hotel in Bakara Market. In barracks, the US Task Force Ranger and Delta Force soldiers discuss and prepare for their mission, with attention particularly focused on the Ranger's new leader Sergeant Eversmann (Josh Hartnet), who expresses a moral belief in US involvement in Somalia. During the assault, Somali forces shoot down two Black Hawk helicopters and a brutal firefight ensues on the ground until the following morning; the conflict is remotely led and overseen from headquarters by Major General William F. Garrison (Sam Shepard). The camera follows numerous American soldiers into the battle, watching some of them die; CWO Michael Durant (Ron Eldard) is captured and interrogated by Abdullah 'Firimbi' Hassam (Treva Etienne), and some soldiers escape to a Pakistani-run UN safe-zone. Eversmann reflects on his experiences, drawing on the wisdom of a brave Delta Force veteran, Sfc. Norm 'Hoot' Hootle (Eric Bana).

Black Hawk Down implies the mission is a tactical mistake on the part of Washington, but there is little indication that the authorities' motivations emerge from, or are even consistent with, private interests. Written captions at the start of the film establish that the US government sent the military to Somalia to stop the indigenous people from killing each other – and from starting to kill international forces – leading the 'response' from the 'world'. We are told that 'behind a force of 20,000 US Marines, food is delivered and order is restored [in Somalia]' and that US policy is to oppose a 'warlord' who is using 'hunger' as a 'weapon' against his own people. The official narrative was further elucidated in the film's companion documentary, *Good Intentions, Deadly Results*, which explicitly states that 'the most ambitious humanitarian mission in modern history' unfortunately 'ended in bullets, missiles and death', and that the moral of the story is that 'no good deed goes unpunished'.

This narrative was in marked contrast to that of African Rights' co-director Alex de Waal, for instance, who pointed out that when the US troops arrived in Somalia the fighting had ended in all but one province in the south, and that according to the Red Cross and American Friends Service Committee, 80–90 per cent of the aid was getting through.[20] This raises the possibility that the war had other or additional unmentionable motivations, such as to stimulate US arms sales,[21] distract public attention from the US's inability and/or unwillingness to solve the Balkans crisis with a PR coup,[22] acquire oil resources,[23] or even because UN Secretary General Boutros Boutros-Ghali harboured a longer-term rivalry with Aidid's Habr Gidr clan.[24]

The opening scene suggests that Somali citizens – victims of the Aidid militia – might be positioned to receive considerable sympathy in this film. However, the viewer is not permitted to engage with them. The scene is shot from the distant perspective of the US Black Hawk helicopter, as though the people on the ground are characters in a computer game. The script appropriately describes them in undignified, objectifying terms: 'hordes' of Somalis 'swarm' onto the truck to 'grab' the sacks of grain.[25] And, although they need help, there is no indication that they actually appreciate receiving it.

Military action is largely seen through the eyes of Eversmann and Garrison, who reflect official thinking on the US campaign. Eversmann – the 'everyman' – explains his attitude toward the Somalis: 'I respect them. Look, these people have no jobs, no food, no education, no future. I just figure that, I mean, we have two things we can do. We can either help or we can sit back and watch the country destroy itself on CNN.' Although the other soldiers display much less awareness of the political implications of their mission, they instinctively hold benevolent, interventionist views comparable to those of Eversmann and Garrison. When Eversmann cries, 'Did you see that?' in response to the Aidid-sponsored massacre in the opening minutes of the film, Durant requests to intervene militarily, but he is not permitted due to UN regulations.

Similarly, while Atto indulges in incorrect stereotypes about Americans (for instance, he wrongly assumes that the Texas Garrison is from Arkansas and calls the KO Corral the 'OK Corral'), Garrison is witness to the facts of life in Somalia that speak for themselves so loudly that they are written by the omnipotent narrator at the start of the film. Paradoxically then it is the American general who, after a six-week posting, gives the more credible account of events in Somalia – alleging genocide – even though he happens to be a leading figure in the invading military force. The real-life Atto in fact complained to the BBC about the film's portrayal of his arrest, saying that his colleague Ahmed Ali had suffered injuries to both his legs and that his single car – not an imposing motorcade as the film depicts – was shot at least fifty times by US forces. He also claimed that people died during the attack.[26] On the DVD commentary, Ridley Scott and Jerry Bruckheimer admit that shots were fired at the motorcade and that Atto and his entourage then fled into a building to which the US laid siege, an incident which was omitted from the film.

Although the US causes civilian casualties, this is not its intention. We continually hear warnings about the UN rules of engagement ('You do not fire unless fired upon!'), and the military does not ever abandon these rules, even to the point of absurdity. Furthermore, their own sense of decency prevents them from killing armed and dangerous women and children, at least not without the appropriate expressions of misery and heartache. US Major General Anthony C. Zinni, who directed operations in Somalia, said that women and children constituted two-thirds of the 6,000–10,000 Somali casualties that resulted from clashes with UN peacekeepers or in fights between rival Somali factions during the four months of US intervention in the summer of 1993.[27]

Bowden's book sensitively reflects this concern about US behaviour. He describes Somali characters as having understandable motivations for their resistance and meaningful relationships with their friends and families.[28] Bowden explains that the Somalis had seen six raids, prior to 3 October, where the US troops often killed people indiscriminately.[29] During the first raid, the US accidentally arrested nine UN employees. On 14 September, the US assault force stormed the home of a man who turned out to be a close ally of the UN and was being groomed to lead the projected Somali police force; this led to 38 erroneous arrests.[30] On 19 September, after a bulldozer crew of engineers from the 10th Mountain Division was attacked by a band of Somalis, US troops fired into the crowd that had come to see the shooting, killing nearly a hundred people.[31] Previously, on 12 July, the UN authorised what became known as the 'Abdi House raid' in which the UN tried to take out Aidid's leadership, instead massacring at least fifty Somali leaders drawn from across the political spectrum and thus pushing the country to the extreme.[32] Bowden chronicles events that do not tally with the film's portrayal of American squeamishness about killing[33] and otherwise intimidating women and children,[34] including an incident where 'massive Ranger volley literally tore apart [a Somali woman] ... It was appalling,' says Bowden, 'yet some of the Rangers laughed.'[35]

It is by far and away the American soldiers who receive the most sympathetic treatment in the film of *Black Hawk Down*. They are shown to be under tremendous stress – it is they who are the frustrated victims of the first scene (described above) because they are unable to display their benevolent spirit due to UN rules of engagement. The attractive young recruit Private First Class Todd Blackburn (Orlando Bloom) falls in slow motion from a Black Hawk helicopter to his death. Later, Corporal Jamie Smith is shot and in a graphic and gruelling scene, Sargeant First Class (Sfc) Kurt Scmid (Hugh Dancy) must clamp Smith's femoral artery. Over Smith's bloodcurdling cries of pain, we observe in close-up as the grotesque operation goes horribly wrong and Eversmann must lie to the dying man to mitigate his misery. This scene, where Smith ends up discussing his parents before his death, together with Sfc Randy Shughart's call home, which rings off just as his wife picks up the receiver, also helps to connect the violence that the US military is enduring in Africa with the suffering of families.

Although Operation Restore Hope was in reality an all-American operation, the film's cast is varied in nationality – McGregor is Scottish; Bana is Australian; Isaacs is English – which subtly renders the struggle a multilateral one. By this reading, the film is not just a US military disaster but a tragedy for Western civilisation itself. By the end, the idealistic Eversmann has become influenced by Hoot's attitude, that no one 'back home' understands the motivations of military men, which are based around camaraderie only, political values being unimportant in battle. Eversmann's transformation, then, further elevates the military above both the enemy and even Western civilians. The soldiers' rather less edifying attributes, such as parading around naked, using blow-up plastic sex dolls and masturbating in a parachute – as depicted in the book[36] – are conveniently excised for the silver screen. More traditional pastimes are depicted. Similarly, at the Pentagon's direct request, the film-makers toned down its depiction of the military hunting a wild boar by helicopter, though it had been filmed[37] and discussed in the book.[38]

Black Hawk Down provides a depiction of American suffering and innocence that is extreme even by Hollywood standards, juxtaposed with an evil or otherwise worthless enemy population. Film historian Lawrence Suid argues that the film is 'by no stretch of the imagination ... an argument to get back into Somalia ... if anything, it's the exact opposite!'[39] Suid's point is right in a narrow sense, namely that the film shows some of the dangers of US intervention for Americans. Still, *Black Hawk Down* implies that the US military can literally do no wrong and that where the US does choose to fight it must win at all costs, or else risk giving succour to the enemies of civilisation. Suid's further comment, that the film shows 'for our efforts, we were slaughtered',[40] again points to the inability of certain commentators to recognise what were, at best, serious moral ambiguities over US intervention. Closing captions inform us that the US withdrew from Somalia after the battle and, watching it in the immediate post-9/11 world, it is hard to avoid the reading that such a 'cut and run' approach led to blowback against America.[41]

The film-makers, including Bowden, often emphasised how *Black Hawk Down* was not a political film.[42] Such a claim is especially hard to take seriously from Bowden, since his own book presented a much more nuanced picture of the situation in Somalia. Indeed, Bowden reveals that the US threatened Somalia with an enormous, dramatic attack, in the event that Durant not be released unharmed by his captors. He quotes US Ambassador to Somalia Robert Oakley as sending a message to Aidid, that 'Once the fighting starts again, all this pent up anger is going to be released. This whole part of the city will be destroyed, men, women, children, camels, cats, dogs, goats, donkeys, everything ... That really would be tragic for all of us, but that's what will happen.'[43] Another lesson to be drawn from Bowden's book – though not his film – surely is about the capacity for ferocious violence by powerful nations when situations spiral out of their control, including during 'humanitarian' missions.

TEARS OF THE SUN

The Pentagon-backed *Tears of the Sun* took a similar line. While simultaneously claiming that the Navy SEALs are 'anonymous heroes'[44] and 'Little America protecting Big America',[45] its director Antoine Fuqua repeatedly protested that he did not think his film was pro-war.[46] Certainly, the film's sympathies leaned that way, as would have been rather more obvious had Fuqua run with any of its less poetic working titles: *Man of War*, *Hostile Act*, or *Hostile Rescue*.[47]

In the film, the US sends a unit of Navy SEALs led by Lt. A.K. Waters (Bruce Willis) to Nigeria to extract a US citizen, Dr Lena Fiore Hendricks (Monica Bellucci), who works in a Christian mission. Nigeria is undergoing civil unrest and Islamic Fulani troops are ethnically cleansing the Christian Igbo and killing any foreigners who get in the way. Kendricks refuses to leave without her patients, so Waters tricks her onto the helicopter. On their way out, they see the mission destroyed below and Waters makes the decision to turn around and help them all. Waters discovers that one of the Nigerians in the group, Arthur Azuka (Sammi Rotibi), is the sole survivor of the country's previous ruling family, hence making the group a high-value target. With Islamic troops in pursuit, Waters tries to obtain official help from his superior, Captain Bill Rhodes (Tom Skerritt) but he refuses to sanction US involvement in a civil war. Waters gives his men the choice of staying or leaving and they decide to stay. At the climax of the film, Waters reaches the Cameroonian border having incurred some losses and US jets destroy the enemy with napalm.

Initially, *Tears of the Sun* shows US military authorities as un-heroic, implying that they are not necessarily informed by values and principles. Waters' first appearance, emerging from a helicopter on a battleship, is notable for its lack of heroic signifiers. The music is downbeat, haunting, uninspiring. Waters then appears as a hostile presence in Africa, emerging without warning behind a missionary and clasping his hand around her mouth. Even when Kendricks spits in his face, his demeanour remains unchanged, implacable and resolute.

However, Waters' unit comes to realise the moral importance of their engagement as Waters becomes increasingly uncomfortable with his assigned role, which seems to be pushing him towards a nervous breakdown. This is symbolised by the Seals' facial transformations, from heavy black camouflage at the start to undisguised faces at the end, exposing their individuality as the mission proceeds. Although there is one rhetorically dissenting voice (Kelly Lake), the Seals decide to work together for the goal of the majority. Ellis 'Zee' Pettigrew (Eammon Walker) begins by warning Waters that he is deviating from his orders but Waters' actions inspire Zee to equate the struggle for black rights in the US with the struggle for black rights in Africa.

This new imperialism, *Tears of the Sun* implies, is morally justified because contemporary America and its military are informed by deeply entrenched values of democracy and multiculturalism.

For the vast majority of the film, the Fulani appear as a feeble and exposed childlike mass, incapable of governing themselves. They sing together seemingly in happy ignorance (despite being hunted by indigenous forces), while the Americans lead them quietly, seriously. During the jungle trek, the Fulani are weak and wounded, inexplicably carrying a carpet, as though incapable of leaving behind their simple comforts. (Meanwhile, the non-indigenous white female Kendricks remains alert and pristine even as she carries a toddler.) One woman gives an old herbal remedy to Zee and tells him a brief story of her victimhood. There is little else by way of back-story for any of the indigenous personnel. Only once does a Nigerian actually do anything actively to help – a few seconds of camera time is devoted to an unnamed Nigerian man shooting a machete-wielding Fulani who is attacking Waters. Their dialogue is decidedly limited, despite their ability to speak English. They remain totally dependent on the US and after the battle they gush praise and thanks to Waters despite his previous betrayal.

Ultimately, *Tears of the Sun* excuses initial US failures to help foreign victims by demonstrating the inherent difficulties and dangers of intervening militarily in a foreign country. However, this apparent need to curb the application of benevolent force is shown to be deeply upsetting to US authorities, especially to those military figures closest to it. The film indicates that by intervening militarily the US will suffer losses but will benefit spiritually by living up to its inherently good values. As in *Windtalkers* (2002), by the end of the film this intervention is associated with the Almighty Himself, which builds on earlier religious references: the mission, the murder of the priest, and the 'spiritual' score. Awe-inspiring jet-fighters soar into battle, accompanied by rising music and religious chanting. Kendricks literally breathes 'Oh God', as though having a religious experience and, at the flick of a switch, they engulf the enemy below in a sea of hellish fire. At the climax, having emerged triumphant from the battle, Waters finally gives the jaunty *Die Hard* (1988) smile – all busted up, face streaming blood – as a Nigerian women sings his praises. He is relaxed, assured, his spirit purged. He has found the role for which he, and by extension the US, were made: applying righteous force.

Fuqua explains that he was prompted to make the movie by two documentaries: *Cry Freetown* about Sierra Leone, and *Delta Force* about Nigeria. In these films, as he describes it, 'Shell Oil Company [is] running pipelines through villages like what you saw in the film, and when people would complain, the police would show up and they would cut the hands of people [*sic*].'[48] The villages appeared in *Tears of the Sun*, but despite his apparent social conscience, Fuqua omitted any mention of Western oil corporations. Ironically, Fuqua quotes Edmund Burke in the film's closing caption – 'the only thing necessary for the triumph of evil is for good men to do nothing'[49] – and, on set, he kept a copy of a book depicting harrowing images from Rwanda. The book was called *The Silence.*[50]

BEHIND ENEMY LINES

The Political Film Society nominated *Behind Enemy Lines* (2001) in its Exposé category but actually the film obfuscates the historical events on which it was loosely based, namely, the downing of US Air Force Captain Scott O'Grady over Bosnia in 1995. The film received full Department of Defense cooperation and the film-makers admitted to resultant script changes, commenting 'they don't want you to embarrass the military if you're going to use their stuff'.[51]

In the film, Lt. Chris Burnett (Owen Wilson) is a Navy pilot on the USS *Carl Vincent*, which is deployed in the Adriatic Sea and conducting aerial patrols over Bosnia. Burnett is cynical about his role in what he feels is – for the US – a meaningless war, and so hands in his resignation to his Commanding Officer Admiral Leslie Reigart (Gene Hackman). In one of his final flights over the supposedly demilitarised zone, Burnett diverts from his flight plan to take some photographs. Concerned that the Americans might discover they're hiding mass graves in the area, the Serb Army, led by Miroslav Lokar (Olek Krupa), shoots down Burnett's plane. Lokar then orders his brutal assassin, Sasha (Vladimir Mashkov) to execute Burnett's co-pilot Stackhouse (Gabriel Macht) and pursue Burnett through Bosnia. Burnett calls for an airlift but NATO Commander Admiral Juan Miguel Piquet (Joaquim de Almeida) prevents Reigart from sending in his troops, citing the fragility of the diplomatic agreement NATO has recently made with the Serbs. Burnett must hike several miles to a safe-zone and, during this journey, he is embroiled in the ethnic conflict in areas that *should* be safe-zones. Burnett arrives with a Bosnian Muslim companion, Babic (Kamil Kollarik) at the safe-zone, but NATO has abandoned its rescue mission, believing Serb lies that Burnett is dead. Burnett decides to recover the photographs of illegal Serb fortifications from the crash site so that Stackhouse's life will not have been lost in vain, and Reigart decides to lead an exclusively American rescue mission without Piquet's approval. US helicopter gunships kill Burnett's Serb pursuers as he scrambles under fire to acquire the photographs before being winched to safety. Burnett asks Reigart to return his letter of resignation, Reigart retires honourably, and Burnett's data leads to Lokar's arrest.

Sky News's real-life presenter Aeronaut Van Lynden fills the role of the film's narrator, informing us at the start that the US has established a ceasefire that 'appear[s] to be holding'. Later, Van Lynden clarifies that the NATO mission has been an 'ultimately unsuccessful chapter in the [NATO] alliance's history'. Van Lynden therefore assumes benevolent intent on the part of the US and that the chaos in Bosnia is contributory evidence that the US has been politically unable to impose its good will.

When Piquet criticises Reigart's decision to leak Burnett's status to the media, the film appears to challenge Reigart's and America's moral righteousness, as Piquet points out that a risky mission to save one pilot could shatter the entire peace agreement. On the DVD commentary, director John Moore comments that Piquet 'wins' the scene, as Reigart throws his papers across the room in frustration.

However, both Reigart and the film itself seem to forget the scene ever happened and it is exclusively US force which ultimately secures justice. Piquet becomes the villain: not only does he smear the American national character but also repeatedly orders Reigart not to rescue Burnett. Instead, Piquet orders his own belated mission, which he abandons because the Serbs falsely report Burnett's death at the hands of Bosnian Muslim renegades. Piquet does not interrogate the veracity of the Serb claims with the same level of suspicion as he questions Serb reports of Stackhouse's death. The film also establishes the injustice of Piquet's stereotyping by tracing the moral conversion of its hero, Burnett, who embraces the new principles he has learnt in the heat of battle and makes a daredevil dash under heavy fire to grab the digital photographs that will condemn the Serbs.[52] The disagreement between Burnett and Reigart is less about the need to apply US power than it is about how to deal tactically with the power structures that limit US power in the Balkans, with Burnett exuding the youthful energy and impulsiveness that dismisses the NATO authorities. They come together over more fundamental principles, notably the value of American servicemen and the importance of using American force for humanitarian reasons, regardless of international constraints.

The US places a high premium on human life. All the Americans – but not Piquet, who is an unspecified European – feel the loss of Burnett acutely. However, through Burnett, the US also learns the value of saving the lives of their Bosnian Muslim allies. When Burnett arrives in Hac, Bosnian Muslims are furious that the US has abandoned them to the Serb military. Their implication is that the US government has other interests at heart than the fate of Bosnian Muslims. As it transpires, though, the audience sees that it is the rest of the world – that is, the Europeans and international organisations – who are unwilling to back up their agreements with force. The US is unfairly left to take the blame from the victims on the ground because it is unable to apply its benevolent force due to the constraints imposed by its allies and the fierce resistance of their enemies on the ground. As Madeleine Albright famously put it to Colin Powell, 'What's the point of having this superb military that you're always talking about if we can't use it?'[53]

In reality, Captain Scott O'Grady had been blown a considerable distance from the crash site, where he concealed himself in the forest. Admiral Leighton Smith, chief of the US forces in Europe, immediately told the NATO liaison officer to inform the UNPROFOR commander General Janvier in Zagreb that 'We've had an F-16 shot down, I'm coming to get him. When I find him, I'm going to pick him up. Don't anybody get in my way because if you do, I will kill you.' The same message was delivered to the Serbs, with the addition 'I'm not kidding and I'm not asking permission.'[54] Though he had members of his own forces held captive by the Bosnian Serbs at the time, the chief of UN General Bernard Janvier was 'completely cooperative' on the process of agreeing to a combat rescue mission and put pressure on Bosnian Serb Army Chief of Staff Ratko Mladic to return the pilot alive.[55] NATO established radio contact with O'Grady, determined that he was alive and not in captivity. Smith sent a rescue force consisting of no less than forty aircraft and sixty US marines aboard the US *Kearsarge* in the Adriatic. At the last minute, the operation was technically re-designated as a NATO and not a solely US mission. Since each had different rules of engagement

– NATO missions do not permit 'pre-emptive fire' – this caused some confusion but Smith made his philosophy clear: 'If you even think somebody's going to shoot at you, take 'em out.'[56]

The film-makers maintain that *Behind Enemy Lines* was pure fiction but O'Grady, at least, took exception and sued.[57] Regardless, the film was a peculiar rendering of the US role in the Balkans, as throughout the 1990s it had been characterised by the relative invulnerability of its aircraft and considerably less international constraints than the film suggests. Even during NATO's most intense military campaign – the 79-day mass bombardment of Serbia during the Kosovo campaign in 1999 – losses were extremely low.

After 9/11, 20th Century Fox brought forward the release date of *Behind Enemy Lines*, using a promotional poster featuring Burnett charging forward, furiously firing a pistol against a background of two towers of light surrounded by clouds of smoke. The promise is thus made to the viewer: the superpower will be shown roused and angry – a therapeutic response to the destruction wrought by al-Qaeda's 9/11 attack.

Moore said that working on *Behind Enemy Lines* 'gave us the chance to interact with the guys, the pilots, mechanics and technicians ... I made the movie for them', he says.[58] Them, of course, and their masters at the Department of Defense.

COURAGE UNDER FIRE

The Pentagon refused to provide full support to *Courage Under Fire* (1996), as it was unhappy about the film's cynical portrayal of the military,[59] but the film barely departs from the standard portrayal of the Gulf War as a good war fought against worthless Arabs.

Courage Under Fire begins in Kuwait at the start of Operation Desert Storm. The US advances and, in the chaos of an Iraqi ambush, Lt. Col. Nathaniel Serling (Denzel Washington) orders his tank to fire on another tank which turns out to be American. The military authorities refuse to investigate the incident and assign Serling to a desk job, where he must study the merits of a posthumous Medal of Honor nomination for medevac pilot Captain Karen Emma Walden (Meg Ryan). In flashback, we see several versions of Walden's final hours. It first appears that she made a spectacular rescue of a downed helicopter crew, then held her own crew together to fight off the Iraqis after her helicopter crashed. The US government is pushing for a positive outcome to Serling's review in order to reap the political benefits of having their first female recipient of the award. However, Serling finds some inconsistencies in the soldiers' testimonies, which leads him to question what really happened.

The main suggestions of US motivations for its action in the Gulf are spelled out in the opening few minutes. Over stock news footage of US jets taking off and the Iraqis shooting anti-aircraft fire, we hear President George H.W. Bush enunciate the official reason for the war: 'The 28 countries with forces in the Gulf area have exhausted all reasonable efforts to reach a peaceful resolution … have no choice but to drive Saddam from Kuwait by force.' Cue the image of a camera-mounted laser-guided missile slamming into a building. US force is thereby associated with humanitarian methods and accuracy, even though it has since emerged that the vast majority of US weapons used in the war were not in fact laser-guided.[60] We then cut to unchallenged images of chanting Iraqis with guns and fade into an image of Saddam Hussein, accompanied by a sinister downturn in the musical score. Whilst Bush aims for the rational 'liberation of Kuwait', we hear Saddam offer the apocalyptic promise of 'the mother of all battles'.

Iraqis are all faceless enemy combatants. The allies are nowhere to be seen, even though it was the British who sustained the largest 'friendly fire' toll during Desert Storm.[61] The Americans are the innocent victims. The Iraqis fire first on the US soldiers, ambushing them as they advance. In response, US soldiers do return fire on Iraqis but enact a swift cease-fire, after which they take large numbers of prisoners alive despite the real-life reports of 'turkey shoots' against retreating Iraqi soldiers and civilians.[62] Later, another Iraqi creeps up on Walden's unit, causing the confusion that results in Walden's shooting – again excusing American action due to the hostility of the Other. Much of this positive impression of US forces comes from the centrality of Denzel Washington, a black man known for playing sympathetic roles, who here exudes a sense of responsibility, from his guilt over the death of his friend to the fact that he speaks perfect Arabic when ordering the Iraqis to surrender. One US soldier, recounting his story, checks himself guiltily when he calls the Iraqis 'fuckers'. Serling smirks at the inappropriate tone, as if it was unusual, but ultimately signals his approval of the term ('You were right the first time'). The benevolence Serling demonstrates throughout the film is therefore rendered an ingrained American trait or habit, but that does not mean we should infer that the lives of Iraqi victims have any intrinsic worth. Indeed, Washington begins his battlefield advance with the cry 'Let's kill 'em all, let's eat 'em up.'

American suffering continues after the war is over. One of the soldiers runs away and turns to heroin, another commits suicide. Serling himself temporarily loses his family and his alcoholism spirals out of control. There is little indication of the information, provided in *Three Kings* for example, that Iraqi troops were sometimes buried alive in their trenches by US tanks.[63] In fact, the tank battle is shown to be quite evenly matched, resulting in the orderly capture of prisoners of war, with the chaos of the situation only having a shockingly negative impact upon Americans, not Iraqis (who sneakily 'ambushed' the Americans).

To conclude, *Courage Under Fire* presents America as the unique significant victim of the Persian Gulf War. The film does criticise government manipulation of the war for public relations – ultimately suggesting that honesty is the best policy – but this is not the same as interrogating the mythical benevolence of US power. The heroes of the film are American military men who are comfortable with their role in the war, aside from specific unsound judgements that led to American deaths. Walden herself is awarded the Medal of Honor posthumously for being a truly militaristic hero, living up to the Marine's credo 'leave no man behind'. In all this, US motivations for deploying force are reduced to the simplistic value-laden idea that the US was opposing Iraqi aggression and depletes the malign effects of that deployment to a few friendly-fire victims, ignoring the wider massacre of tens of thousands of Iraqi soldiers and civilians.

JARHEAD

Jarhead (2005) is an adaptation of the autobiography of US Marine and Gulf War veteran Anthony 'Swoff' Swofford (Jake Gyllenhaal), a 'jarhead' (slang for Marine) Gulf War veteran. The film follows Swoff's journey, starting from brutal Marine Corps boot camp and Camp Pendleton. Staff Sergeant Sykes (Jamie Foxx) invites Swoff to his sniper course. Iraq then invades Kuwait and Swoff's unit is sent to the Gulf in 1990. The film follows his sexually and professionally frustrating experiences and those of his colleagues, and takes in a march through the grim geography of the conflict. Swoff and Troy are finally given a combat mission, but another team of Marines appears and calls in an air-strike, causing Troy to break down with despair. Wandering around in a daze, Swoff and Troy discover a Marine victory party and they finally get a chance to fire their weapons – but only in celebration.

Jarhead is another example of a film showing the various miseries of warfare for an invading force, with scant attention paid to foreign victims or the real reasons for the campaign, despite its general air of cynicism. Rather, it concerns the miseries of the Marines who are not permitted to claim their first kill. In this sense, *Jarhead* is akin to *Behind Enemy Lines*, though the former does not resolve this narrative problem with such violence. Director Sam Mendes said, 'This is not about giving myself the opportunity to say, "Sam Mendes thinks George Bush should get out of Iraq." A movie should dredge up something deeper in you than just opinion.'[64] Mendes complained about others on the set promoting the film as apolitical: 'The very act of making this film in this climate *is* political. I'm sort of amazed that people can't see that.'[65]

In *Total Film*, Jamie Graham's insightful review effectively rebuts Mendes' point, explaining that the film should have been 'sharper, smarter, angrier, funnier'. Graham observes that in the book Swoff cheers the chopper attack scene in *Apocalypse Now* and then admits he wants to rape, pillage and burn. In the film, he cheers the scene but 'while the implication is there, the extent of his savagery is muted'.[66] Graham goes on to argue that Mendes was wrong to omit Swoff's commentary while his colleagues simulate sex with another jarhead, Kuehn. 'We aren't field-fucking Kuehn,' writes Swofford (2006), 'we're fucking the press pool Colonel and the sorry, worthless MOPP suits and the goddamn gas masks and canteens with defective parts and President Bush and Dick Cheney and the generals and Saddam Hussein ... ', and so on.[67] 'This should have been *Jarhead*'s defining soliloquy, its "Choose Life" chant', says Graham in a reference to the opening minutes of *Trainspotting* (1995), but instead it is regrettably 'consigned to the wastepaper basket, replaced by the nagging feeling that Hollywood didn't have the balls to be so overtly political given the current climate'.[68]

The 'current climate' was surely a factor in Mendes' tame rendering, though it should be added that such remoulding comes as standard when politicised narratives pass through Hollywood's machinery.

BODY OF LIES

When Ridley Scott released *Body of Lies* (2008), Iraq and the Middle East were yet again fetishised as a land of violence, deception and torture, in contrast to the US, which is characterised as being 'incapable of secrecy because [it is] a democracy'. The film is not about the legitimacy of US actions, which are taken as read, but rather about how we can make better use of foreigners to implement the War on Terror more effectively – 'what we need to learn to get it right', as the film's writer David Ignatieff puts it (DVD commentary).

Similar assumptions were made in Robert Redford's *Lions for Lambs* (2007), whose liberal flavour briefly made it the *bête noir* for conservative movie critics, even while it ignores the humanitarian situation on the ground in Afghanistan, sympathises with 'heroised' US troops under attack, and suggests they should be aided by more serious American news media and liberal leaders.

CONCLUSION

It is perhaps predictable and appropriate that when making a War Film producers will encourage the audience to identify with American soldiers. More controversially, this has led to the framing of popular perceptions not just of the 'good war' against fascism in the 1940s but also for more recent, more controversial US actions like Somalia and Iraq.

Major studio productions of critical, classic War Films like *Apocalypse Now*, *Full Metal Jacket* and *Casualties of War* have dried up in favour of products like *Tears of the Sun*, *Black Hawk Down* and *Behind Enemy Lines* – all receiving heavy involvement from the Pentagon and all embellishing American suffering by championing the use of US power for what are presented as humanitarian ends. Challenging War Films do exist – as in *Redacted* (2007) and *In the Valley of Elah* (2007) – but typically only by independents at lower budget levels, as we shall see later.

Amongst the major productions, the limits of criticism are revealed in films like *The Thin Red Line*, *Jarhead* and *Courage Under Fire*. All show some dehumanising aspects of war – but for US troops, not their worthless foreign victims.

4
COMEDY

As a genre, comedy has an ambiguous relationship with US power. On the one hand, to maintain a humorous tone, the sympathetic portrayal of actual victims in comedy remains taboo and stereotypes are employed for comic effect, as with the backward Kazakhs in Sacha Baron Cohen's mischievous *Borat* (2006), for instance. Indeed, some of the most radical films from previous eras are quite dismissive of other cultures and victims. For instance, even the celebrated 'antiwar' film *M*A*S*H* (1970) made little comment on the US presence in Korea or its consequences for non-Americans.

On the other hand, satirical comedy is built around societal criticism, epitomised by Stanley Kubrick's classic *Dr Strangelove: Or How I Learned to Stop Worrying and Love the Bomb* (1964), which depicted the apotheosis of a self-destructive and amoral foreign policy apparatus even while employing stereotypes such as drunken Russians.

The film ends with the accidental triggering of a global nuclear war by a tiny US elite, who have been informed by Dr Strangelove that they can flee the conflagration to underground mine-shafts where they will be able to copulate with a selection of highly attractive women in order to repopulate the planet.

There is, in short, tremendous potential for subversion within comedy.

In the contemporary era, however, the conformist tradition has won out, with pictures like *True Lies* (1994) placing the emphasis on US authorities, particularly their militarised forms, as straightforward heroes. Others, such as *Team America: World Police* (2004) endorse US power more obliquely, employing an ironic style to avoid such obvious political bias. Only lower-budget, independent productions have been able to push the ideological boundaries a little further.

TRUE LIES

Jamie Lee Curtis dismissed allegations of racism in the Pentagon-supported *True Lies* by saying 'It's just a funny film. It's funny. It has no ramifications for me. It's funny, funny, just funny',[1] typifying mainstream commentary about the film. In truth, *True Lies* celebrates the application of US power whilst rejecting duplicitous foreign cultures all the way from Egypt to Western Europe. Republican Bob Dole endorsed the film.[2]

In *True Lies*, Harry Tasker (Arnold Schwarzenegger) works for Omega Sector (presumably part of the CIA) and pretends to be a computer salesman. Ignorant of his profession, his bored wife Helen (Jamie Lee Curtis) becomes romantically involved with a car salesman, Simon (Bill Paxton), who masquerades as a spy to attract women. Just at the point Harry is about to reveal all to Helen, Islamist terrorists kidnap them and reveal a plan to destroy several US cities with nuclear weapons.

Harry and his colleague Gib (Tom Arnold) are the heroes who save the world. Omega is an ultramodern, technologically advanced part of the US national security apparatus, presented as 'The Last Line of Defense' in a country surrounded by anti-American bullies. It is led by Spencer Trilby, played by an eyepatch-wearing Charlton Heston, every inch the stalwart warrior who insists upon high standards of intelligence and professionalism.

In contrast, Salim Abu Aziz (Art Malik) is the 'real psycho' leader of a particularly nasty splinter group called Crimson Jihad. Salim's language is unimaginative, rude, and peppered with banal rhetoric, in contrast with the inventive language used by the wisecracking Schwarzenegger and his comedian co-star. Although Crimson Jihad is the principal enemy in the film, it is merely the spearhead of a more wide-ranging Other that threatens to engulf the United States: its missiles are smuggled out of Kazakhstan and imported from 'all over the Middle East', including Iran, Iraq and Syria 'as everybody knows'; the suggestion is that state sponsorship of global terrorists with genocidal intent and multiple, deliverable nuclear-tipped missiles is a plausible scenario, which was not the case when the film was made and remains fantasy well over a decade later.

True Lies also denigrates European culture: the opening scene is set in an old mansion at Lake Chapeau in Switzerland, surrounded by guards with machine-guns and Alsatians. Inside, sophisticated and wealthy Europeans dance to a violin concerto. We can see that this ancient culture, which excludes Americans, is a mask for something more sinister, just as the ancient Egyptian statues are used to conceal and smuggle nuclear weapons.

The principal sympathetic victim of the film is Harry, a husband and father who is upset because he thinks his wife is cheating on him, and who then must try to save his wife, daughter and the world almost single-handedly. Salim's pain, in contrast, is a constant source of slapstick and bathos, as he struggles to impose his backward beliefs on a modern world: when videoing his threat to America, the battery runs out on his camera; when threatening to turn the key in his nuclear weapon, he finds the key is missing. The film ends with Harry bashing Salim's testicles against his DOD-supplied fighter jet and blasting him into a helicopter attached to a missile.

The film also aims its comedy at weak Americans: Simon, in particular, is a complete joke – an ignoble coward and wannabe Lothario pretending to be a heroic spy. In this sense, the film is an 'equal opportunities offender', although viewers might note that ignoble cowards and wannabe Lotharios do not constitute a racial, ethnic, or religious group. Interestingly, when Helen asks Harry if he has ever killed anyone he replies with the impeccably deadpan 'Yeah, but they were all bad', providing a glimpse into what the film abjectly refuses to do elsewhere: consider the sympathetic treatment of anyone outside of the militarised American establishment.

True Lies exalts US violence, showing that it is highly effective in creating a better world and exposing the true face of foreigners. The macho sex fantasy works so well for Harry and Helen that they continue to indulge in it after the terrorists have been defeated: the final scene shows them on a joint mission in a European embassy, similar to the film's first scene but with a curious difference – the Arabs are now conspicuously absent and the Americans are, triumphantly, safe and in full view.

The importance of simplistic and contemptuous depictions of foreigners was indicated by the decision not to make a sequel to *True Lies* after 9/11, despite the script having been already written. As Curtis put it, 'terrorists aren't funny anymore'.[3]

HOT SHOTS!

Reviewers treated the *Hot Shots!* films (1991, 1993) exclusively as genre parodies, akin to *Top Secret* (1984) and *Airplane* (1980), that 'raise[s] stupidity to an absolute science'.[4] The original *Hot Shots!* closely lampooned *Top Gun* (1986) and the sequel concentrated on the *Rambo* series. In *Hot Shots! Part Deux*, the US – represented by CIA operative Michelle Rodham Huddleston (Brenda Bakke) and Colonel Denton Walters (Richard Crenna, reprising his role from the *Rambo* series) – ask retired field operative Topper Harley (Charlie Sheen) to lead a rescue mission into Iraq to rescue the last rescue team, who went in to rescue the last rescue team who ... went in to rescue hostages left behind after Desert Storm. Topper turns them down but when his friend Walters himself is similarly kidnapped – just as in *Rambo II* – Topper joins a US Special Forces unit to complete the mission.

The original *Hot Shots!* does allude to the Machiavellian behaviour of the arms industry in that two American arms dealers attempt to sabotage the Air Force's planes so that the President will use their company instead. On discovering their duplicity, Benson (Lloyd Bridges) punches him in the face and says 'You dare call yourself an American? It's scum like you that put a taint on our military' – which is literally his only line in the film that is not part of a joke. The system works.

Having shown that he is a likeable fool who can swing a fist, Benson reappears in the sequel as the US President, drawing on popular images of Ronald Reagan and George H.W. Bush. Nor does his bumbling incompetence stand in the way of success, as he is still able to target and personally defeat Saddam in a 'light sabre' battle without creating collateral damage, in a way that was duplicated by the idiotic Commander Lassard (George Gaynes), who duels with the Russian mafia kingpin in *Police Academy: Mission to Moscow* (1994).

Iraqi civilians are simply absent, their military men are cannon fodder for our heroes, and Saddam himself is characterised as a prissy, lisping transvestite. By the end of *Part Deux*, Saddam has turned into a half-man, half-dog and is killed by a falling piano as our heroes fly off into the sunset with the rescued hostages. Although the people of the Middle East are supposedly under threat from Saddam in the film, *Hot Shots! Part Deux* focuses exclusively on the victimhood of the American military. Topper is a depressive drop-out whose girlfriend has left him, while Commander Arvid Harbinger (Miguel Ferrer) is breaking down because he can no longer kill – a 'problem' (albeit packaged ironically) that Topper ultimately helps resolve. Topper and Arvid then embark on a killing spree that the film claims makes it the 'bloodiest movie ever', a tongue-in-cheek reference to the ever-escalating violence in Action Adventure pictures. Although a direct parody of *Rambo*, there is little indication that *Hot Shots!* is trying to break down its chauvinistic viewpoint and, as Geoff King observes when discussing *Hot Shots!*, 'parodies can exist quite happily alongside their straight cousins, profitably spoofing the originals without threatening their existence'.[5]

Overall, the narrative of the *Hot Shots!* series is pretty ghoulish, particularly with hindsight, as the US killed thousands of people – including retreating forces that were 'militarily irrelevant' according to a senior Army source[6] – in the Persian Gulf War that occurred just before the release of the first film and only two years after the release of the second. *Hot Shots!* uses this backdrop for a string of gags that rely on poking affectionate fun at some of the most nationalistic films of recent times. One can only imagine the American reaction to a light-hearted comedy in which the US endures a series of devastating attacks and where the President is depicted as a cross-dressing nutcase.

SOUTH PARK

South Park: Bigger, Longer and Uncut (1999) was a successful spin-off from the popular cartoon TV series, starring four boys – Cartman, Stan, Kyle and Kenny – all voiced by the creators Trey Parker and Matt Stone. In the film, parents in the town of South Park, led by Sheila Broflovski (Mary Kay Bergman), protest against a scatological film 'Asses of Fire', whose stars are Canadian comedians Terrance and Phillip. Broflovski has a public argument with the Canadian Minister for Movies, using racial slurs. Canada's protests at the UN are rebuffed by the US representative. Canada bombs the US, killing the Baldwin family. President Clinton retaliates, is usurped by his new Minister for War, Broflovski, and the situation deteriorates into all-out war. The US organises a military show during which Terrance and Phillip will be executed. Kenny discovers that when the blood of Terrance and Phillip hits American soil, Satan – allied with Saddam Hussein – will be able to rule Earth. Can the boys stop the execution in time?

The plot was a reworking of Michael Moore's low-budget ($12 million) *Canadian Bacon* (1995) – considered here by way of comparison – in which the US President (Alan Alda) and his advisers decide to start a new Cold War to stimulate the economy and distract Americans from problems at home. In the absence of genuine enemies, the US finally decides to demonise Canada, following a televised brawl between rival Canadian and American fans at an ice hockey match. Niagara's Sheriff Bud B. Boomer (John Candy) buys into the propaganda and leads various sorties into Canada. Meanwhile, American arms dealer R.J. Hacker (G.D. Spradlin) blackmails the President for one trillion dollars to prevent his 'Hacker Hailstorm' from firing all the US's missiles at Russia.

South Park: Bigger, Longer, and Uncut presents the military as racist at an institutional level, suggests that US military power is disproportionate and ignores peaceful solutions (at one point, a radio announcer tells us that Canada has begged for peace but 'naturally we are not listening'). That aside, the film gives little indication that private interests exert influence on policy. Rather, American actions are generally depoliticised. The US–Canadian spat begins because Terrance and Phillip use four-letter words. This escalates because Broflovski says Canadians are 'all the same' with their 'slitty eyes' and 'flapping heads' (actually, not a typical slur but an in-joke about the poor quality of the animations). When Canada complains at the UN, the US simply says 'fuck Canada'.

In contrast, *Canadian Bacon* is more politically engaged: while the idiotic Boomer and his friends are motivated by negative stereotypes, the civilian and military authorities are not. The President and his advisers want a new Cold War, not a hot one, as a convenient arrangement to benefit dominant societal interests, particularly the current administration and the arms industry. The President desperately begs his Russian counterpart to recreate Cold War antagonism but, when this is rebuffed, he decides instead to apply a slick media campaign to demonise Canada. He will not nuke his northern neighbour, though, even to prevent the 'Hacker Hailstorm' from firing, because that is where he goes on holiday. The film even goes as far as to have the President send a CIA team to bomb a hydroelectric plant in Niagara, which they intend to blame on the Canadians, drawing an explicit parallel with the 1964 Gulf of Tonkin incident, in which many believe America bombed its own ship to provide a *casus belli* for US escalation of the Vietnam War.

South Park: Bigger, Longer, and Uncut's most sympathetic victims are the four boys. They recognise that Terrance and Phillip's film is just harmless fun; they want their parents to love them instead of going away to fight ridiculous causes; they are threatened with censorship, including the insertion of V-chips in their brains to prevent them from swearing, and they are aware of the impending rise of Satan and the dangers of war. Kenny himself is ignored on his deathbed, sent to Hell, and finally sacrifices himself for the world. The film positively revels in the death of the Baldwin and Arquette families. The film is, in short, a repudiation of nationalism and a call for people to identify instead with the values of justice and toleration.

Yet, the existence of *Bigger, Long and Uncut*'s primary enemy, Saddam Hussein, creates a confused sense of dissent. On one hand, by using this real-life villain, the film to some degree legitimates the need for US power. Saddam is the very embodiment of cruelty and deception. He is – literally – worse than Satan, exalting in the use of torture and seeking global power for its own end. Throughout, Saddam insists 'I can change' and even sings a song to this effect, which uses Arabic imagery and musical styles. Saddam's threat actually brings the US, including the military, to its senses: 'What have we done?' cries the Colonel, as though emerging from a trance. Tim Jon Semmerling comments that the film 'makes us reflect on our overuse, to the point of silliness, of the "evil" Arabs in order to produce fear'.[7] Nevertheless, Semmerling concedes that the film also pushes the idea that the Arab can only be destroyed by extreme measures (Saddam is cathartically impaled on a stalagmite in Hell) – in this case by harnessing the power of Cartman's profanity – which finally results in a fully harmonious community.[8]

Canadian Bacon goes considerably further in interrogating US power. The most vilified character in the film is Hacker, a key part of the American elite. The Canadians, ostensibly the film's external enemies, are portrayed as comically civilised people: their authorities write love letters to their prisoners, get caught up in a discussion about politeness when trying to arrest Boomer, and insist Boomer rewrites his anti-Canadian graffiti to include French translations. *Bigger, Longer, and Uncut* is a film that challenges various assumptions in mainstream political discussion, particularly the need to control freedom of speech to 'protect' children. Its approach to US power though is much more ambiguous: it certainly criticises the propensity of American institutions towards violence and suggests that the American military is overzealous and racist, but it hints that evil threats to America – albeit exaggerated – do exist out there.

TEAM AMERICA: WORLD POLICE

Trey Parker and Matt Stone's political ideology was thrown into sharper focus by their all-marionette production *Team America: World Police* (2004). In this film, the super-secret Team America tracks down a group of Islamist terrorists who are coordinated by the evil North Korean dictator Kim Jong Il and allied with a group of Hollywood celebrity anti-war activists including Tim Robbins, Sean Penn, Samuel L. Jackson, Matt Damon and the 'giant socialist weasel' Michael Moore (the latter's puppet was stuffed with ham). Team America insults caricatured indigenous populations and destroys much of Paris and Cairo in its efforts to avert a huge terrorist attack; the team ends up killing the celebrities (though Michael Moore self-detonates) and forces Kim – who turns out to be an alien bug-like creature – to flee to outer space.

The film brilliantly parodied American nationalist cultural products, such as the *Thunderbirds* franchise and the output of Jerry Bruckheimer and Michael Bay. Songs include the bombastic 'America, Fuck Yeah!' and '*Pearl Harbor* Sucked, and I Miss You'. As such, the film established a cynical and knowing tone, but ultimately revealed itself to be highly conservative. Perhaps this could have been offset a little had Parker and Stone turned their guns on the political establishment as well, but an earlier draft of the script which depicted George Bush and John Kerry was abandoned because they didn't think it worked on an emotional level.[9]

According to Stone, 'Nobody should listen to our views on foreign policy, because we don't know what the hell we are talking about.' Rather, the film was about 'what it feels like to be an American for the past two years – and for the past 30 years for that matter. We are in this weird position: are we proud to be American or not?'[10] Whatever the intentions of the film-makers, A.O. Scott observed in the *New York Times*: 'When Team America blows things up in other countries, they do it by accident, in the course of their sloppy but zealous fight against the people who want to do it on purpose. This is not a trivial moral distinction, and it is one the film hangs onto in impressive earnest.' Scott comments that *Team America* may be 'hyperbolic' but it is 'not sarcastic' and is indeed 'one of the more cogent – and, dare I say it, more nuanced – defenses of American military power that I have heard recently'.[11]

According to Megan Lehmann, writing in Rupert Murdoch's *New York Post*, *Team America* 'ultimately offers up a remarkably sensible, even optimistic, worldview that lets some air out of the inflated state of the current political climate'.[12] Indeed, although Parker and Stone may not think they know what they are talking about with regards to foreign policy, the film's message also reflects a fundamental assumption of many international relations scholars. For instance, James Gow, Chair of International Peace and Security at Kings College, claimed the film 'offers the best vehicle for understanding the dominant security issues of today': the US is a 'dick' but at least 'dicks fuck assholes'.[13] Of course, this ignores the fact that the US actually provides key diplomatic and logistical support to various 'assholes', including Saudi Arabia, Angola, Chad, Colombia, Ethiopia and Uzbekistan – a contention which appears not to concern Parker and Stone, not to mention the vast majority of the entire entertainment community.

TROPIC THUNDER

A comparable political tone was delivered by *Tropic Thunder* (2008), which satirises shallow and idiotic movie stars who are thrust unwittingly into a real war. Any consideration of the film's approach to US power was overshadowed by concerns from a coalition of activists about the film's repeated use of the word 'retard'.[14] In terms of international politics, *Tropic Thunder* was less significant than *Team America* as it showed no soldiers and was not set in a contemporary war zone. Still, the villains remain part of the Eastern Other, based in Asia's infamous drug-producing region the Golden Triangle, where a barbaric child soldier leads a gang of heroin dealers.

Although the film received no Pentagon assistance, it was associated quite closely with military figures: technical advisory company Warriors Inc was on set with several ex-US military figures to help with the look of the film (DVD commentary). Then, on 3 August 2008, the film's stars Ben Stiller, Jack Black and Robert Downey Jr visited Camp Pendleton for a special screening to Marines and sailors in partnership with the Navy Morale Welfare and Recreation (MWR), the Marine Corps Community Services (MCCS), and the USO. 'We were really excited to show this movie to the military personnel who do so much for our country', said Stiller at the event.

A week later, Downey Jr said to an interviewer, 'I'm working for the Department of Defense. If something alarming goes down, I might have to enter my co-ordinates and be picked up by helicopter.'[15] He seems to have been joking, but after *Iron Man* and *Tropic Thunder*, the line was becoming increasingly blurred.

CHARLIE WILSON'S WAR

Charlie Wilson's War ennobled US efforts to arm the Mujahideen in 1980s Afghanistan, based on a book by George Crile. Although the *Investors Business Daily* complained that the film was evidence of liberal bias in Hollywood because it did not specifically celebrate Republicans' efforts in Afghanistan,[16] most commentators who examined its politics recognised that *Charlie Wilson's War* was highly supportive of the Reaganite initiative. Michael Johns, former

Heritage Foundation foreign policy analyst and speech-writer for George W. Bush, praised the film as 'the first mass-appeal effort to reflect the most important lesson of America's Cold War victory: that the Reagan-led effort to support freedom fighters resisting Soviet oppression led successfully to the first major defeat of the Soviet Union'. The CIA's Hollywood liaison Paul Barry called it a 'genuinely ... positive portrayal of CIA accomplishment'.[17]

An earlier, substantially different draft of the script suggests that the film-makers originally had significantly more radical intentions, but these were unacceptable to powerful forces which ensured the film was sanitised for their own ends. Pakistan's former honorary consul to the US Joanne Herring hired legal legend Houston attorney Dick DeGuerin to rattle NBC Universal, successfully ensuring changes, including her previously smutty dialogue.[18] Perhaps more significantly, though, it was the real-life CIA itself, in the form of on-set 'adviser' Milt Bearden, former CIA case officer and chief of station in Pakistan, that galvanised the most crucial changes.

In the film, maverick Congressman Charlie Wilson (Tom Hanks) meets the aforementioned Joanne Herring (Julia Roberts), who persuades him to visit the Pakistani leadership and support the Afghans' struggle against the Soviet Union. Visiting an Afghan refugee camp, Wilson is deeply moved but frustrated by the CIA's low-key approach. Wilson befriends maverick CIA operative Gust Avrakotos (Philip Seymour Hoffman) and his understaffed Afghanistan group to develop a different strategy, notably by supplying the Afghan Mujahideen (holy warriors) with Stinger missiles to counter the Soviet helicopter gunships. The CIA's anti-Communist budget grows from $5 million to over $500 million and the Soviets are repelled. The film is bookended with Wilson receiving a major commendation from the CIA but we realise at the end that his pride is tempered by his fears for the future, as 'the crazies have started rolling in [to Afghanistan]' and Charlie has found little Congressional support for rebuilding Afghanistan.

The film represents the US winning a key military victory against the Soviet Union, which prefigured its collapse. Wilson, Herring and Avrakotos are the pioneers that work around the existing softly-softly US strategy, characterised by having 'the Afghans ... walking into machine gun fire 'til the Russians run out of bullets'. Wilson and Co. are all-American heroes without whom the world would be 'hugely and sadly different'. But when Charlie tries to maintain US commitment to Afghanistan, he is given the cold shoulder. 'No one gives a shit about a school in Pakistan,' a

Congressman tells him and, when Charlie corrects him he receives the response 'Afghanistan? Is that still going on?'

Meanwhile, the Russians are portrayed as brutal imperialists, gunning down hopeless Afghans whilst discussing marital infidelity. The Mujahideen are pitiful victims of what the Russians call the 'killing season', although, as they receive greater American support, they begin to resemble the gun-toting warriors familiar from contemporary news coverage of Islamist terrorists.

The final draft of *Charlie Wilson's War* suggests that US support for the Mujahideen went only to the faction led by Ahmad Shah Massoud, the moderate Afghan leader who was assassinated on 9 September 2001. However, according to Bearden – who actually delivered some of the weapons himself in the 1980s – only a tiny fraction of the available money went to Massoud, while huge sums were delivered by the CIA via its ally in Pakistan, the ISI, to a vicious fundamentalist called Gulbaddin Hekmatyar.[19] Indeed, Ed McWilliams, the former US special envoy to Afghanistan, confirmed the widespread assumption that the US itself gave Hekmatyar – subsequently 'specially designated' by the US as a 'global terrorist' allied with Bin Laden – the bulk of its aid, and that Bearden tried, with some success, to prevent warnings of the coming maelstrom from reaching Washington.[20] As Hekmatyar did appear in the earlier version along with a pointed reference to al-Qaeda,[21] it seems likely that when Bearden said that the film would 'put aside the notion that because we did that [supply arms] we had 9/11', he was tacitly referring to such cuts.[22]

The original script also emphasised other complexities in US foreign policy, as we can see from the following extracts. Charlie angrily chastises Israelis for their war on Lebanon in 1982:

> *Charlie*: Sabra and Shatilla, I just saw it. I thought the press accounts had to be blowing it out of proportion so I went to see it myself. Oh my God, Zvi … what the fuck happened?
> *Zvi*: Exactly what you've been told happened. Lebanese Christians came in and began slaughtering the Palestinians.
> *Charlie*: This was supposed to be a surgical strike against the PLO. There are mass graves back there, the place is still on fire. They just told me the body count's up to 900, it's three days and they're still pulling bodies out. 900 civilians.[23]

After being stonewalled by the Israelis, Charlie points out 'Your sentries let the Lebanese soldiers in. [a beat] Didn't they. They watched while it happened.'[24] Zvi eventually tells him 'I don't lose much sleep over dead Palestinians.'[25]

Gust reveals he has developed serious concerns about his actions in Afghanistan. He translates for Charlie the latest speech by a fictionalised cleric named Mohammad Haroon Hamid, who claims 'The day will come when we will rule America ... the day will come when we will rule Britain and the entire world.'[26] Gust complains, 'This guy's two son-in-laws are the leaders of the al-Konar arm of the Mujahideen. We gave them 44 million in weapons and supplies and I oversaw their training myself. We might want to be a little more careful about that.' He adds that the president of Pakistan 'has been skimming quite a bit of American taxpayer money for ... an Islamic bomb'.[27]

Gust also breaks down the idea that the Soviets were simply genocidal invaders:

> *Gust*: This is a two-year-old report. It's from the Red Cross. They were gathering statements from Afghan refugees regarding Soviet atrocities in their village. This woman said the Russian soldiers came in, gathered them in a semi-circle and you know what they did?
> *Charlie*: What.
> *Gust*: The Russians forced them to learn how to read and write.[28]

Gust wryly notes, 'I'm not worried, though, 'cause I know if Islamic fanaticism ever gets outa hand, Joanne Herring and her friends will rise up to meet it with Christian fanaticism and then we've got ourselves a ballgame. And I wouldn't be concerned except we've just sent enough weapons over there to kill everyone on both sides.'

These kind of comments, whispered backstage at the CIA awards ceremony in Charlie's honour, disrupt the more simplistic triumphalism that characterises the awards in the final version.

The tone of the finished film is summed up by the jokey end-caption from Charlie, which declares 'These things happened. They were glorious and they changed the world ... and then we fucked up the end game.' 'Charlie did it', declares the banner at the CIA's award ceremony. The tone of the original script was more Strangelovian. Similar to Crile's book, it ends with Wilson hearing a 'teeth-jarring explosion'[29] at the Pentagon on 9/11 – a chilling scene in which the link is firmly established between US policy and its consequences – but which was also excised.

Director Mike Nichols intimated that the scenes discussed above had been filmed but that he had left to them to 'curl up on the floor and die'.[30] The DVD contained no deleted material.

No draft of the script acknowledged the US's part in deliberately provoking the Soviet invasion. In a 1998 interview with French news magazine *Le Nouvel Observateur*, former National Security adviser Zbigniew Brzezinski revealed he had 'no regrets' about the US having provided 'secret aid to the opponents of the pro-Soviet regime in Kabul' to encourage Moscow's intervention through a 'secret operation' in an effort to give the Soviet Union its own 'Vietnam War' in an 'Afghan Trap'.[31] No one raised the issue that a 1982 Congressional Financial Disclosures document suggests Charlie Wilson actually had several hundred thousand dollars' worth of holdings in petroleum companies, whilst the film explicitly has him declare a modest salary. And, despite the revelatory 'behind-the-scenes' impression given by the film, the whole CIA operation in Afghanistan remains largely classified.[32]

YOU DON'T MESS WITH THE ZOHAN

In *You Don't Mess With the Zohan* (2008), Israeli Army commando Zohan Dvir (Adam Sandler) quits his job to follow his dream of hairdressing in New York. His Palestinian terrorist enemies catch up with him while property developers are trying to depopulate the Arabs and Israelis from Zohan's part of town; as a result, he must fight for his life, his new Palestinian girlfriend and his hair salon.

'Getting a kick out of *You Don't Mess With the Zohan* demands lightening up', explained one reviewer.[33] Rob Schneider – an Californian actor who plays a Palestinian terrorist – says 'we're an equal opportunities offender' and that the film isn't 'mean spirited'.[34] Screenwriter Robert Smigel claimed, 'we tried to be equally offensive to all sides',[35] but that 'some people ... whether your intention is pure or not ... are going to find something to be angry about.'[36] Daniel Treiman, who wondered if Adam Sandler might just be 'Our greatest Jewish mind', reassured 'those worrying that Sandler is tarnishing Israel's image abroad, fear not: The film's Arab characters don't come off any better. So it's a tie.'[37]

In the film, the Palestinians' hero – Zohan's arch-enemy – is Phantom, a crazy, egotistical terrorist played by John Turturro, well known for his depictions of crackbrained characters. Phantom is comically maligned in the most extreme ways, including when he claims Mariah Carey's singing is 'beautiful like a scud missile soaring to its target' and when, in a parody of *Rocky* (1976), he eats live chicks and punches a cow. Phantom appears to be completely uninterested in actually helping his community – he excuses himself stealing a boat from one of his people by saying 'sorry, it's for the cause!' and, as he achieves greater celebrity status, he 'buys' wives and plasters images of himself all over his expanding restaurant chain. The film never specifies what Israel's quarrel is with Phantom and in this sense it seems to dub him a terrorist simply by virtue of his being on the wrong side.

Salim (Schneider) is a Palestinian cab driver, stressed out by trying to hold down another job as a catalogue salesman. When an American woman gets into his taxi, she appears to be an archetypal paranoid old white lady who admonishes her co-passenger 'Be quiet! He [the driver] could be a terrorist!' The funny joke is ... Salim really *is* a terrorist.[38] What's more, Salim's taxi-driving friends are also terrorists and together they embark on an idiotic mission to kill Zohan. In doing so, they telephone Hizbollah but an answering machine apologises that the organisation has 'currently suspended our terrorist supply network because we are in negotiations with Israel', adding reassuringly, 'We will resume as soon as negotiations break down.' Unfortunately for Salim, he is so illiterate and stupid that when he tries to make a bomb to kill Zohan, he purchases Neosporin antibiotic ointment instead of liquid nitrogen. Later, he botches a business deal with Phantom for twenty of his wives in exchange for one touch of his 'pee pee'. Elsewhere, the calamitous Salim screams insults like 'stupid cow', 'I curse you and I curse your hair' and 'die in hell!' Why is Salim so upset? Because years ago Zohan stole his goat.

In stark contrast, Zohan is a brilliant commando who even the terrorists think is 'very cool'. In the film, Israel tries to avoid collateral damage, hence Zohan's one-man mission to the Lebanese border to try to recapture Phantom. In fact, the worst thing an Israeli has done, according to the film, is steal the aforementioned pet goat. A young Israeli counter-terrorist meets Zohan at a nightclub and tries to convince him to return to the fight. Zohan explains, 'I couldn't take all the fighting anymore. What's it all for?', to which the kid replies, 'Are you crazy? If I could blow a terrorist inside out like you, this is all I would do.' In the original script, the kid enthuses, 'The way you ... made Malami Benazir eat his own shit in '97? I can't believe I'm meeting you, man.'[39] Too strong for the final take, it seems.

As we follow Zohan's story, we are invited to feel sorry for this man who is hounded by his vengeful enemies when all he wants to do is make hair 'silky smooth'. Ultimately, Zohan becomes an almost Christ-like figure, who decides to turn the other cheek even as Phantom hits him repeatedly and says 'Fight back!'. Zohan has risen above violence so, while Phantom pleads with the crowd 'Where's the hate?', Zohan works on bringing the communities together. He is also specifically Westernised – like the Israelis in *Munich* – fitting into American society and even shown conducting a community nightwatch, rather like the kind of home-front activity Karl Rove requested be promoted in the Bush administration's meetings with Hollywood in 2001.

Zohan also shows a general antipathy towards greedy big business. Grant Walbridge (Michael Buffer) wants to get rid of all the 'foreign people' in the area to build a giant shopping mall and roller-coaster. He hires white-trash thugs who hate Israelis, Palestinians and puppies to use violence to clear out the residents.

Yet it is the Palestinians who receive by far the greatest attention and who are discussed in terms that link them closely with the real world. Notably, a Palestinian demands of an Israeli shopkeeper: 'Give it up [your shop], like you gave up the Gaza Strip', insinuating that Israel had claim to Gaza and ignoring the fact that Israel still occupies Gaza's borders and airspace, and controls its imports and exports. Meanwhile, Dalia blames the troubles on 'extremists' and 'hate' on both sides which is 'over there' and 'crazy'. The conflict between the Phantom and Zohan renders the Israeli–Palestinian problem as a personalised cartoonish fight between invincible superheroes. Elsewhere, Palestinian children throw rocks at Zohan, explicitly echoing the famous images of the intifada that demonstrated the seemingly futile but spirited responses of a community to occupation. In response, Zohan catches the rocks, turns them into the equivalent of a balloon animal and throws it to the amazed children who say 'wow!'.

The mentality of the producers goes some way to explain how such ideas permeated a mainstream Hollywood film. Sandler said:

> When I was a kid, I always heard about the Israeli army and this tiny little country and how everyone around them wants them gone and every time somebody comes after them, they take care of business. As a Jewish kid, you were proud of that: 'All right, they are trying to take out the Jews and the Jews ain't gonna let it happen.' So I just admired them.[40]

Schneider seems to have a less charmingly infantile approach. When asked if the film will be shown in a country like Syria, he responded sardonically, 'We're still in talks with Sony Damascus.'[41]

Zohan ends happily: Israelis and Palestinians unite to repel Walbridge, whose wife's breasts explode. The block is turned into a collectively owned mall called the 'Peace and Brotherhood Fire Insurance Mall', in which Phantom opens a shoe store and Salim runs a 'ride the goat' business. Zohan and Dalia are married and Zohan's parents signal their approval of both his hairdressing and his bride. Dalia's Palestinian parents are conspicuously absent.

Treiman dismissed concerns about the movie's politics: 'Who really goes to an Adam Sandler film for the purpose of being educated in the nuances of the Israeli–Palestinian conflict?'[42] But did anyone go to *Zohan* to be *mis*educated? And should we laugh along if a Palestinian jokes about forcing Israelis to eat their own shit?

Early in the film, *You Don't Mess with the Zohan* reveals its politics in a nutshell. A bearded, sword-wielding, black-bereted Arab asks Zohan 'So we are the bad ones?' and protests at Zohan's disinterest: 'It's not so cut and dried!' Zohan knocks him off a balcony but the debate continues with the Palestinian shouting 'we settled here for hundreds of years'. Zohan gets the last word, shouting with sarcastic venom over the corpse, 'Good point. None of my ancestors ever stepped foot in this land. No, you're right.' The not-so-'pure' intentions of the film-makers are, for a moment, unable to remain concealed behind the levity.

AIR AMERICA

Do any major Comedies challenge US power at more fundamental levels? *Air America* (1990) certainly makes the attempt, on a pretty thin budget of $30 million. The film shows that despite President Nixon's public denials, the CIA was constantly flying planes around Laos during the war in Indochina. Moreover, this is part of a cynical venture not to win the war but to profit from it by selling heroin and guns – as historians have indeed demonstrated was the case.[43]

Billy Covington (Robert Downey Jr) joins the US side as Gene Ryack (Mel Gibson) is attempting to skim off some cash from his cargo. Senator Davenport (Lane Smith) goes to Laos to investigate these tales of corruption but the Army makes him realise that his political career will be over if he reveals the truth – namely that the CIA is buying in the illicit goods from the Laotian military – so he attempts instead to scapegoat the 'rotten apple' Robert

Downey Jr. As Gibson departs, he cheers up those he is leaving behind by reassuring them, 'There will be another war coming to a theatre near you soon', meaning there will be more opportunities for profiteering. The film ends on an uplifting note, as Ryack jettisons his 'nest egg' cargo in favour of saving a group of refugees.

THREE KINGS

Three Kings (1999) used a narrative device similar to *Air America*'s to satirise the Persian Gulf War. The *New York Times* said *Three Kings* conveyed 'the amorality and chaos of the situation [in Iraq]' with 'strong implicit criticism of the Bush [Sr] Administration's wartime policy'.[44] McCrisken and Pepper explain that the film undermines the popular view that the Persian Gulf War was fought like a bloodless 'video game'; it raises questions about what the war actually achieved, and rejects the 'simple racism' of films like *Black Hawk Down*.[45] The film-makers did not request Pentagon assistance and actually called upon the advice of Jack Shaheen, who has written extensively about Orientalism in Hollywood film, to help reduce stereotypes (a role he felt resulted in a positive film).[46] Hala Maskoud, president of the American-Arab Anti-Discrimination Committee, said of the film: 'We're happy that for once we are not stereotyped by Hollywood ... It shows the Arab and Muslim in their complexity, with feelings and normal aspirations.'[47]

During the production of the film, director David O. Russell apparently experienced institutional indifference at Warner Brothers, aside from his lone source of support, production chief Lorenzo di Bonaventura. Sharon Waxman reports that at one stage *Three Kings* was adapted to suit the studio, including giving clothes to some depicted Iraqi prisoners and toning down a rape scene.[48] Often the film-makers would be told that the project was 'weird. You people are all weird', prior to its completion and subsequent critical acclaim.[49] This ambivalence was aslso reflected in Warner's decision to fund *Soldiers Pay* (2004) – Russell's follow-up documentary about the poor treatment of US troops in the Iraq War – only then to ditch it as an accompaniment to the re-release of *Three Kings* just before the election.[50]

Three Kings is set in Iraq just after the 1991 US invasion and during the failed Shia-led uprising against Iraqi President Saddam Hussein's Sunni Muslim-led government. Four US soldiers – Major Archie Gates (George Clooney), Pfc. Conrad Vig (Spike Jonze), Sfc. Troy Barlow (Mark Wahlberg), Sgt. Chief Elgin (Ice Cube) – find a map leading to Saddam's hidden gold in a village near Karbala in northern Iraq. During their search for the gold, Gates' unit becomes embroiled in the uprising. They rescue several prisoners and break the US–Iraq ceasefire. Barlow is captured by Iraqi forces and Captain Said (Said Taghmaoui) subjects him to torture and interrogation. An Iraqi resistance leader, Amir Abdullah, whom Gates's unit rescues and whose wife is executed by Iraqi soldiers, realises that Gates's unit is not officially working for the US military and so negotiates a deal with Gates in which they will work together to rescue Barlow, split the gold, and get the Iraqis over the border into Iran. They successfully rescue Barlow but at the border, US military authorities headed by Colonel Ron Horn and Captain Doug Van Meter prevent the Iraqis from escaping, which will likely mean their imminent execution by Iraqi soldiers. Gates's unit decides to give the stolen gold to his superiors to return to Kuwait who, in exchange, lead the civilians past the border guards.

The film implies that US actions are informed by narrow interests, not values. Gates lectures his unit on the significance of 'necessity' in determining human actions; we see the bloody results of the US betraying the Iraqi revolution; Gates is only successful in rescuing the Shia when he offers Horn the stolen gold. Nevertheless, although the heroes (Gates's unit) also begin their quest with purely selfish interests – stealing the gold – the closer they get to real Iraqis and the actual battle the more they become heroic, benevolent and less self-interested. Furthermore, the reasons given for the US betrayal of the Iraqi uprising are vague and could be construed as at least partially laudable, with Colonel Horn silencing Gates's protest by raising the spectre of a new Vietnam.

The film does not establish facts which would disrupt the idea of US benevolence more seriously. Isolated newspaper articles reported Iraqi initiatives offering various forms of compromise, such as leasing out control over two uninhabited mudflats assigned to Kuwait by Britain, and the resolution of a dispute over an oil-field that extended two miles into Kuwait over an unsettled border.[51] The *New York Times* similarly reported that the Bush administration blocked the 'diplomatic track' for fear that it might 'defuse the crisis'.[52] While *Three Kings* indicates that members of the US authorities are self-interested – seeking, for example, promotions – this ignores the influence of important systemic economic and political forces such as the US's desire to dominate the UN and override international law. For instance, we see the desert awash with oil but aside from the tacit implication that it is significant, there is no exploration of the idea that the US was there to defend and extend the rights of the US and its corporations to control and profit from oil.[53]

Iraqi soldiers do not suffer like the Americans or the rebels. Indeed, most of them are fairly standard movie villains, operating as tools of Saddam Hussein, the epitome of evil. Gates tries to avoid killing any Iraqis at all. His plan is to scare the Iraqis into giving up the gold, with his men keeping the safeties on their guns. Gates is only compelled to deploy physical force after the Iraqis fire first and his approach acts as a metaphor for the film's position on the whole war: the US is reacting to Iraqi aggression (the invasion of Kuwait), even if it did pursue some non-specific concurrent interests in doing so.

There is some ambiguity in the representation of victims, which is unusual in Hollywood film. First, we see images of burnt and buried Iraqi corpses strewn along a stretch of road, and prisoners of war being 'processed' like objects. Secondly, there is some attempt to generate sympathy for a specific Iraqi: Captain Said is presented partially as a victim of US power, a humanised, complex character who does not fit into binary categories of good vs. bad Arab. He tries to bargain with Gates, but points out that Saddam will kill his family if he and his soldiers simply abandon their posts. Said mirrors Barlow. They both are/were family men with a wife and small daughter. Indeed, they were also both trained by the US military and funded by the US government. Said also speaks about his son who was killed by US bombs. He asks Barlow to imagine how the American would feel if his own daughter were bombed – hardly the 'happy violence' that characterises most Comedies and many other films. Both scenarios are visualised, inviting viewers to sympathise with the Iraqi. Thus the film situates this character not simply as victim or oppressor.

Nevertheless, Said is ultimately still a villain, much more obviously than he is a victim. He does torture Iraqis, and Barlow, quite graphically, for example, forcing him to drink crude oil (a scene against the wishes of the on-set adviser Jack Shaheen); Said is also directly associated with the disturbing images of prisoners tied to metal bed frames. Ultimately, the film suggests the US has done the right thing in opposing Iraqi aggression. Barlow even has the last word on the matter, claiming that 'Too much bombing is crazy but not saving Kuwait.' The objection raised is that the US has adopted inappropriate tactics to achieve this commendable end, namely not taking the fight all the way to Baghdad.

The Iraqi Shia are more humanised figures. Family man Amir Abdullah (Cliff Curtis) says that they just want to make business without the threat from Saddam. In one scene, two men have a discussion with Vig, Elgin and Abdullah. Gates does not even appear here; it is the Iraqis who are foregrounded. They somewhat humorously lead Vig into saying he was 'trained to kill all Arabs' and then they laughingly tell him he has a 'terrible haircut'. The Iraqi Shia are truly, if briefly, humanised figures. That said, aside from such moments, they are generally passive, unable to help themselves, and dependent on the Americans to lead them.

The Americans receive the greatest sympathy in *Three Kings*. Vig represents the frustration of US soldiers in an emotionally unsatisfying war. He wants to wear night goggles and blow up footballs because he did not see any action during the war; he imagines an Iraqi victim's head being blown off in a cartoon-like manner. Vig is later shot dead. The Shia embalm and wrap his body and agree to carry the body to an Islamic shrine in Iran, therefore giving the American heightened status. The audience is encouraged to feel most sympathy for Barlow, who goes through a particularly gruelling change. He is the 'everyman' figure – an office worker and family man who is reluctant to put himself in harm's way. He is shot several times, then captured and horrifically tortured. Later, Iraqis shoot Barlow yet again and he has an operation which will keep him alive for a few hours. We suffer with Barlow, too, when he is a perpetrator of violence: in the opening scene, Barlow, confused by the rules of engagement, decides to shoot an unarmed Iraqi. The bullet tears through the Iraqi's neck, where normally one would expect a clean cinematic kill. In this scene, the Iraqi seems to be a victim but the film dwells on Barlow himself, who looks distressed for what he felt he had to do. The American soldier remains the victim even when he stands over the body of a dying Iraqi, who is treated essentially as a comic foil.

Three Kings is an unusual ideological product in Hollywood terms, which begins to break down the official history of the Gulf War. Nevertheless, the film presents the US military as the victim of the government's implementation of inconclusive policies in Iraq, notably the early termination of military force. The film does not discuss the impact of dominant US interests, while implying that the US was operating on principal in its reaction to Iraqi aggression.

These limitations have significant implications because, as it stands, the film suggests that the problems of Iraq can be solved, and only solved, by the application of US force. In 2002–03, the

Bush administration was able to use such humanitarian rhetoric to support an assault on Iraq which was based on the same powerful interests and assumptions of benevolence that informed US actions in 1990–91, creating more of the same victims. Indeed, director Russell sheepishly indicated *Three Kings* ideological consistency with the 2003 Iraq War. On meeting future US President George Bush Jr in July 1999, Russell said he was making a film that would question his father's legacy in Iraq. Bush shot back: 'Then I guess I'm going to have to go finish the job, aren't I?'[54]

CONCLUSION

Major modern Comedy films have not tended to reflect the more vibrant satire available elsewhere in Hollywood history and the entertainment community more broadly. On the 1990s stand-up circuit, Bill Hicks became known as 'Chomsky with dick jokes',[55] railing against the US wars on Iraq and drugs. Although Comedy Central appears once to have compelled *The Daily Show*'s (1996–) host Jon Stewart to apologise publicly for 'dumb, stupid' comments about President Truman (Stewart called him a 'war criminal'), the programme has regularly presented quite challenging perspectives on America's role in the world.[56]

Amongst the major film productions, though, the line has been much tighter and Hollywood's sense of humour has marched firmly in step with the regiments of the state. There are exceptions, but even a smart comedy like the well-intentioned *Three Kings* draws upon strong strands of neoconservative thinking on Iraq. Products like *Team America* and *You Don't Mess With the Zohan* play the 'plague on both your houses' card, but as much as the film-makers cast themselves as being above the fray and independent of state interference, they are supporters of reactionary politics at fundamental levels. The knee-jerk politics of other films, like *True Lies*, were happier to wear their brutishness on their sleeves. Perhaps most disturbing of all was *Charlie Wilson's War*, which was quietly rewritten to suit the interests of the national security apparatus, thereby passing up the chance to produce what at least had the potential to be the *Dr Strangelove* of our generation.

5
Action Adventure

Action Adventures are perhaps most liable of all film types to present simplistic takes on US foreign policy, ignoring trenchant thought in favour of thin back-stories, melodrama, violence and spectacular effects. As a rule, Action Adventures 'heroise' US central power structures clearly and reflexively, as is exemplified by films like *The Hunt for Red October* (1990), *Executive Decision* (1996), *Air Force One* (1997), *Sum of All Fears* (2002) and *Eagle Eye* (2008) – all of which were provided support by the Pentagon. Other Action Adventures, such as *Outbreak* (1995), *The Peacemaker* (1997) and *Collateral Damage* (2002), are relatively more politically engaged but still focus on the benevolent intent of US troops and policy-makers and show the overall benefits of US violence, as we shall see.

Certain franchises warrant little comment, particularly as they are so widely known. For example, few would deny that the politics of the James Bond or *Mission Impossible* films are anything other than firmly in the camp of Western governments. Both have featured villainous 'rogue agents' but ultimately always maintain the integrity of national security organisations, as in the conclusion to *Quantum of Solace* (2008), where it is pointedly mentioned that the CIA has fired the cynical agent and promoted the affable Felix Leiter. Occasionally, the producers of these series have worked with such organisations to make the films, which is why the producers of *Tomorrow Never Dies* were compelled by the Department of Defense to remove something as petty as a joke about the US 'losing Vietnam' from the script.[1]

Nevertheless, the genre remains open to possibilities for more critical content and the thin back-stories are not necessarily obliged to follow establishment lines, as in products like the *Bourne* franchise. Other films have depicted relatively apolitical characters and scenarios – as with *Speed* (1994), in which mid-level police officers must stop a bomb aboard a bus, the bomb being wired to explode if the bus slows down to 50 miles per hour. Such products are a reminder that successful, exciting, high-concept films do not need to involve high-level politics at all.

Other Action Adventures also employ back-stories that disparage the US government but it would be quite a stretch to see these as films with any kind of leftist agenda on US foreign policy. *The Long Kiss Goodnight* (1997) involves a group of CIA operatives who plan to frame a Muslim for the detonation of a chemical weapon on US soil, in order to guarantee increased defence budgets; in *Under Siege 2* (1995) an American-made super-weapon blasts away thousands of Chinese people; *The Shooter* (2007) discusses the massacring by the US of villagers in Ethiopia for corporate gain. However, the victims of these films are, of course, never actually shown on screen – where are the Chinese victims in *Under Siege 2*? Where is the contextualisation of US 'false flag' operations in *The Long Kiss Goodnight*? Where are the Africans in *The Shooter*? Where, indeed, is the acknowledgement that the US has been a long-term ally of Ethiopia in the War on Terror?

'TOP GUN II'

One of the most notable cases of Defense Department cooperation on a film in this genre was with *Top Gun* (1986), in which Navy pilots push themselves to the limit in high-velocity training. The actor Barry 'Wolfman' Tubb claimed that on set 'It was just nuts; riding motorbikes through [hotel] hallways, chasing girls down on the beach, having parties. All those things you can imagine went on.'[2] *Empire* magazine reported that after one of their 'animal nights', the now notoriously focused Tom Cruise threw up over a car and on another occasion, Don Simpson – regularly wired on coke and not a swimmer – almost drowned when the stunt team threw him and Jerry Bruckheimer into the pool after a naked Kelly McGillis.[3] The Pentagon acknowledged the film 'helped with recruiting like crazy'.[4]

Ironically, though, plans for 'Top Gun II' were reportedly ditched in the early 1990s when hundreds of Navy pilots hit the front pages for allegedly molesting and mauling 87 women at the Navy's Tailhook Association annual convention. The Pentagon's own investigation into 'Tailhook' cited *Top Gun* by name and reported that 'some senior officers ... told us that the movie fuelled misconceptions on the part of junior officers of what was expected of them and also served to increase the general awareness of naval aviation and glorify naval pilots in the eyes of many young women.'[5]

Consequently, the Navy's response to the script for 'Top Gun II' was 'get the hell out of here'.[6] A proposal too rich even for the Pentagon's blood.

AIR FORCE ONE

Despite the obvious tendencies for the genre to present highly aggressive narratives, let's examine some major Pentagon-backed movie presentations to see exactly how they do so. In *Air Force One*, Russian terrorists led by Egor Korshunov (Gary Oldman) take over the presidential plane, Air Force One. President Marshall (Harrison Ford) remains undetected on board and fights to rescue his family and the hostages. Whilst Korshunov executes prisoners, the White House must decide whether or not Vice-President Kathryn Bennett (Glenn Close) should assume the presidency. Korshunov captures Marshall and threatens to kill his wife and daughter unless Marshall prevails upon the Russian government to release Kazakhstan's ultra-nationalist General Radek from jail.

Many of the US leadership figures in *Air Force One* are truly heroic and the President himself is adulated as an action hero – resuscitating the image of the Vietnam vet in the process. Marshall castigates himself and his country for not acting earlier to halt the genocide caused by Radek's previous rule in Kazakhstan. When Marshall improvises his speech in Moscow – 'Never again will I allow our political self-interest to deter us from doing what we know to be morally right' – he is not saying that existing US policy is non-benevolent. Rather he is implying that US deployment of military force is by definition always benevolent but that, regrettably, force is not used enough because political will is lacking until more tangible US interests are in jeopardy. This is the film's criticism of US foreign policy, as far as it goes.

Even Defense Secretary Walter Dean (Dean Stockwell), whom the film shows advocating the wrong tactical decisions, is trying to promote common values. He qualifies his statements about destroying the plane ('I hate to say this but …') in contrast to the callous Russian Petrov ('fifty lives means nothing in the grand scheme') and he is driven by the desire to prevent an even worse outcome for ordinary people.

At the climax, Marshall's noble intent is put to the ultimate test: with only time enough remaining for one more person to leave Air Force One before it crashes, Marshall must decide whether to crash into the sea with Caldwell or save his own skin. Without there being any realistic choice, the narrative problem is immediately and conveniently resolved as the traitorous Secret Service Agent Biggs (Zander Berkeley) shoots Caldwell dead. Meanwhile, Biggs himself is the only American bad guy and the film assiduously refuses to offer any explanation for his treachery, thereby making opposition to the President appear all the more unfathomable.

Sympathetic attention in the film is directed almost exclusively at the US military and civilian authorities. Marshall makes brief mention of refugee camps and how 200,000 Kazakhs were killed under Radek's regime, but this all remains off-screen. The film also alludes very briefly to some problems facing Russia, which Korshunov claims has been turned over to 'gangsters and prostitutes'. In the film, though we do not actually see any Russian people other than the terrorists, we are not positioned to trust anything Korshunov says, and our only images of Russia – stunning shots of Red Square – are of considerable opulence, de-legitimating the notion that post-Communist Russia had become the basket-case Korshunov describes. Rather, the spread of US power and capitalist values seems to have worked out for the common good.

The US executive branch is particularly sympathetically portrayed. The camera dwells on Marshall's pained reactions to deputy press secretary Mitchell's (Donna Bullock) killing; he feels for Doherty when he learns of his death; we stay with Marshall throughout his agonising attempts to stand up to Korshunov. Furthermore, *Air Force One* shows us that the victimisation of the US executive leads to the victimisation of literally the whole world, as the consensus is that relations with Russia and its satellite states are one step away from being plunged back into a war-like mentality, epitomised by Korshunov and Radek.

Curiously, although American leadership figures are portrayed as possessing the highest values and being morally above reproach, some military men are simultaneously disposable. Caldwell is quite matter-of-fact that Marshall should live, instead of him, simply because Marshall is president. Likewise, at least two Special Forces men have plummeted to their deaths in the presidential plane. The film traverses this potentially deflating ending by pushing the case that the military are incredibly noble and important people but – simultaneously, unquestionably – much less important than the President, which further dignifies his office and demonstrates the film's extreme devotion to traditional established US authorities.

The Department of Defense provided full cooperation for the film, but did not have much to change in the script. Instead, the Air

Force spent some time making changes to ensure the other armed services were removed almost entirely from the product.[7]

In conclusion, *Air Force One* does not just assume and depict US exceptionalism – it positively advocates acting on it as policy. There are even several references to a bellicose Saddam Hussein, who the President is admirably dealing with by deploying battleships. The film questions US power only in that it is not applied frequently or forcefully enough, and it shows the US repeatedly interfering in the affairs of sovereign nations, including breaching other nations' airspace and ordering the assassinations of their would-be leaders. Ironically, this behaviour is shown to be absolutely necessary to protect common values and democratisation, as Eastern democracies are so fragile, underdeveloped and dependent on US kind-heartedness.

EXECUTIVE DECISION

When the Pentagon-supported *Executive Decision* (1995) was released, it seemed to fit the political *Zeitgeist* of the mid-1990s, which gave us the 'clash of civilizations' paradigm.[8] In this film, Islamist terrorists hijack a commercial airliner. While the initial consensus at the Pentagon is that the terrorists, led by Nagi Hassan (David Suchet) are exerting pressure on the US to release their ostensible leader, El Sayed Jaffa (Andreas Katsulas), intelligence consultant David Grant (Kurt Russell) convinces them that the hijacking is more likely an attempt to crash the plane, packed with nerve gas, into Washington. An anti-terror squad, led by Travis (Steven Seagal) boards the airliner using a prototype Remora aircraft with stealth technology. Travis falls to his death during the audacious attempt to link the two planes, leaving Grant in the hold of the hijacked airliner with the remainder of Travis's team. While the US government releases Jaffa in the hope that it might appease the Islamists, the team discovers and eventually defuses an enormous chemical bomb packed with nerve gas.

Curiously, the notion that a terrorist attack on the US's East Coast would surely target the government itself is not discussed, whilst in reality of course the government was obliged to take aversive action to maintain continuity, hence Vice-President Dick Cheney's dash to an 'undisclosed location' following 9/11. Instead, the debate in the film is framed in terms of how the executive can save the greatest numbers of ordinary people, regardless of its own safety. The 'executive decision' forms the agonising central focus of the film. The solution is some method of high-tech violence. Negotiation, as shown through the Senator Mavros character, is tantamount to suicide.

Executive Decision is populated with ordinary, scared American victims who regain their dignity only through contact with the US military. For example, both pilots make gaffes which suggest the anti-terrorist squad might be boarding, notably by failing to cover up the alarm light when the team attaches the Aurora to the airliner. However, when the co-pilot searches the hold to discover the cause of the flashing light, Captain Rat (the keenly patriotic Latino-American) covertly shows him the Stars and Stripes sewn onto his military uniform. From this point onwards, the co-pilot lies convincingly to the terrorists about the reason behind the alarm light. Similarly, Grant is a goofy civilian CIA agent, but he saves the day with military support. In the final stand-off, a baffled Nagi asks Grant 'Who are you?', expecting him to be some kind of hero. 'I'm no one', says Grant, and this is not false modesty. Grant is a normal person who works well as part of an effective, democratic militarised system. This is why Travis's death, while unusual, fits well into the narrative and ideological construction of the movie.

In contrast, the Islamist leader Nagi Hassan (David Suchet) seeks to dictate a 'dramatic statement'. His al-Thar ('Revenge') movement uses other-worldly justifications for their kamikaze actions. Most of the terrorists on board the plane believe that their mission is to blackmail America into releasing their original leader El Sayed Jaffa from US custody though Jaffa himself is more moderate. But the film suggests it is Nagi and the Marriott bomber who represent the new irrational spirit that has come to dominate the Palestinian struggle.

In conclusion, *Executive Decision* fantasises about a revitalised relationship between soldier and civilian, which belies the militarism ingrained into corporate Hollywood's take on international security. By the final scene, Grant and Rat are able to salute each other in a sign of mutual respect when previously Grant was derided as a James Bond wannabe. As a uniquely free, multicultural, democratic system – which does not ever negotiate with terrorists – America is able to overcome the death of its lead hero (and, indeed, the absence of its president), in stark contrast to the Other's dictatorial hierarchy built on lies and deception.

Executive Decision also gives the lie to the Bush administration's self-serving claim that it could not have predicted the 9/11 attacks (although it demonises the Palestinians rather than al-Qaeda). National security adviser Condoleezza Rice said, 'I don't think anyone could have predicted that these people would take an airplane and slam it into the World Trade Center'[9] and that 'Hijacking before 9/11 and hijacking after 9/11 mean two very different things.'[10] Perhaps Rice could have paid attention to the numerous intelligence reports on the subject, including one as early as 1995 when an accomplice of Ramzi Yousef – mastermind of the 1993 World Trade Center bombing – admitted that he learned to fly at US flight schools and had plotted to crash a hijacked aircraft into the CIA's headquarters.[11] Either that, or she could have done what millions of other people did – kick off her shoes, order some snacks and watch *Executive Decision.*

STEALTH

Reactionary narratives like those of *Air Force One* and *Executive Decision* were not just the result of pre-9/11 insularity in the US. Take the Pentagon-backed *Stealth* (2005), for instance, which imagines a heroic elite team of US Navy pilots killing assorted terrorists and warlords throughout the world, explicitly without creating collateral damage even when destroying huge buildings in downtown Rangoon, Burma. The action takes in Tajikistan and North Korea as well as a gratuitous holiday scene amongst the beautiful waterfalls of Thailand, which worked as a nice advertisement for military life. The film seemed to set itself up for a longer-running franchise, but this was scotched when the film turned out to be one of the worst flops of all time, making just $32 million on a $140 million investment.

CLEAR AND PRESENT DANGER

Other films laid greater claim to being critical, though almost invariably this only ever consisted of unsubstantial points. *Clear and Present Danger*, made with full Pentagon cooperation, is based on the novel (1990) by Tom Clancy, a hard-right Washington insider. It was co-scripted by self-confessed 'zen-fascist' John Milius, who was also behind films like *Conan the Barbarian* (1982), *Red Dawn* (1984), *The Hunt for Red October* (1990) and *Flight of the Navigator* (1991).

In *Clear and Present Danger*, US President Bennett (Donald Moffat) orders National Security Adviser James Cutter (Harris Yulin) to establish the secret and illegal 'Operation Reciprocity', implementing a hard-line policy against a Colombian drug cartel,

Cali. Cutter employs the help of CIA Deputy Director of Operations Robert Ritter (Henry Czerny) and they use government money to bankroll a secret army. Together, they set up acting CIA Deputy Director Jack Ryan (Harrison Ford) as the fall guy for their actions, but Ryan battles to save the troops and the truth.

Clear and Present Danger depicts the US military in reflexively positive terms – reluctantly obeying their shady civilian masters and engaging in daredevil operations that neutralise nefarious drug dealers and destroy their infrastructures.

More interesting is the film's depiction of civilian authorities, for although it undoubtedly deplores the undemocratic tactics of the villainous Bennett-Cutter-Ritter triumvirate, all three are genuinely trying to defeat the drug cartels, which are a 'clear and present danger' to US national security, and to reduce the flow of narcotics into the US. The culmination of their plan comes when Cutter makes a treaty with the villainous Felix Cortez (Joaquim de Almeida), whereby the latter would run the cartels without US interference in exchange for a dramatic cut of supply to the US and regular arrests for US propaganda purposes. This is certainly a deal with the devil but is arguably well intentioned, reflecting the Bennett-Cutter-Ritter view of the moral world as being shades of 'grey' rather than the 'right and wrong' equation preferred by Ryan.

The original script framed US policy in less favourable terms but fell foul of the Pentagon's marker pen. For instance, the President says of the Colombian drug lords, 'Those sons-of-bitches ... I swear, sometimes I would like to level that whole damn country – and Peru and Ecuador while we are at it.'[12] The offending line was removed, along with any presidential references to 'payback', 'Bustin' some butt' and his calling the dealers 'monkeys and jabaloneys'.[13]

No version of the *Clear and Present Danger* script cared to mention anything about the real-life effects of the US relationship with Colombia, the most salient being that while Colombia receives more US arms and training than any other nation in the world (with the exception of Israel and Egypt), it also has the worst human rights record in the hemisphere.[14] Commenting on Colombia in 1994, the year the film was released, Amnesty International reported that at least a thousand people had been illegally executed with impunity 'by the armed forces or paramilitary groups operating with their support or acquiescence', while 'disappearances' and 'torture' were increasingly widespread.[15]

In *Clear and Present Danger*, the prevalence of other powerful characters – principally Ryan and Admiral James Greer (James Earl

Jones) – suggests that the US political system also produces honest men who can rein in the kinds of abuses of protocol by the Bennett-Cutter-Ritter trio. In fact, the majority of American characters who work within civilian power structures are remarkably amiable: FBI Director Jacobs (Tom Tammi) even gives his secretary Moira Wolfson (Ann Magnuson) two days off just because she is in love. On his deathbed, outgoing CIA Deputy Director Greer emphasises the importance of the oath of allegiance public officials take to the American people, which Ryan dramatically sees through by shouting down the President in the Oval Office.

Bennett, Cutter and Ritter are therefore the exceptions, not the rule; what is more, they know it. Although they talk tough, they are under constant threat from the benign system, embodied by Ryan and Greer and symbolised by Congress. At the climax, we see close-ups of Bennett, Ritter and Cutter, all with blood-drained faces, desperately calling after Ryan who, with patriotic musical strains playing, solemnly swears to tell the truth in front of a congressional hearing. While the outcome is left open, Bennett-Cutter-Ritter's panicky manipulation suggests that they know Ryan will emerge triumphant. Power is only abused by minority elements and these are forced to act in secret, perpetually fearful of the system's all-pervading decency.

The principal victims of the film are Americans, especially the military and the majority of the civilian government. Ryan is shown under constant stress, trying to do the right thing while dodging political intrigue. At another stage, he and his government companions are ambushed from above by machine-gun-wielding terrorists. The terminally ill Greer struggles heroically to maintain the good name of the CIA. In a key scene, director Phillip Noyce intercuts Greer's sombre state funeral with images of the military coming under heavy fire from drug barons in the jungle. As Bennett mouths formal platitudes, the enemy soldiers kill US troops to the tune of 'America The Beautiful', traumatising the sole survivor – the patriotic Latino-American Domingo Chavez – and thus resuscitating the 'stab-in-the-back' myth from the Vietnam War. It is a narrative straight out of *Missing in Action* (1984–85) and *Rambo* (1982–).

At one point in *Clear and Present Danger*, US bombs kill some children who are family members of the drug dealers. Even here, the film makes a point of showing that the US military has not noticed the children. At the last minute, Clark sees them and hesitates in shock, implying that he would not have authorised the attack had he known they were present, but the missile is already on its way.

One of the unidentified boys' teddy bears shows up in the rubble on the television news later that day, prompting a visibly distressed Cutter to terminate the military mission. And so, ironically, this scene in which the US kills children actually serves to demonstrate compassion amongst America's leadership.

Following this, we might ask some reasonable questions. Where is this abundance of sensitivity from the US national security apparatus towards the people of Latin America in the real world? Did an operative's tears smudge the ink of the Pentagon's Special Forces counter-insurgency manual, which states that establishing 'death squads' in places like El Salvador and Nicaragua is particularly effective because it 'forces the insurgents to cross a critical threshold – that of attacking and killing the very class of people they are supposed to be liberating'? Did US leaders visibly crumple with the shame of sponsoring these death squads? As a priest in El Salvador described:

> People are not just killed [by the death squads] ... they are decapitated and then their heads are placed on pikes and used to dot the landscape ... Men are not just disemboweled ... their severed genitalia are stuffed into their mouths ... women are not just raped ... their wombs are cut from their bodies and used to cover their faces. It is not enough to kill children; they are dragged over barbed wire until the flesh falls from their bones, while parents are forced to watch.[16]

The answers are all too obvious, except to a Hollywood hooked on schmaltz, wilfully ignorant of reality and in thrall to power.

THE SUM OF ALL FEARS

In another Tom Clancy adaptation, *The Sum of All Fears*, the Russian President suddenly dies and is succeeded by Nemerov (Ciarán Hinds), a man whose politics are virtually unknown. The change in leaders sparks concern among US officials, so CIA Director Bill Cabot (Morgan Freeman) recruits a young analyst, Jack Ryan (Ben Affleck), to supply insight and advice on the situation. Meanwhile, a world-wide cabal of neo-Nazis steal a nuclear weapon that was accidentally discarded by Israel during the 1973 war with Egypt and Syria. In an attempt to trigger hostilities between Russia and the US, they smuggle the bomb into Baltimore and detonate it during a football game. On Air Force One, the President prepares to retaliate against Russia, but Ryan contacts Nemerov and encourages him to back down.

As an institution, the CIA is shown to have a purely de-escalatory influence – implementing the Strategic Arms Reduction Treaty (START) and finding information to facilitate conflict resolution with Russia. When the President and his advisers do apply force, it is with heavy hearts and purely as a way of demonstrating 'deterrence', in the hope that this will encourage the Russians to back down. They never apply excessive violence and are ultimately successful – with Ryan's help – in avoiding nuclear warfare.

Not surprisingly, the members of the neo-Nazi cabal are afforded no sympathy in their deaths. What is more striking though is that they are all mercilessly executed by the CIA and Russian secret police, without collateral damage, and the executions are intercut as part of an uplifting opera-backed climax where Russia and America sign peace accords. Far from questioning these presumably illegal assassinations, the film invites us to see their direct perpetrators, a CIA agent and a former KGB officer, as friends of our hero Ryan. The KGB officer actually coyly congratulates Ryan on his engagement of marriage despite seemingly having no way of knowing it had happened (short of the implied illegal surveillance). In sum, the film celebrates and makes light of the enormous covert powers of a globally operating US national security state and its allies – endorsing its methods, dismissing its victims.

In contrast, Cabot dies a tragic and heroic death whispering significant final words; the President emerges from the nuclear blast and gets straight back to running the country. Ryan himself is the most implausible and comforting figure of all: the idealistic CIA agent who shrugs off a nuclear blast and then unravels an international criminal conspiracy before hacking into the Russian President's private communication line and persuading him to stand down his nuclear forces – all in an afternoon's work.

Far from belonging in the Political Film Society's 2003 'Peace' category, the Pentagon-assisted *Sum of All Fears* provides blanket endorsement for the legitimacy of US power. Emphasising the difficulties of applying force in a world without perfect intelligence further excuses the executive for what would be – had Ryan not saved the day at the last minute – the destruction of millions of people in a nuclear war. It is US leadership itself, not even the nuked citizens of Baltimore, that suffer most obviously in a world of genocidal enemies and it is only they, the dignified and heroic leaders of the free world, who are ultimately able to stave off disaster and pave the way for peace and stability.

In this context, it is notable that CIA Director George Tenet gave the film-makers a personal tour of the Langley HQ; the film's star, Ben Affleck, also consulted with Agency analysts, and Chase Brandon served as on-set adviser.[17] Affleck is now married to Jennifer Garner, who worked with the CIA on her TV series *Alias* and who even made an unpaid recruitment ad for the Agency.[18]

Whether the CIA secured script changes is, as usual, hard to know. It was reported though that the Pentagon secured a script change to show that a US aircraft carrier under attack was not destroyed but rather just damaged, in line with the organisation's reluctance to appear vulnerable.[19]

Such tampering was barely noticed, in part because the press made a hubbub about the identity of the film's villains. Clancy's book *Sum of All Fears* (1991) ends with the President deciding to kill the Iranian leader by nuking the city of Qom, though Ryan blocks the move because he considers the collateral damage would be too great. He advocates assassination instead.[20] Not that Ryan is averse to threatening to nuke Iran himself, as when he is US President in 1996's *Executive Orders*.[21]

For *The Sum of All Fears*, however, after intense lobbying by CAIR, the film-makers agreed to change the identity of the baddies – a rare success for an outside organisation. Even so, several commentators including the *New York Times* criticised the film for not going with the original villains. The *Times* chastised the film industry: 'Neo-Nazis no longer suffice as villainous sitting ducks, and Hollywood may finally have to come to grips with the real issues that can't be reduced to black-and-white caricatures',[22] as though Hollywood's addiction to Arab and Muslim villains is any less a parody of itself.

COLLATERAL DAMAGE

Collateral Damage (2002) feigned to challenge such simplistic stereotypes. In the film, Colombian terrorists led by Claudio 'The Wolf' Perrini (Cliff Curtis) conducts a terrorist campaign in the US, which kills the wife and child of Gordon Brewer (Arnold Schwarzenegger), but misses the primary targets, CIA agent Peter Brandt and the Under-Secretary of State for Latin American Affairs. Brewer goes to Colombia, is captured by the Wolf and meets the Wolf's apparently repressed wife, Selena (Francesca Neri). They enter an alliance and the CIA rescues them by destroying the Wolf's compound. Back in Washington, DC, Brewer realises Selena was a villain all along who has used him to trick her way into a federal building in order to bomb it.

In the film, Brandt's sweepingly violent tactics are shown to be unhelpful as he uses Brewer's kidnapping to justify an assault on the terrorist compound. Brandt, though, is unusual. At a systemic level, the CIA and US authorities are less irresponsibly gung-ho and for a good reason, namely avoiding the destruction of US relations with Colombia (something with which Brewer appears reluctantly to agree). In the midst of this inter-agency wrangling, the grieving Schwarzenegger fills the part of an idealised American leader by trying to neutralise the source of the problem, the Wolf, without causing collateral damage. 'I will only kill you,' Brewer tells the Wolf in Schwarzenegger's idiosyncratic tone. The film wraps up with Brewer receiving the Presidential Medal of Freedom, bringing Schwarzengger the star and the government ever closer.

The film does make some brief allusions to the suffering of non-Americans. Selena tells Brewer that the Wolf became a terrorist when US-backed paramilitaries came and killed people in their village, including their child. However, as we learn later, Selena is a liar and a killer. Why should we trust what she says at all? Curiously, there is also a Canadian involved – Sean Armstrong – played by actor John Turturro, who was actually born in New York. Armstrong will say anything and betray anyone to escape jail, where he is imprisoned for lewd conduct. Yet when Brewer helps him escape, Armstrong good-naturedly provides him with information voluntarily, as though snapping out of a trance. It is as though Armstrong has finally remembered his – or Turturro's – American roots after spending too long in the company of nasty foreigners.

The film characterises Colombia on the whole as a war zone where 'half the country want to kidnap you; half the country want to kill you', illustrated by a lethal on-screen bus hijacking. Such characterisations are pretty sweeping, although they do reflect the deteriorating security situation in real-life Colombia. Selena appears to have fallen under the benevolent American wing so it is an even worse act when she betrays not just Brewer but also us, the audience. Furthermore, in a film specifically about collateral damage, Selena (presumably with the Wolf's tacit consent) is distinct in that she is prepared to leave her own young son to die from a bomb she has set herself, for a cause that is never sketched out. And, in case anyone was wondering if perhaps the guerrillas have an identifiable and achievable emancipatory goal, this is ultimately dashed by Selena's war cry ('It's never over!'), as though, for the Colombian leftists, warfare is an end in itself.

In the *Washington Post*, Stephen Hunter wrote that *Collateral Damage* is 'from a world where moral equivalence and promiscuous empathy were still the colours of the day',[23] but misses the fact that the film raises 'moral equivalence' only to dismiss it. Nor was the film's 'empathy' terribly 'promiscuous': while *Collateral Damage* was in production, the US was involved in Plan Colombia – a $1.3 billion, principally military, aid package. The international community had opposed Plan Colombia and Congress had tried to ensure that the Colombian armed forces improved human rights. President Bill Clinton simply 'waived most of the[se] conditions on the grounds of US national security interests', a decision 'deplored' by Amnesty International in yet another year where hundreds of Colombians were killed by their own leaders.[24]

Earlier versions of the *Collateral Damage* script had depicted Libyan terrorists – that old chestnut – instead of Colombians,[25] so the final cut, by Hollywood standards, was a triumph of creativity.

Schwarzenegger himself was refreshingly unabashed about how the film should function ideologically:

> You want to make it entertaining and make it heroic, because that's what people want to see. They want a positive outcome. They want revenge. People are very loud and clear about what they want. When we tested our movie in November, they wanted to see a positive ending, they wanted us to kick the butts of the terrorists. Because in real life it's all so complicated. You know? Where are they? Have we found them all? We've found some of them. But bin Laden is still out there, some other guys are still out there. So there's still a dissatisfaction. But in a movie you close the deal. You close the chapter. Movies bring a certain kind of closure, a fantasy that makes people feel good afterwards.[26]

Schwarzenegger in fact acknowledged explicitly some of the trends within such retrogressive, even racist, products:

> It's no different than during the Second World War or the Vietnam War. That's how John Wayne became the big hero, along with Kirk Douglas and all those guys. Doing war movies and kicking the Germans' butts and calling them 'Krauts' and all this stuff. It was great, great entertainment. They showed the Americans, losing

fewer lives, you know, and usually there's a personal focus on a guy. People like to see those things under those circumstances.[27]

THE PEACEMAKER

The Peacemaker was promoted as a cerebral Action Adventure that considered the nature of US power in a new security environment. The film was the first to be released by Dreamworks SKG and is based on the book, *One Point Safe*, by journalists Andrew and Leslie Cockburn. Between them, Andrew and Leslie have written books critical of the US–Israeli relationship, the secret war in Nicaragua and Donald Rumsfeld.[28] So, one would be forgiven for expecting their filmic work to provide some kind of challenge to official US narratives but in fact it remains consistent with Pentagon-CIA mythology.

In *The Peacemaker*, disaffected elements of the Russian military led by General Alexsandr Kodorov (Aleksandr Baluyev) steal nuclear weapons and detonate one of them in the Urals. White House nuclear expert Dr Julia Kelly (Nicole Kidman) and Special Forces intelligence officer Lt. Colonel Thomas Devoe (George Clooney) travel to Austria and then throughout the world trying to find the nukes, which Kodorov is smuggling into Iran. However, Bosnian Serb radical Vlado Mirich (Rene Medvesek) escapes with the final bomb which he delivers to his half-brother, Dusan Gavric (Marcel Iures), a disillusioned Bosnian politician, who intends to detonate it at UN headquarters in New York. Kelly and Devoe track him down but their SWAT team is unable to take him out. Kelly and Devoe find Gavrich and confront him. He commits suicide and Kelly defuses the bomb.

The US places a high premium on human life in the movie. As terrorists transport a nuclear weapon into Iran, Devoe warns his own assault team 'whatever you do, do not shoot any civilians' and then literally points out who can be killed. As the film reaches its climax, the US's insistence on careful targeting is put to the test. Devoe's marksman will not take a shot at Gavrich because a little boy is dangerously close to his sites. The marksman, wailing 'Oh God', emphasises just how deeply entrenched these common values of human rights within US power systems are: even when Devoe repeats an explicit order in an effort to prevent a nuclear explosion on US soil, the authorities do not ultimately risk the life of a child.

Devoe can be brutal, of course, but only against the usual villains. Under these circumstances, his violence is endorsed with relish.

George Clooney explained that in the original script, his character lets an unarmed villain pick up a gun so that they can 'do battle' on even terms. Clooney recalls telling the director '"I think this guy dies. You water it down if I arm him again. He just killed my best friend in front of me. I'm playing a military expert. So he dies", and I wanted it to be execution-style ... this isn't *Die Hard*.' Clooney also revealed that he based his character on Jack Nicholson's abusive general from *A Few Good Men*. The left-wing activist's major script input, then, was not to add even a line that questioned US policy but rather to show his character's brutality in a heroic and sympathetic light.[29]

Victims of US enemies are subject to much greater support than those of the US and, naturally, the enemies are demonised. In the case of *The Peacemaker*, this is particularly interesting because it was received and promoted as a film that created a more realistic and sympathetic enemy than is the norm. Producer Walter Parkes noted, 'We knew that if we could show that our "villain" has a moral imperative – even if what he's doing is utterly horrific – we'd be approaching what might otherwise have been a traditional action movie in a fresh way that would set it apart from the genre.'[30]

However, the 'tragic' depiction of Gavrich amounts to little more than a series of brief clichéd scenes – beside his wife's graveside in the pouring rain, screaming in the street like a comic-book villain, portraying the tortured pianist. Ultimately, Gavrich is a take on the traditional 'Bond villain', complete with the threatening TV address, the twisted ideological desire for apocalyptic violence and the elaborate master plan.

In contrast, overwhelming sympathetic attention is directed towards centres of US power, embodied by the hounded Devoe and Kelly, who are shown to be under constant threat and stress. It is New York itself though – the hub of US and UN power – that is the ultimate sympathetic (potential) victim. Civilian and military authorities keep reminding us that the device could destroy 'ten blocks', cause 'half a million deaths', 'destroy half of downtown Manhattan'. The city is depicted on a map as a huge target, coloured red to mark the expected nuclear fall-out should the bomb explode. Time literally stands still during the search for Gavrich; he sets the nuke at ten minutes but the film takes a full twenty minutes for the countdown, thereby prolonging the viewer's agony on behalf of the New Yorkers.

For a painfully long time, no one – including the supposedly empathetic Kelly – had even figured out that New York was the terrorists' target. New York is emblematic of American benevolence, we are invited to believe, so why would anyone possibly want to destroy it? Surely the '44th parallel' target they discover refers to Sarajevo or some other city that is actually part of the malign outside world – deadly cities where opulent Russian Mafia front companies send their goons out into the streets with guns blazing and where the police appear to have taken a permanent holiday. Cities like Vienna.

Quite apart from this inanity, the film ignores parts of *One Point Safe*, not to mention the broader debate about nuclear proliferation. Although *One Point Safe* largely concerns a small group of US policy-makers fighting bureaucracy to prevent nuclear proliferation, it does provide some criticism of US nuclear weapons policies. For instance, the Cockburns refer to the impact of corporate forces on US behaviour, reporting that a deal between the US and Russia for the US to buy five hundred tons of highly enriched uranium from Russian nuclear warheads was stalled at the US end because the US Enrichment Corporation found it more economically beneficial to enrich uranium for sale to the power industry itself rather than buying the Russian warheads.[31]

Other commentators draw attention to the Pentagon's Space Commission, which is in charge of coordinating US space military operations. Its major document, *Vision for 2020*, sets out plans for the deployment of offensive weapons in space, including nuclear weapons.[32] *Vision for 2020* speaks directly to its government sponsors, saying its aim is 'dominating the space dimension of military operations ... to achieve "full spectrum dominance"' over the planet for the benefit of US 'commercial, civil, inter-national [*sic*], and military interests and investments'.[33] Another Pentagon report resuscitates Nixon's 'Madman' theory by advocating that Washington present a 'national persona' which is 'irrational and vindictive' when US 'vital interests are attacked', because 'it hurts to portray ourselves as too fully rational and cool-headed'.[34] The provisos about US benevolence are discarded when elites talk amongst themselves, in these cases at least, but when the same information is filtered though the Hollywood system anything unsavoury is removed and an image of impartial US benevolence remains.

To conclude, *The Peacemaker* shows the US to be well within its rights as benevolent global leader to apply military force wherever it sees fit, as it is the only country with the means, good nature, and competence to do so. This is quite at odds with the political views of a very large range of analysts, seemingly including those who produced the film. It is a testament to the strength of the Hollywood ideological machine that even where a film is produced from left-wing sources and is promoted as a thoughtful new form of Action Adventure film with sympathetic enemies, it still manages to present an exceptional America juxtaposed with intransigent enemies that must be destroyed for the good of the planet.

Director Mimi Leder commented that 'we are a vulnerable world and we need to protect ourselves. That is a message I hope gets across with the film.'[35] On these terms, the film succeeds – it does indeed sound like we need to 'protect ourselves' from the entire Middle East, particularly Iraq (which, in the back-story, Devoe prevents acquiring chemical weapons) and Iran. The solution advocated is targeted state-sanctioned violence, which proceeds without negative consequences. America is, after all, the Peacemaker.

THE *RAMBO* FRANCHISE

Action Adventures produced post 9/11 have followed similar trends, all the more pronounced in certain cases. In *John Rambo* (2008), our eponymous hero – based in peaceful Thailand – rents his jungle boat to a group of Christian missionaries who plan to provide aid to the Karen people of Burma. Rambo kills river pirates who threaten the crew and, once the missionaries arrive, they fall into the clutches of the sadistic Major Pa Tee Tint. Thai officials hire mercenaries to rescue the Americans and Rambo ends up saving the day.

The narrative is so predictable as to require little comment. Suffice it to say that the film's tagline is 'Heroes never die ... they just reload'; the trailer highlights Rambo's philosophy of 'When you're pushed, killin' is as easy as breathin'', and Rambo literally wipes out more people in this sequel than he did in all the previous instalments combined (236, by one count). To top it all off, a committed Christian pacifist learns the error of his ways after seeing Rambo in action and bashes in a Burmese lowlife's head with a rock.

The earlier films had been accompanied by a welter of merchandise, including toy dolls, shoot-'em-up computer games, and a spin-off kids' television show *Rambo and the Force of Freedom* (1986), demonstrating the franchise's cartoon-like attitude to political violence.

The charity Burma Campaign welcomed the attention that the film brought to their issue and Stallone blasted the regime in numerous interviews. Perhaps, though, Stallone would have worried the junta more seriously if his film had included any information about US complicity in Burma's dictatorship that escaped the sanctions placed upon it for human rights abuses. After natural gas was found in 1982, a consortium which included the US company Unocal (later bought by Chevron) and France's Total-Final Elf built a pipeline between 1994 and 1998. During Clinton's presidency, companies already doing business with Burma were exempted from international sanctions. Britain's Premier Oil finally pulled out in 2002. Sales of natural gas are the largest source of revenue for Burma's government; gas exports accounted for half of the country's exports in 2006.[36] Maybe the junta would have seemed less steady on its feet had the film revealed any of this. Instead, it continued to butcher its people and brushed off Stallone as a 'fat lunatic'.[37]

TAKEN

Post 9/11, the tendency towards endorsing new levels of extreme violence was not confined to the ongoing *Rambo* series. Hollywood began to make state-backed torture ever more mainstream. In 2007, the US military's West Point Academy joined with human rights campaigners at a major face-to-face meeting with the producers of *24* to ask them to stop making torture repeatedly look so effective.[38] *Man on Fire* (2004) depicts an ex-CIA operative who takes revenge on a Mexican gang that kidnapped a child in his care.

Similarly, in *Taken* (2009), Liam Neeson plays another retired CIA operative who uses his old buddies to track down his daughter after she is kidnapped by slave traders in Eastern Europe, subjecting them to execution, including merciless electrical torture. Neeson finishes his spree by gunning down an Arab sheik who is about to impose his oily fatness on innocent little Kim, before whisking her off for singing lessons with a famous pop star. Ahh, Bless.

OUTBREAK

So, have any Action Adventure films been able to break out of the ideological strait-jacket? *Outbreak* (1995) makes some limited attempts. The film is about a deadly super-virus, which Major General Donald McClintock (Donald Sutherland) wants to destroy by massive bombing campaigns against any infected conurbation, including in the US. Colonel Sam Daniels (Dustin Hoffman) tries to find other means to defeat it.

Through the McClintock character, *Outbreak* suggests that elements of US authorities serve private interests rather than the common good for foreign policy goals. McClintock comments contemptuously how 'revisionist historians' are questioning the legitimacy of the US nuclear attacks on Japan in 1945. His point, although briefly stated, is accurate. Information has emerged that now interrogates the necessity of using nuclear weapons on Japan, including the apparent fact that Japan's leaders were prepared to surrender before Hiroshima was attacked.[39] The scene where Daniels convinces the pilots not to bomb the town therefore becomes a revisionist fantasy – albeit a metaphorical one – for averting Hiroshima. We see American families torn apart by the threat of disease and feel real terror as their obliteration nears, but we are also invited to see them as stand-in Japanese – and indeed, Africans – too.

There is considerable ambiguity as to McClintock's motivations: does he think it is the only way to prevent further deaths? Is he trying to cover up his previous crime in Africa? Or is he trying to cover his tracks in helping develop biological weapons for the government? Meanwhile, the presence of other powerful characters – namely the rest of the US military – suggests that the system also produces dutiful men who are willing and able to rein in unwelcome mavericks like McClintock.

Americans remain the main sympathetic victims. In the opening scene, where McClintock destroys the African village, it is American soldiers we see dying, imploring 'Get me out of here, man!'. Treatable infectious diseases kill millions of Africans every year so it is striking that the film goes all the way to that continent to show dying white people. The centrepiece of the film is an American town under threat – a fictitious event, in contrast to the real-world threats of, say, Ebola and HIV, which have decimated parts of Africa.[40]

So, although *Outbreak* does mention nefarious US interests and receives some sympathetic allusions to non-American victims, these are not the major emphases of the film. The focus, in fact, is that the US military heroically saves thousands of people after a virus gets out of control and that although elements within it may adopt brutal tactics – that may or may not be intended to benefit private interests – as an institution the military is able to root out such regrettable aberrations itself and correct its mistakes. Participant Picture's low-budget *The Crazies* (2010) uses a similarly US-centric set-up, but more hard-headedly depicts a government escalating its destruction of American towns in an attempt to contain its own biological weapons leakage.

Outbreak shares several similarities to *The Siege* (1998), which imagines an extra-judicial military crackdown that occurs in Manhattan when Islamist terrorists begin a bombing campaign. Despite this challenging portrayal, Muslims from all parts of American society remain thoroughly villainous. The FBI arrests Bruce Willis's Colonel, though he was trying to do the right thing for his country.

THE *BOURNE* FRANCHISE

The most politically critical Action Adventure was the *Bourne* series (2002–). The narrative begins with fishermen discovering the naked body of a man. The man, who has no idea who he is, finds out he is an assassin called Jason Bourne (Matt Damon) brainwashed by the CIA under an umbrella operation called 'Treadstone' and then, later, 'Blackfriar'. Bourne had been knocked unconscious into the sea when one of his missions went wrong and now CIA is attempting to kill him to cover up their complicity in state-sanctioned murder.

Doug Liman, director of the first film, *The Bourne Identity* (2002), explained that he had jettisoned almost everything from the original Cold War-era novels except the premise. He did this not only to modernise the story but also 'to bring it in line with my politics, which are definitely left of centre. I wanted to create a backstory for the film that really talked about American foreign policy ... without cramming my political beliefs down people's throats' (DVD commentary). He had been inspired, he explained, by his father, Arthur L. Liman, who was chief counsel to the Senate committee investigating the Iran-Contra affair.[41]

The studio, Universal, was remarkably willing to take risks with the movie, notably by hiring Liman, but even in this case the desire to dumb down was evident. Liman clashed with the studio repeatedly, with him wanting to spend time and money on character development scenes, whilst they demanded more action sequences. Although the shoot was ultimately a success, it was, in Liman's words, a 'fucking nightmare'.[42] 'Universal hated me', Liman explained. 'I had an archenemy in the studio. They were trying to shut me down.'[43]

In the *Bourne* series, the CIA is presented as a villainous bureaucracy gone too far. The back-story is that the dictator of a small African country, Nykwana Wombosi (Adewale Akinnuoye-Agbaje) is threatening to expose CIA operations in Africa unless it helps him back into power. It turns out that Wombosi has just survived an assassination attempt and CIA management is trying to find out if any of their men were stupid enough to have done such a thing. Unfortunately for deputy director Ward Abbott (Brian Cox) and Treadstone co-ordinator Alexander Conklin (Chris Cooper), they were in on the assassination attempt. For a moment, then, it seems as though the film will go down the usual route and show how the system corrects itself and expunges a few 'bad apples'. But as the series progresses, self-interest and the need for secrecy are shown to be rife throughout the Agency, including the deputy director Noah Vosen (David Strathairn), the Mengele-style doctor Albert Hirsch (Albert Finney) and even the CIA director himself Ezra Kramer (Scott Glenn).

The CIA even ends up eating its own: Bourne, Abbott, Nicky, and so on. 'When you start down this path,' asks Landy, 'where does it end?' Noah replies brutally 'It ends when we've won.' The franchise suggests that such a victory is not at all in the interests of the public, as the film's CIA spends most of its time acting like the Mafia rather than a protective force.

Paul Greengrass directed the subsequent *Bourne* films along similar lines to Liman's original. Greengrass explained on the DVD commentary to *The Bourne Supremacy*, 'We can't trust the authorities ... and we have to search for our own answers as Bourne is searching for his, and those answers are on the street.' He adds that government, especially secret government, 'have not told us the truth' about the Iraq War, begging the question why Greengrass saw fit to publicise the government's version of events for 9/11 in *United 93* (2006).

Ultimately, of course, the nefarious parts of CIA are brought down from within, namely by an alliance between Bourne and Landy. At the end of *3 Days of the Condor* (1975), Robert Redford is paranoid that the major newspapers will not print the proof he has that CIA has been trying to kill him as part of a secret operation to invade the Middle East. None of that in *Bourne*, where Landy simply faxes some offending documents and says coolly to Vosen, 'You better get a good lawyer.' And, of course, aside from the assassinated Wombosi, we see little indication of the impact CIA is having on foreign victims.

Still, *Bourne* is a remarkable piece of work which functions in many ways as the antithesis of the masculinised Bond series.

Aside from some foaming at the mouth from the likes of Bill O'Reilly,[44] *Bourne* has not seemed to concern right-wing commentators as much as many films in other genres. The CIA's

Hollywood liaison Chase Brandon even appeared in one of *Identity*'s DVD extra features, congratulating the realism of the Bourne character and adding it was 'really quite a thrill ride and really well done'.[45] Ultimately, in a genre that foregrounds titillation and surprise, even a product that hacks at the chains of conformity can only be taken seriously on the grounds of entertainment. It will take more than just the *Bourne* films to overturn Hollywood's lazy reliance on mainstream political ideology in the products it produces. The CIA's official chief historian also alluded to its relative unimportance when comparing it to *The Good Shepherd*, which 'warrants attention because [it] markets itself as the ... hidden history of CIA', whereas products like *Spy Game* and *Bourne* are 'transparently total fiction'.[46]

CONCLUSION

Despite the common caricature of Action Adventures as being mindless, nationalistic and violent, the genre is really little different to any other in terms of its level of critical political content. Films like *Outbreak*, *The Shooter* and *The Long Kiss Goodnight* presented critical viewpoints on US power, although playing up the hyperbolic escapism helped them to avoid controversy. *Bourne*, it must be said, dipped its toe into political controversy.

Traditional depictions of US power – as in *Executive Decision*, *Air Force One*, *Clear and Present Danger*, *Sum of all Fears* and *Stealth* – continued to dominate the genre. All presented the US in glowing terms and suggested that a hostile external world can only be brought to heel through the imposition of great force. Invariably, they turned to the Pentagon for major hardware assistance, which imposed further political limits on what could be said. *The Peacemaker* and *Rambo*, however, give some indication of how the national security services rarely need do more than oil the machinery when working the dream factory.

6
Science Fiction

Science Fiction can accommodate rather simplistic narratives depicting morally unambiguous fights between the US and space aliens, from *War of the Worlds* (1953, 2005) to the Pentagon-assisted *Invaders from Mars* (1986), as well as numerous instalments of Buck Rogers and Flash Gordon. Still, as the Science Fiction genre tends to take place in dystopic worlds, it does also have a tendency to provide more cerebral warnings of the dangers of power and technology, hence the 1968 classic *Planet of the Apes*, for instance, in which we are shown the apocalyptic results of superpower rivalries.

High-cost feature films from the past two decades, like *Stargate* (1994) and *Independence Day* (1996), have gone more down the Buck Rogers route and place the emphasis on militarised US authorities, or their thinly veiled equivalent, as world-saving heroes. Franchises like *Transformers* (2007–), *Iron Man* (2008–), *G.I. Joe* (2009–) and ultimately even the initially independent *Terminator* (1984–) did likewise with Pentagon backing and oversight.

It is striking that even relatively critical Science Fiction films from Hollywood history have been de-radicalised during the remake process. Tim Burton's 'reimagination' of *Planet of the Apes* (2001) removed some of the more radical commentary on US power: in the more recent film, the ape planet is not actually revealed to be the irradiated Earth but rather more straightforwardly a distant globe where US astronauts and their monkeys crashed thousands of years previously. Similarly, in the remake of *Godzilla* (1998), the Japanese monster is created by a genetic mutation following French nuclear tests and then destroyed by the US armed forces. Bearing in mind that the original film suggested that it was US military testing that triggered the rise of the beast and that Godzilla this time attacks the US (rather than Japan), it is all the more peculiar a set-up to absolve US responsibility for the irradiated beast's rampage.

Still, let's focus on those films which depict US power most directly.

INDEPENDENCE DAY

In *Independence Day* the US military and President Thomas J. Whitman (Bill Pullman) discover that several city-sized alien spaceships are heading towards Earth. The aliens obliterate New York, Los Angeles and Washington, and US deployment of nuclear weapons fails to penetrate the alien ships' defences. Whitmore, scientist David Levinson (Jeff Goldblum) and US Marine Corps Captain Steven Hiller (Will Smith) go to Area 51 and devise a successful counter-attack using a computer virus and the aliens' own technology, with the President himself heading a US-led world coalition.

The *New York Times* opined that *Independence Day* has 'a genial it's-only-a-movie attitude that sets it apart, quite emphatically, from other blockbuster action movies' and means it 'scarcely has any' social relevance.[1] The Pentagon certainly disagreed, as it engaged in lengthy negotiations with the producers over the script. Following Department of Defense criticisms, producer Dean Devlin told them he was willing to undertake revisions to ensure that the film will 'make *Star Wars* and *Top Gun* look like paper airplanes ... If this doesn't make every boy in the country want to fly a fighter jet', he declared, 'I will eat this script.'[2]

For the Department of Defense, though, sticking points had remained, including the film's characterisations of a weak US military as well as its depiction of Area 51 – a secret military testing ground rumoured to use extra-terrestrial technology gathered from the 1947 Roswell incident.[3] The Pentagon suggested, apparently with a straight face, that the film-makers eliminate 'any government connection' to Roswell and Area 51 and instead have a 'grass roots civilian group ... protecting the alien ship on an abandoned base',[4] in a vain attempt to skirt around one of America's most enduring modern myths.

Independence Day frames the US's deployment of force as being informed by common values, articulated by the President in his pre-battle address as being 'freedom' for mankind, 'not from tyranny, oppression, or persecution ... but from annihilation'. Prior to this realisation, the US tries everything to prevent war and collateral damage. The President encourages his people to 'reserve judgment' about the intentions of the aliens and resists the advice of the Defense Secretary to attack the alien craft. Even in the face of the alien destruction of Earth, in the President's mind lingers the possibility that the bad behaviour of the aliens is not due to their being intrinsically evil. The President does order a defensive, conventional attack but holds off from using nuclear weapons until he is positive that the aliens are beyond moral redemption. When the aliens explicitly repudiate peace, the President is finally able to say, guiltlessly in line with common values, and with macho venom the words the film has encouraged the audience to think from the beginning: 'Nuke 'em.'

The *Independence Day* aliens are vanquished through the wonder of US exceptionalism, about which we are reminded from the opening shot of the US flag on the moon to the final images of 4th of July celebrations.[5] Two British soldiers enthusiastically receive the American message of a counter-attack, speaking in the quintessentially English accent associated with the previous 'good war', the Second World War. The unity of Arabs and Israelis is made possible by US leadership. While the US insists that its own domestic boundaries remain intact, its President decides that its values, ideals and even Independence Day itself will be extended globally, thereby erasing what Gregory Jay calls the 'postcolonial condition' and returning the 'happy primitives to their place in the world'.[6]

Michael Rogin points out the deep-set misogyny that accompanies American actions. The three female career professionals are 're-subordinated to their husbands'[7]: power-suited Connie is in khakis and flannels, demoted, remarried, and jumping into Levinson's arms like a besotted cheerleader as he chomps on a cigar, while Whitmore's First Lady was killed in the alien attack on Los Angeles, a consequence of disregarding her husband's request that she leave immediately once the threat became apparent, and Jasmine has been married off into a higher economic stratum.

Indeed, if one is prepared to consider a popular metaphorical reading of the film for a moment, there is a somewhat Freudian tone to the film when the sexually abused pilot flies a suicide mission into the mother ship's suggestively open undercarriage. This was surely cinema's first faintly metaphorical world-saving revenge rape assault, though remarkably it was not the last: five years later, the heroes of *Evolution* (2001) recycled the idea and destroyed an alien invader by pumping gallons of product-placed Head and Shoulders shampoo up its fundament.[8]

Republican Presidential candidate Bob Dole summed up *Independence Day*'s prevailing ideology in terms that reflected his own sophisticated instincts: 'We won, the end. Leadership. America. Good over evil. It's a good movie. Bring your family, too.'[9]

STARGATE

Dean Devlin and director Roland Emmerich made a previous feature, *Stargate*, which legitimates the use of American power in similar terms to *Independence Day*. The film fantasises about a masculinised US, specifically projected onto the US military. It violently rejects a demonised Other, but places even greater emphasis than *Independence Day* on the US role in leading oppressed nations to freedom, specifically by invoking images and narratives of the Persian Gulf War.

In *Stargate*, the US military takes Egyptologist Daniel Jackson (James Spader) to an underground military base where he is shown a secret alien device called the Stargate. He joins a team led by the suicidal Air Force Colonel Jack O'Neil (Kurt Russell) through the Stargate portal and across the universe to a planet remarkably akin to popular Western images of ancient Egypt, including deserts, pyramids and slavery. On arrival, they find a pacified tribe called the Nagadan, ostensibly led by Kasuf (Erick Avari) but cruelly dictated to by Ra (Jaye Davidson), who pretends to be a sun god. Ra captures the team and intends to destroy Earth by sending O'Neil's hydrogen bomb back through the Stargate. Jackson and O'Neil escape, encourage the Nagadan people to rise up against their rulers, and detonate the weapon in Ra's spaceship.

The US military travels through the portal for two apparent reasons: to further scientific discovery and to neutralise any potential 'threat' from the other side. Yet when the Americans meet the Nagadan, they instinctively alter their mission to humanitarian intervention, specifically by encouraging the overthrow of Ra's regime. Nor is this through any controversial use of US force: it is Ra who strikes first, thereby bringing the innocent Americans into a fight not of their choosing.

The ancient Egyptian leaders are brutes and can therefore be dispatched by the Americans with quips like 'Give my regards to King Tut, asshole.' Meanwhile, the ordinary people are kind, hospitable and clueless – a colonial stereotype symbolising what one commentator neatly calls a 'childlike representation' of a population that 'desperately seeks guidance of a western superior in order to achieve their own potential'.[10]

Stargate highlights the Nagadans' curiosity, naivety, illiteracy, and their desire to imitate American actions and values. Appropriately, they are played by non-white, non-Western actors. In one scene, a Nagadan boy, Skaara (Alexis Cruz) mimics O'Neil by smoking a cigarette, but on doing so the smirk on his face is predictably replaced by coughing. Floyd Cheung argues that the humour in this scene is associated not only with Skaara's young age but also with his society's inexperience.[11] The situation is similar with regard to the submissive concubine, Sha'uri (Mili Avital): whilst Jackson is able to learn her language, she cannot reciprocate and offers herself sexually instead.

In the *Journal of Popular Culture*, Margaret Malamud sees the Nagadan as a metaphor for a clichéd Islamic world which shows 'a static culture forever mired in the past, awaiting American redemption'.[12] This is certainly persuasive: the city's inhabitants perform bodily movements associated with Islamic prayer rituals; the people dress like Bedouins; the town's architecture resembles a nomadic tent-city; women are covered by clothes and subordinate to men, and the desert landscape is populated by camels. Ra himself wears the regalia of a goddess rather than a god (drawing on Jaye Davidson's role as a transsexual in *The Crying Game* (1992)), inhabits the body of a boy and wears a corset associated with sado-masochistic imagery. Malamud draws the parallel with one of the ways the Western media demonised Saddam Hussein in the run-up to the Persian Gulf War, namely by dwelling on his purported sexual perversity and excesses, and his use of children as human shields.[13]

The Americans inspire Kasuf, a jittery weakling who refuses to fight for his rights, finally to head the cavalry in a violent insurrection against Ra. The natives dress themselves in US uniforms and carry US-supplied guns, one of them putting on a helmet while smoking a cigar – they are members of another denigrated sub-race that is the lucky benefactor of US power. The film climaxes with the US obliterating Ra's spaceship with its hydrogen bomb, successfully avoiding the creation of any collateral damage by first having it teleported into outer space, in line with the myth of the laser-guided 1991 Gulf War bombing campaign. Indeed, if *Stargate* is to be understood as a metaphor for the Gulf War, it would have been more accurate for the Americans to encourage Kasuf and the Nagadan to rise up, then refuse to help them whilst allowing the defeated Ra to use weapons they could easily have banned (helicopter gunships in the case of Iraq) to crush the rebellion and ensure their old ally, Ra, remained in charge.

Genuine sympathetic attention is reserved for the US military and its scientific attachment. We first see O'Neil seemingly suicidal at home and discover that his son accidentally shot himself dead with a gun that O'Neil had left lying around. O'Neil is so depressed that he is content with the mission, even when they cannot reactivate the Stargate and it seems they may be stuck in the desert permanently. We are therefore pleased for O'Neil when he makes the decision to destroy Ra while preserving himself. Jackson is also a sympathetic figure – a bumbling Egyptologist with theories no one believes so that, when he decides to stay in their world after Ra is dead, it seems as though he has finally found a home.

We are invited to rejoice, therefore, that the invading US forces – after screwing, drugging, patronising, arming and nuking an indigenous population – are finally happy.

TRANSFORMERS

Military assistance with the *Transformers* film franchise (2007–) is helping to generate particularly unambiguous, effective and widely distributed propaganda for the state, including for all aspects of the armed forces. Prevalent themes include anti-appeasement, the life-enhancing qualities of fighting for a cause and the high-tech efficiency of the US armed services. 'Why does the military let me use their stuff?' asks its director Michael Bay. 'Because they look good at what they do in my movies ... I really admire them for the service they do for their country' (DVD commentary).

The second film in the *Transformers* series, *Transformers: Revenge of the Fallen* (2009) was 'probably the largest joint-military movie ever made' boasted Army Lt. Col. Greg Bishop, and it crucially linked up all aspects of the military as rarely done before. It is careful to 'internationalise' the US war effort ('We've got Jordanians!') and the US valiantly defends Arab villagers in Qatar – site of a military base. Bishop added, 'I suspect most American citizens could never accurately describe what it is like to be a soldier in today's army. They get their perspective of the army through the media, so our job is to educate the American people on who we are. At the end of the day, they are the stockholders.'[14] Bishop's logic is admirably tortuous: the Armed Forces are obliged by the people to 'educate' them about how wonderful the Armed Forces are. This is to be achieved through the public purse.

Bay also includes scenes which take a cheap shot at the French (commenting on their cuisine) and a pair of wacky, animated characters called Skids and Mudflap, commonly identified as racist stereotypes.[15] Toys sold in the millions and General Motors used it as a 'once in a lifetime opportunity' to draw young people into the car market with extensive product placement.[16]

IRON MAN

Meanwhile, the Pentagon-assisted *Iron Man* franchise (2008–) was only marginally more sophisticated. Air Force Captain Christian Hodge, the Defense Department's project officer for the production commented that the 'Air Force is going to come off looking like rock stars.'[17] In the film, Tony Stark (Robert Downey Jr), head of a Lockheed-style arms manufacturer, travels to Afghanistan to showcase his new weapons system to US commanders. Stark's military convoy is ambushed by terrorists who torture Stark and force him to build weapons for them in their mountain-cave complex. Instead, Stark tricks them by building a prototype metal super-suit, which he uses to kill his captors and escape. Back in the US, Stark declares that his company needs to get out of the weapons business because he now has 'more to offer the world than making things blow up'. He then builds a souped-up model of the suit, becomes 'Iron Man', and embarks on a mission to kill terrorists in Afghanistan.

The emotional appeal of *Iron Man* rests on the idea that Stark, the self-confessed 'Merchant of Death', has changed his carefree attitude to arms manufacturing. Several reviewers fell for this curious conceit: the film was variously described as having 'a sprinkle of anti-war and redemption themes', being a 'pacifist statement', 'militantly anti-war profiteer', and Iron Man himself is a 'pacifist superhero' who 'shuns arms manufacturing ... [to] save Mankind'.[18] These readings of the film ignore the blatant fact that Stark actually continues to build weapons, only they are now more hi-tech and produced covertly as part of his own bodily attack-armour. Stark becomes, literally, a weapon of mass destruction, and this is shown to be great news as long as such capabilities remain only in American hands. Stark regrets that he has seen 'young Americans killed by the very weapons I created to defend them', which seems to be what he means when he says he 'had become part of a system that is comfortable with zero-accountability'.

Beyond this desire to avoid killing people on his own side any more, Stark's road to Damascus has been short indeed and the film remains little more than the usual fantasy about the US being able to blast away its enemies with impunity.

TERMINATOR

Other Science Fiction films laid greater – but still dubious – claims to progressive politics. Consider the *Terminator* franchise, variously described as 'anti-nuclear'[19] and 'anti-authoritarian'.[20] This was indeed the tone of the first three films, but by the fourth the series had been co-opted by the Department of Defense, with the result that it was a much more direct champion of the US military. Here, I focus on the 2003 and 2009 sequels, which tell us most about the franchise's approach to the US's role in the wider world.

Rise of the Machines (2003) is set in the present day, just as the US military computer system Skynet has become self-aware and is spreading a global virus as part of its plan to launch a devastating nuclear attack against humanity. A team of human survivors send a reprogrammed T-101 Terminator (Arnold Schwarzenegger) back in time from the future to protect John Connor and Kathryn Brewster because they are destined to lead a successful war against the machines. Meanwhile, the machines send back a female T-X Terminator (Kristina Loken) to kill John and other potential members of the human resistance.

In *Rise of the Machines*, US deployment of nuclear force is portrayed as a major miscalculation caused by blind faith in technology and militaristic authority. At the heart of the military industrial complex is the feeble Robert Brewster – programme director of Cyber Research Systems' (CRS) autonomous weapons division who is bullied by his Pentagon superiors into deploying Skynet.

Rise of the Machines provides little justification for the creation of such an extensive and sophisticated military-industrial complex. No designation, for instance, of the 'threats' from North Korea and Iran, pointedly referenced in *Transformers* and *Iron Man II*. There is also the hint that the build-up has something to do with a culture of 'funding' in the Pentagon, which alludes to the importance of powerful economic self-interests like CRS. Indeed, Skynet itself is reminiscent of the space-based weapons systems famously championed by the US since the early 1980s, when President Reagan poured billions into 'Star Wars' technology. The *Terminator* franchise views with suspicion these technological developments and, in *Terminator 2: Judgment Day* (1991), our heroes even triumphantly demolish a major military-industrial facility.

That said, the critique provided by *Rise of the Machines* is very limited. As always, our sympathies are with the Americans, from the vagrant Connor to the military commander Brewster. Additionally, in terms of the political philosophy espoused by the franchise, it rises little beyond Luddism and survivalism. Nor is there any indication that in the real world, at the time of the film's production and release, the US was engaged in controversial hostilities in Afghanistan and

Iraq and was reconfiguring its nuclear weapons policy to permit their usage in the event of 'surprising military developments' and other new circumstances.[21]

The nuclear war, when it finally comes in *Rise of the Machines*, has an air of inevitability which essentially provides closure. In the scene 'Mission Complete', our heroes are safe, the T-X destroyed, other bunker dwellers are getting in touch on the airwaves as we see the missiles shoot into the air over golden cornfields and explode in beautiful mushroom plumes from outer space. The final words of the film – 'The battle has just begun' – position the viewer to imagine the future of these characters and, indeed, the series did continue in *The Sarah Connor Chronicles* TV series (2008–09).

By the fourth movie, *Terminator: Salvation* (2009), the franchise had made a clear shift towards supporting establishment narratives, despite its earlier reservations. The Department of Defense provided its assistance and the film was shot at Kirtland Air Force Base.[22] A central theme is whether John Connor (Christian Bale) should prioritise striking a decisive military blow against the machines or rescue some captured humans, who are entombed – with shades of Auschwitz – by the Terminators.

For a world that is set just fifteen years after a global nuclear holocaust, the survivors are fancifully healthy, not to mention hairy. Indeed, people hang around the streets of Los Angeles, a US submarine patrols underwater and the US Air Force still functions above ground. Radiation poisoning seems to be of little concern, even though two further nuclear explosions occur during the course of the film.

Meanwhile, in the real world, the Doomsday Clock, which has for over sixty years symbolised the nuclear threat level as assessed by the *Bulletin of the Atomic Scientists*, currently stands at six minutes to midnight – midnight being 'catastrophic destruction'. None of this seems to be an issue for director Joseph 'McG' McGinty Nichol as he normalises the unthinkable.

During periods of heightened popular concern about nuclear weapons, films like *On the Beach* (1959), *The Day After* (1983) and the British-made *Threads* (1985) presented bleak, uninspiring worlds following nuclear conflict and as such they demonstrate the serious consequences of conflict. Even the flash-forwards from the first three *Terminator* films hinted at a horrible futurescape of pain, deprivation and *ad hoc* guerrilla warfare. In contrast, producer Jeffrey Silver explained that the Department of Defense gave 'fantastic cooperation [to *Salvation*] because they recognized that in the future portrayed in this film, the military will still be the men and women who protect us, no matter what may come'.[23]

Salvation's sanitised depiction of nuclear war again indicates how film-makers may omit politically disturbing material – even stretching narrative credibility beyond breaking point – for the benefit of their institutional backers.

REIGN OF FIRE

In many ways, the template for *Terminator: Salvation* was *Reign of Fire* (2002), which had imagined the human race threatened by dragons, of all things. As with *Salvation*, Christian Bale plays a resistance leader fighting for survival in a post-nuclear world (the authorities had tried unsuccessfully to nuke the dragons ... perhaps a sequel will show them trying to kill fairies with white phosphorus). Although the film is set in northern England, a high-tech American military squadron of brave dragon-killers turns up and convinces the hunkered-down Brits to fight to win, despite the risks of open warfare. Naturally, the US/UK use of force is successful and leads to a bright new tomorrow.

STAR TREK

The *Star Trek* series and spin-off movies are set hundreds of years in the future and recount the adventures of the USS *Enterprise*, a starship that is part of Starfleet, the military service of the United Federation of Planets. Commentators have long recognised the importance of US foreign policy themes in the ongoing *Star Trek* franchise, ever since the first TV series appeared in 1966.[24] Nicholas Evan Sarantakes uses original production documents to add weight to his argument that *Star Trek* constantly offered thoughtful critiques of US involvement in international affairs by means of allegory.[25]

The most overtly political of the Star Trek movie franchise was the 1991 instalment, *Star Trek VI: The Undiscovered Country*, which has obvious parallels with the end of the Cold War – widely recognised by reviewers – and, indeed, the film's writer and star Leonard Nimoy (Dr Spock) said he wanted to make the film about 'the Berlin Wall coming down in space'.[26] While the film is indeed a thoughtful critique of Cold War politics, it operates within narrow ideological parameters and only departs a fraction from what one commentator called *Star Trek*'s 'reactionary nostalgia' to change the world.[27]

In *The Undiscovered Country*, the Klingons discover they have an estimated fifty years remaining before they will have completely depleted their ozone layer. Their only choice is to join the Federation, which will mean an end to seventy years of hostility. Admiral James T. Kirk (William Shatner) and crew are called upon to help in the negotiations but peace talks go badly. A mysterious attack on the Klingons appears to emanate from the *Enterprise*, killing Chancellor Gorkon (David Warner) of the High Council. In an attempt to prevent the situation escalating out of control, Kirk and Commander Leonard McCoy MD (DeForest Kelley) beam aboard the Klingons' attacked vessel, but are tried and convicted of assassination. They are sent to Rura Penthe, a freezing gulag, but manage to escape and discover that elements of both the Klingon and Federation societies led by Klingon General Chang (Christopher Plummer) had conspired to perpetuate war between the two races, using stealth technology to frame Kirk. Chang tries to lead a direct attack on the *Enterprise* but is destroyed, and the Klingons and humans unite at a peace conference.

The American Federation is a collection of diverse worlds and cultures that respect, tolerate and celebrate their differences, and the USS *Enterprise* is a military ship on a peaceful mission to 'explore strange new worlds, to seek out new life and new civilizations'. Although the crew of the *Enterprise* has strong negative feelings towards the Other in the form of the Klingons (Kirk initially voices the opinion that the Federation should let the Klingon society die), they do not act upon these. Indeed, Kirk and McCoy put themselves in grave danger by beaming aboard the Klingons' ship to try to save Gorkon's life. By the end of the film, Kirk, McCoy and the others have learnt that their negative feelings towards the Klingons were too judgmental.

There are some indications that private interests are involved in shaping US actions. The plot to kill Gorkon and therefore perpetuate the war between the two races is hatched by 'everyone who stands to lose from peace'. This directly links the US application of power with its dominant interests. However, none of the guilty US characters are physically depicted and we are just provided with a short list of names. Rather, the focus is solely on the maniacal Chang, who rants about the pleasures of warfare as he attacks the *Enterprise*.

As expected, the enemy receives little sympathetic treatment. Even where the Klingons are depicted in submissive forms, they are not sympathetic. At Kirk and McCoy's show trial, the Klingons are shrouded in darkness and shouting like a herd of animals. Similarly, in the gulag, they have no independent voices; they simply wander around, beating things up and grunting. Their arrogant leadership contains a faction led by Chang which wants to go down fighting and is prepared to kill its own people to achieve that nihilistic end. The Soviet analogy is also morphed with an allusion to Chinese communism: David Bernardi points out that Chang is a 'throwback to the stereotype of the diabolical Chinese', drawing on images of the 'yellow horde' and Fu Manchu.[28]

The allusions to the real world paint an American-centric view of the Cold War. In reality, the Soviet Union did not destroy its natural ecosystem, whilst the US was the world's worst polluter until 2007 (when China officially took the crown).[29] Chang's assertion that 'we need breathing room' is openly equated with Adolf Hitler's desire for *Lebensraum*, whereas the Soviet Union actually fought against Nazi Germany. Furthermore, the argument that Washington defeated Moscow by forcing it to overspend in the arms race (also reflected in the movie) is hotly contested, with many historians and political analysts pointing away from this Reaganite position and to the importance of grassroots pressures and the progressive policies of elements within the Soviet leadership.[30]

The American Federation authorities are, of course, much more sympathetic than the Klingons. Kirk's anger at the Klingons is the result of their murdering his son. He gazes at photographs of the boy and speaks wistfully of his life. Although the film makes allusions to 'mirror-imaging', for example, by literally showing Kirk fighting a vision of himself, this is not to equate humans with the Klingons. In fact, the crew of the *Enterprise* overcomes its hostility towards the Klingons, despite being badly treated throughout the film.

Ultimately, although elements of the Klingons are shown to be willing to make peace with the Federation, they only do so reluctantly and because they have destroyed their own hopes for survival. Or, as Bernardi puts it, 'The Klingons and humans get along because the Klingons agree to be more like the Federation.'[31] Other elements are shown to lead an unprovoked attack on their own people to prevent peace in favour of a suicidal 'once more unto the breach'. *Undiscovered Country* is a thoughtful examination of the application of US power, but its world-view is divided into a benevolent US and a malevolent Other and the debate centres around how best the US can operate in these conditions to fulfil its inherently decent objectives.

TOTAL RECALL

Which contemporary Science Fiction films can lay claim to challenging fundamental myths about US benevolence? Two egregious cases are *Starship Troopers* (1997) and *Total Recall* (1990), which were both made by the maverick Dutchman Paul Verhoeven. *Total Recall* (1990) depicts a privatised, futuristic solar system, where Vilos Cohaagen rules an airtight city on Mars where he maintains a monopoly of air production. The city's slum workers have been turned into mutants due to their living within cheaply produced domes that do not adequately protect against cosmic rays, which the thin atmosphere cannot block. The heroic Arnold Schwarzenegger character activates an ancient alien artefact, which creates a breathable atmosphere throughout Mars.

Total Recall, therefore, provides a fairly explicit warning against established power systems. The society depicted calls to mind the *Alien* franchise (1979–), in which The Company exerts a nefarious governmental influence, although *Total Recall* is more focused on this political set-up than on the threat from a predatory extra-terrestrial. Verhoeven also implicates the media in the corporate manipulation of society. Despite being one of the most heavily product-placed movies of all time, Verhoeven mischievously placed some of the requested advertisements into the red-light district on Mars, to considerable irritation.[32] He did the same thing in *Robocop* (1988), which briefly inserted a television commercial for his own fictional family board-game 'Nuke 'Em', whose tagline is 'Get them before they get you!'

STARSHIP TROOPERS

Verhoeven ventured into a more fundamental and sustained attack on US militarism and conformity in his *Starship Troopers* (1997). Some commentators didn't seem to grasp Verhoeven's subtle critique: in the *Washington Post*, Rita Kempley complained that 'Verhoeven's tone, which varies from camp to cynical, is so inconsistent that it's impossible to decide whether he's sending up the Third Reich or in love with it.'[33] Also in the *Washington Post*, Stephen Hunter (1997) criticised the film as 'spiritually Nazi, psychologically Nazi. It comes directly out of the Nazi imagination, and is set in the Nazi universe ... Unlike films from a civilized society that see war as a debilitating, tragic necessity ... this movie sees it as a profoundly moving experience.'[34]

On the DVD commentary, Edward Neumeier explains that he wrote the *Starship Troopers* screenplay 'with Noam Chomsky in mind', and director Verhoeven said the movie was a critique of post-Second World War US foreign policy, with particular reference to the Persian Gulf War. This is in marked contrast to Robert Heinlein's 1959 book of the same name, which was a fictitious account of an infantryman's experiences infused with Heinlein's own strident militarism.

The film tells the story of three friends – Johnny Rico (Casper Van Dien), Carmen Ibanez (Denise Richards) and Carl Jenkins (Neil Patrick Harris) – who enlist in the Earth's Americanised military. Johnny is assigned to the mobile infantry, where he embarks on a ruthless training programme. He eventually decides to quit, but at that moment, horrific giant bugs from planet Klendathu launch a devastating attack on Earth, destroying Johnny's home city and killing his parents. Johnny decides to stay and fight and the film concludes with the infantrymen successfully winning a key battle and capturing a commanding 'Brain Bug'.

US institutions in *Starship Troopers* are motivated by a desire for societal control and victory, and its military personnel seek only sex and glory. This is reflected in Verhoeven's casting of lead actors from *Beverly Hills 90210* (1990–2000) and *Melrose Place* (1992–99) who were well known for their bland sex appeal. Macho bonehead Johnny joins the military to try to get together with the career-driven Carmen, who has her eye on a more successful man, leading to particularly poor test-screening responses to her character, which Verhoeven appears to have ignored.[35] Carl becomes a military colonel and – garbed in a Gestapo-esque trenchcoat – explains proudly that he makes cynical life-and-death decisions about the fates of hundreds of people each day, inverting actor Neil Patrick Harris's most famous role as the geeky teenage doctor in the TV series *Doogie Howser MD* (1989–93).

As with *Robocop* and *Total Recall*, Verhoeven inserts satirical news broadcasts throughout the movie, laden with fascistic imagery: gleeful children are handed guns by avuncular soldiers and stomp on tiny bugs to do 'their bit' for the war effort; a newscaster casually mentions that the bugs may just be retaliating because humans moved into their territory; the hulking, immobile Brain Bug is stabbed painfully and gratuitously in what appears to be his rectum, and a short scene shows Johnny and his team cheering one victory like riotous thugs.

A deluge of other films better warrant the fascistic associations heaped on *Starship Troopers* by the *Washington Post.*

AVATAR

James Cameron's blockbuster *Avatar* turns the usual colonial paradigm on its head, even though it emerges from the Murdoch Empire. 'The snarling vipers of left-wing Hollywood have been let off the leash', cried the *Sydney Morning Herald*;[36] the *Pacific Free Press* called it 'the biggest anti-War film of all time'[37], and it was widely dubbed as '*Dances with Wolves* in Space'. On the surface, *Avatar* does indeed suggest that armed resistance to America's might is understandable and even noble – a simplistic and rather unnerving message, so one can see why commentators with right-wing sympathies were prickly about the film.[38] Still, a closer examination reveals a more complex picture where the leftist vision is emaciated, thereby explaining why the first comments by Rupert Murdoch himself upon watching *Avatar* were about how exciting it would be to use its 3-D technology when screening Premiereship football.[39]

In the film, set in 2154, the RDA Corporation is mining a distant moon, Pandora, using US Marines for protection while the corporation hunts for a vital raw material called 'unobtainium'. In an attempt to improve relations with the native Na'vi and learn about the biology of Pandora, scientists grow Na'vi bodies (avatars), that are controlled by genetically matched humans. A paraplegic former Marine, Jake Sully (Sam Worthington) becomes an avatar, meets a female Na'vi Neytiri (Zoe Saldana) and becomes attached to her clan in Hometree. Although Jake is supposed to be working for Dr Grace Augustine (Sigourney Weaver), Colonel Miles Quaritch (Stephen Lang) has enlisted him to gather intelligence for a military strike that will displace the Na'vi and reveal the unobtainium that lies beneath their 'Tree of Souls'. Jake eventually commits to the Na'vi and works with their leadership to assemble a resistance coalition, which defeats the advancing corporation when Pandoran wildlife unexpectedly joins their ranks. The military personnel are expelled from Pandora, while Jake and the surviving scientists are allowed to remain. The Na'vi use the Tree of Souls to transplant permanently Jake's consciousness into his Na'vi avatar.

The US government is certainly vilified and phrases in the film like 'shock and awe', 'daisy cutters', 'pre-emptive war' and 'fighting terror with terror' tie the American aggressors quite closely to the real-world Bush administration. The leading bad guy is Colonel

Miles Quaritch (Stephen Lang), who wants to use a pre-emptive strike to defeat the Na'vi and acquire their resources, despite the fact that it will destroy Hometree. He is the muscle behind Parker Selfridge (Giovanni Ribisi), the RDA administrator. And yet despite all this, the film makes clear that the Marines are villainous corporate mercenaries, rather than tools of some future US government. Indeed, Jake makes it clear that although the Marines on Pandora are just 'hired guns', back on Earth 'they're fighting for freedom.' A sop, perhaps, to the American audience, but it makes an important distinction.

The Na'vi are undoubtedly sympathetic victims and, in stark contrast to *Stargate* for example, they are not just passive, backward figures. Rather, they have a coherent voice, proper leadership and take a full role in the defence of their land. Neytiri even kills Quaritch, thereby delivering the decisive blow as he is about to kill Jake's human form. Still, in a similar manner to *Three Kings*, key characters amongst the US invasion force are the leading figures in saving the day for the sake of the Na'vi: the heroic Jake who tames a ferocious dragon which only five Na'vi have done before, the Marine Trudy Chacón (Michelle Rodriguez) who switches sides ('I didn't sign up for this shit'), and Dr Augustine who earns her place in the Tree of Souls. Likewise, even though we are invited to respect the Na'vi, we are not required to identify with them: our heroes remain the humans, and US Marines at that.

Compare *Avatar* to, say, the low-budget South African sci-fi feature *District 9* (2009), which explores similar themes but interrogates the South African power system in a more rigorous manner, notably by depicting the apartheid-style system with cold and brutal realism through the eyes of one of its seemingly unrepentant minions. In contrast, *Avatar*'s central figure is Jake, 'a warrior who dreamed he could bring peace', but who develops through the Na'vi his naturally 'strong heart' and attractiveness to the forest's 'pure spirits'.

As with the other films in this chapter, *Avatar* hides its politics behind the veneer of science fiction – even more so since it used state-of-the-art special effects and positioned audiences to enjoy the 3-D glasses much more than its political content. 'The film is definitely not anti-American', clarified Cameron to the *New York Times*. 'My perception of the film is that the Na'vi represent that sort of aspirational part of ourselves that wants to be better, that wants to respect nature. And the humans in the movie represent the more venal versions of ourselves, the banality of evil that comes with corporate decisions that are made out of remove of the consequences.'[40] Similarly, by pandering to the film's lucrative merchandising potential and by chasing the PG-13 rating, Cameron sanitised the movie in key ways, particularly by having the villainous Quaritch and his men kicked out of Pandora in a happy ending that contrasts starkly with countless examples of such real-world struggles. 'We know what it feels like to launch the missiles,' said Cameron. 'We don't know what it feels like for them to land on our home soil, not in America. I think there's a moral responsibility to understand that.'[41] Cameron may have understood his moral responsibility, but he seems less willing to act on it. Despite campaigners appealing directly to him through a full-page advert in *Variety*, as yet Cameron has neglected to make even a single public utterance in support of the 'real-life Na'vi' Dongria Khond tribe in India, whose people and environment are being uprooted by Vedanta, a British mining corporation.[42] *Avatar* is a significant shift in emphasis politically towards open criticism of US brutality, but it's restrained as discussed above and relies more on exploiting a global feeling of cynicism about the superpower – reflected in the film's even more incredible overseas takings – than it does on a systematic critique of US action. As such, it even struck a deal with those well-known anti-corporate environmentalists, McDonald's. 'The Big Mac is all about the thrill of your senses,' said the burger chain's US Chief Marketing Officer Neal Golden in an allusion to Cameron's visual spectacular. 'There's so much going on with the Big Mac. We think it's a perfect match for the movie.'[43]

Perhaps the most instructive barometer of *Avatar*'s politics could be found in a *Fox News* interview with James Cameron at the point of the film's release. Since their ultimate sponsors at NewsCorp were one and the same, Fox was unable to unleash its customary baleful hyperbole about 'left-wing' Hollywood. For his part, Cameron appeared unwilling to recant the film's message but was content to couch it in language that sat well with his interviewer, just as he had with the marketers.

Buried several minutes into the interview, the Fox anchor asks the question: 'There's a little controversy about the storyline, whether it has anti-Americanism ... did politics enter into your head at all when developing this storyline or are people just reading into it?'

> *Cameron*: I think they're reading into it and some people are taking away the right message and some people are taking away the wrong message. I just wanna go on the record as saying that I'm very pro-America. I'm pro-military. I believe in a strong

defence. My brother is a former Marine who fought in Desert Storm and we got a lot of friends who are Marines. So I made my main character in this movie a former Marine and he embodies the spirit of the Marine Corps and all that and it's what makes him a warrior even though he's in a wheelchair. He's disabled, he's still a warrior and he takes on every challenge head on as a Marine would.

Fox anchor: Well, you're talking to the father of a Marine so I'm glad to hear you're with the Marine Corps on this.

Cameron: Yeah, exactly … .

With Cameron's all-American credentials established, he goes on to say that the film does contain two 'cautionary message[s]':

> One is against what we're doing as human beings, not as Americans, but as human beings to the environment, to the natural world. And the other one is a cautionary message which I think science fiction does very well which is to pay attention to how we deal with each other as human beings and what are the steps to war and when are our leaders accountable and not accountable and I kinda go after the idea of big corporations in this movie and how they are responsible for a lot of the ills of the world. And I don't think this is anti-America. We have a big technological, corporate civilisation worldwide and we need to make some changes if we're going to survive on this planet.

In response, the Fox anchor nods respectfully, moves on to ask Cameron about sequels, concludes the segment, and then starts talking with his co-anchor about 3-D glasses.[44] A mainstream viewpoint alluding to the dangers of the current global system is given its 45 seconds of airtime on Fox, everyone is happy and no one loses the two billion dollars.

The real significance of *Avatar* is that it is one of these partial exceptions that highlight the rule. As the *Sydney Morning Herald* admitted, those so-called left-wing 'snarling vipers' are unleashed 'in a way previously unmatched in a high-priced blockbuster'.[45] How did *Avatar* crack – if not break – the political mould? Essentially, it was because James Cameron had established himself as one of the most commercially successful film-makers of all time. Until *Avatar* itself, *Titanic* (1997) was the highest grossing film ever, making nearly $2 billion – several hundred million ahead of its nearest competing franchises like *Lord of the Rings*, *Harry Potter* and *Pirates of the Caribbean* – and he has a string of other gigantic hits including the comparably anti-corporate mentality *Aliens* (1986) and *Terminator 2* (1991) as well as the much more regressive *True Lies*. As a result, Cameron had considerable leeway and an unprecedented budget for *Avatar* (around $250 million even without including marketing) that rendered Pentagon cooperation for even the most sophisticated war scenes completely unnecessary. Cameron is, in fact, so powerful that he can thumb his nose at the suits: 'Tell your friend he's getting fucked in the ass, and if he would stop squirming it wouldn't hurt so much', he once told a Fox producer to say to an executive at the studio.[46] Shocking, especially since it's so rare, but Fox doesn't mind a prick of discomfort for that kind of money.

CONCLUSION

Paul Verhoeven's contributions stand out as the major Science Fiction movies that interrogate US interests and put some sympathetic emphasis – with a giant bug-sized nod and a wink – on non-Americans. Products like *Star Trek* are also intelligent but support US foreign policy at the level of fundamental assumptions, while James Cameron's work sometimes makes important but shallow and sanitised adjustments to the usual colonial paradigms. More typically, ostensibly brainless products like *Independence Day*, *Stargate*, *Transformers* and *Terminator: Salvation* closely follow what the celebrated essayist Susan Sontag in 1974 called Science Fiction's 'hunger for a "good war" which poses no moral problems'[47] and fought against monstrous enemies that 'provide a fantasy target for righteous bellicosity'.[48] Perhaps most disturbing is the fact that the media typically treats these products as politically insignificant or even progressive, when all too often they are quite the opposite and, in several cases, have had direct script input from the government to send the unmistakable message: 'use the force.'

7
Political Drama

The Political Drama genre, which focuses on the inner workings of powerful institutions, readily provides opportunities for narratives that challenge the usual assumptions about US benevolence. Film-makers have occasionally done just that, for example, in *Salt of the Earth* (1954) in which male and female Mexican workers strike to attain better conditions from villainous bosses; *Three Days of the Condor* (1975) in which the CIA – with complicity from corporate America including the media – plans to acquire Middle Eastern oil through invasion, and *Salvador* (1986), where a journalist chronicles the horror of living under a US-backed military dictatorship.

Despite the opportunities within the genre for sophisticated character and narrative development, though, corporate-made Political Dramas involving US foreign policy in the past twenty years have still tended to promote reactionary responses. Some pictures did so in clear terms, exemplified by the courtroom drama *Rules of Engagement* (2000). Films like *Kandahar* (2001), in which a woman returns to Taliban-run Afghanistan, were less extreme but nevertheless open enough to be co-opted by George W. Bush for political ends.[1] More typically though, films in this genre continued to depict the US as a benevolent entity but endorsed the use of force in less gleeful terms, hence *Thirteen Days* (2000) and *Spy Game* (2001). A handful of others, notably Oliver Stone's Presidential and Vietnam series, have provided considered challenges to the notion of US benevolence in world affairs.

RULES OF ENGAGEMENT

Let's first focus on *Rules of Engagement*, which the American-Arab Anti-Discrimination Committee (ADC) denounced as 'probably the most vicious anti-Arab racist film ever made by a major Hollywood studio'; the government of Yemen condemned the film as a 'barbaric and racist attack against Arabs and Yemenis', urging all Arab states to boycott it and its studio.[2] CAIR wrote to Secretary of Defense

William Cohen, saying that the film 'seems to justify the killing of Muslim men, women and even children ... it also offers a very negative image of Muslims and Islamic beliefs.'[3] Naturally, with such glowing testimony, the film received unequivocal support from the Pentagon, including the provision of the aircraft carrier USS *Tarawa*, as well as helicopters and personnel (DVD commentary).

In the film, Colonel Terry Childers (Samuel L. Jackson) successfully rescues Ambassador Mouraine (Ben Kingsley) and his family from the besieged US embassy in Yemen but subsequently feels compelled to order his men to wipe out the crowd of protesters below. There is initially some ambiguity as to whether Childers and his Marines were taking fire from the crowd or only from some rooftop snipers. In court, prosecuting attorney Major Mark Biggs (Guy Pierce) argues that Childers murdered the crowd when he should have been shooting at the snipers instead. Childers' old Vietnam buddy-turned-lawyer Colonel Hayes Hodges (Tommy Lee Jones) proves that an Islamist terrorist network operates in Yemen, but not that the crowd was armed and hostile, or that National Security Adviser Bill Sokal (Bruce Greenwood) is withholding evidence to that effect (which he is). Biggs calls one of Childers' old Vietcong enemies, Le Cao, to testify, in an attempt to prove that Childers has a track record of war crimes. However, although Le Cao asserts that Childers illegally threatened to execute him during the war, he also admits that he would have done the same thing had their roles been reversed. Childers is exonerated.

The film represents military authorities in especially glowing terms, embodied by the hero, Childers, who is rendered as a dignified and compassionate human being. Indeed, Childers and Hodges are such decent and magnanimous figures that they never refer to their enemies in racist terms – it is only when a drunken Hodges is at his lowest ebb that he fears Childers may have fallen prey to racial hatred and considered the crowd 'ragheads', 'camel jockeys', or 'fucking gooks'. Otherwise the idea that a Marine may use racist language or have racist thoughts – even when outnumbered by heavily armed Islamist terrorists – is unexplored, unthinkable. Indeed, the film revolves around the deep affection between two men of different races – Hodges and Childers – who emerge out of a racially harmonious army, and who never even raise it as an issue between themselves.

Although the civilian government in *Rules of Engagement* is vilified as selling out the military, it is fundamentally driven by diplomatic necessity rather than narrower interests. Sokal insists that the US must not lose its bases in Saudi Arabia, Jordan and Egypt because the US needs to stay friends with moderates in the region to avoid a bigger war. We are invited to recognise the heroism of the military that enforces US policy, as though force is deployed for noble values, even while the politicians who give those orders adopt tactics that are detrimental to the Marines. Indeed, the government is presented as a restraining force, albeit an imperfect one, which holds to account any excesses by the military for the cause of world stability.

No such ambiguities exist over the American civilian anti-war protesters in *Rules of Engagement*, who are viewed as an ignorant and unruly mob, one of whom starts an unnecessary fight with Childers. The representation of protesters was similar in 2008's *Vantage Point*, in which the US President appears to be assassinated by Islamic terrorists just as he is announcing a celebrated new peace initiative between the Western and Muslim worlds. Strikingly, *Vantage Point* is told from no less than eight different perspectives – not one of them from the throngs of protesters depicted on screen, who carry pictures of the President defaced with banal messages, even whilst we the audience are encouraged to think the President is really a pretty good guy.

Still, in *Rules of Engagement*, as much as we are encouraged to sympathise with Childers' decision to 'waste the motherfuckers', for the first half of the film the implication is that his order in the field could well have been morally and legally wrong. An intriguing premise ... but this ambiguity is dramatically trounced by a remarkable and pivotal scene: Sokal decides to watch the tape. We see CCTV footage of the incident, which shows very clearly that every member of the crowd was armed and hostile. Childers' subsequent separate flashback shows the same thing and even includes a little amputee girl – initially a pitiful sight – viciously firing an AK-47. The film implicates every strata of Yemeni society in the terrorist atrocity – government, police, ordinary men, women and children.

The original scenes of the embassy confrontation clearly show images of unarmed Yemeni being gunned down by Childers and his troops, but the later footage directly, graphically and convincingly contradicts this by showing a hostile crowd on an objective record (the videotape), which the government is then compelled to destroy. The film-makers' cack-handed botch-job – apparently the consequence of showing versions of the movie to test audiences – fundamentally renders the film an unambiguous contest between

US Marines, who make morally righteous judgements, and a world of civilians, who are prepared to lie and – in the case of the Yemenis – kill.

Little context is provided for the weekly Yemeni protests which gives any suggestion they are motivated by social grievances. Just two brief explanations are vocalised, both from Americans. In response to her child's question 'What's wrong, Mommy?', as they cower beneath a desk in the besieged embassy, Mrs Mourain replies, 'The people are upset about some things ... they're trying to get attention ... .' Sokal describes the protests in derogatory terms that are left unchallenged by the rest of the film – the protesters are motivated by 'the usual bullshit about American presence in the Gulf'. 'Presence', instead of 'political, economic, and military impact'; 'The Gulf', instead of 'holy sites' – nothing that complicates the message that the Yemeni are fighting a 'bullshit' cause.

In his review of the film in *The Nation*, Stuart Klawans points out that the government blaming the military is hardly a standard response. For example, in July 1988, guided missile cruiser USS *Vincennes* attacked an Iranian civilian airliner, killing 290 people without provocation.[4] Middle East reporter Robert Fisk explained that the US government issued notes of regret for the loss of human life but never admitted wrongdoing, accepted responsibility, or apologised for the incident. Officially, the US continues to blame Iranian hostile actions for the incident and the men of the *Vincennes* were all awarded combat-action ribbons.[5]

Rules of Engagement was written by James Webb, Secretary of the Navy under President Reagan. It offers a militaristic right-wing viewpoint on US foreign policy: US enemies are contemptible; non-American victims are insignificant and, indeed, in this case, the victims are brutal maligned perpetrators. The film could have been, and perhaps was initially intended to be, a meditation on the moral ambiguities of state violence but during production it became something quite different. At the climax of the film, the final show of solidarity between the two former enemy soldiers – Childers and Le Cao – further morally elevates military men above civilians and whitewashes the enmity between the US and Vietnam, as though indigenous victims of American military attack can and should forgive – even respect – US atrocities if only they can appreciate their benevolent intent.

Rules of Engagement's denouement might be compared to that of *Basic* (2003), in which we are led to believe a unit of Marines have killed each other but who have in fact faked their deaths so they can operate secretly in the war on drugs, an ending similarly prompted by test audiences (DVD commentary). Hollywood's tendency to chase profit within an ideological system here had a profound effect on the ideology of a film and the original intent of its makers. Likewise, in *Swordfish* (2001), a CIA renegade robs billions of dollars, which is eventually revealed to be for financing a private army to kill a 'Bin Laden' figure.

CRIMSON TIDE

In *Crimson Tide*, the rebellion in Chechnya has spread to neighbouring ex-Soviet republics, prompting a massive Russian attack. The US has stopped providing aid and the Russian ultra-nationalist Vladamir Radchenko has denounced this as an act of war and seized a naval base. The US sends in the nuclear submarine USS *Alabama*, under the command of Captain Frank Ramsey (Gene Hackman) and his new XO Lt. Commander Ron Hunter (Denzel Washington). The Pentagon sends a message ordering a nuclear strike on Russia, but the submarine is attacked and the radio systems knocked out. An emergency message received during the battle is only partially received. Ramsey wants to ignore the second message and nuke Russia immediately, while Hunter wants to wait for confirmation. The conflict escalates into mutiny as Ramsey and Hunter fight for control of the *Alabama*'s missiles.

The US civilian government's actions are shown to be for the benefit of world peace. The President, specifically identified as Clinton, has suspended economic aid to Russia because he is 'appalled at the loss of human life'. Although Radchenko threatens to use nuclear weapons on the US and Japan, the US does not retaliate immediately but instead sends in submarines as a defensive force and actually succeeds in not killing anyone at all. The fundamental goodness of US behaviour is thrown into still greater relief through the extreme demonisation of the Russian enemy: Radchenko is shown fulminating at a party conference whose platform is akin to that of the real-life ultra-nationalist Vladimir Zhirinovsky, who gained a sizeable percentage of the vote in Parliamentary elections in the mid-1990s. In reality, though, whilst Zhirinovsky never gained executive office, Radchenko easily acquires power, access to nukes, and then declares that he will use these weapons on the US and Japan in the event that just one Russian citizen is killed.

On the US side, while Ramsey is a capable and inspirational leader, he is liable to aggressive outbursts, takes too literal an interpretation of the rulebook, and reveals a racist streak. Throughout the film, however, the idea of using force, even nuclear weapons, against Russia is never criticised. It merely suggests, through Hunter, that in this instance the Russians might already have been defeated by the conventional military. This is the internal debate for 'Everyman' Lt. Peter 'Weaps' Ince (Viggo Mortensen), with whom the audience is encouraged to identify at the crucial point of the mutiny.

Crimson Tide ends with a caption that explains in the real world, as of 1996, naval commanders no longer had the authority to launch nuclear weapons without the involvement of the President. The caption, in fact, ignores more fundamental criticisms of US nuclear weapons policy, not least the fact that – as independent military analyst Han Kristensen discovered through national security documents declassified under the Freedom of Information Act (FOIA) – that policy permits the first use of nuclear weapons in a wide range of new circumstances.[6] These trends became even more pronounced following 9/11, when the Pentagon published its 2002 *Nuclear Posture Review*.[7] As such, the film uses Hunter as an idealised naval officer to overcome what the narrative suggests is merely a curious technical defect in US nuclear weapons systems.

In conclusion, *Crimson Tide* shows that the US uses its power to police the world, elements of which are willing and able to destroy the United States with nuclear weapons. The film considers no political solution to this problem and makes no indication that the US is part of the problem or able to be part of a non-military solution. Even though the rebels are ensconced in a military base 'between the Chinese and North Korean borders', there is no suggestion that China – the major regional power – might be a complicating factor or that it might be able to help defuse the crisis. Instead, the US places the nuclear option on the table from the outset and the film shows that the good men of the US Navy are rightly ready to push the button to save the potential American victims at the expense of the Russians. Somewhat implausibly, the 60,000 rabid Russian nationalists surrender as soon as they are faced with fighting their own countrymen (conveniently meaning that the Americans do not have to kill a single person) and, simply by threatening nuclear use, the US is able to help bring the situation back from the brink and preserve peace.

Crimson Tide is ultimately an optimistic story, in which the calmer, intellectual black man Commander Hunter is ascendant in a rational military. Hunter and his supporters win the argument, save the day, and Ramsey gracefully retires. In reality, military historian

Lawrence Suid notes, Hunter 'would probably have been jailed or, at the least, given a dishonorable discharge'.[8] Real life does not always offer the comforting solution of a morally sophisticated group of servicemen but let's not let that stand in the way of a nice story.

SPY GAME

Spy Game (2001) supports US power more subtly, with some limitations. It presents an institutionalised strain of self-interest in the CIA – connected with corporate interests – though the rest of its depictions follow the standard lines about US foreign policy. The CIA's Chase Brandon advised on the film for a while but not surprisingly ultimately signalled his disapproval when the final rewrite 'showed our senior management in an insensitive light'.[9]

Spy Game is set in 1991, just as the Cold War has ended. CIA agent Nathan Muir (Robert Redford) discovers that his former protégé Tom Bishop (Brad Pitt) has been arrested by China and is due for execution in 24 hours. A CIA task force headed by Director Cy Wilson (Garrick Hagon) and dominated by Charles Harker (Stephen Dillane) quizzes Muir about Bishop's career in an attempt to unearth information so that the Agency can distance itself from him and avoid an embarrassing diplomatic incident during US-China trade talks.

Muir recounts his history of Bishop from Vietnam in 1975 to Cold War Berlin and on to mid-1980s Beirut. He presents Bishop as an idealistic figure in stark contrast to himself and it becomes apparent that the Chinese have captured Bishop trying to break out a girlfriend (British aid worker Elizabeth Hadley (Catherine McCormack), who had blown up the Chinese embassy in London) from Su Chow Prison. Although estranged from Bishop, Muir breaks all of his own rules about becoming emotionally involved and covertly spends his retirement fund on privately financing a US Special Forces rescue mission for Bishop and Hadley.

The CIA's most senior players are shown willing to sell out their own man in order to secure economic agreements between the US and China. Still, a strong strain of decency runs through the organisation. Most obviously, this is represented by Bishop, played by that idealised model of modern masculinity, Brad Pitt. Additionally however, Muir is a fundamentally good guy, despite appearances to the contrary. When a Lebanese faction supported by the US destroys a building, Muir sees it as a good result – 74 dead, 1 terrorist killed – but Bishop is less happy, seeing such reasoning as 'fucked up' and quits the CIA in turmoil. It is the US which is victimised by its own brutality – it is too sensitive and benevolent to participate in the harsh realities of the world without feeling great pain.

A key scene summarises the essential message of the film, as Muir and Bishop argue about the rights and wrongs of selling out an East German refugee, Frederick Schmidt (Joerg Stadler):

> *Bishop*: Ah, Jesus Christ, you just ... You don't just trade these people like they're baseball cards! It's not a fucking game!
> *Muir*: Oh, yes it is. It's exactly what it is. And it's no kid's game either. This is a whole other game. And it's serious and it's dangerous. And it's not one you want to lose.
> *Bishop*: Nathan, we killed this man. We used him and we killed him. Okay, then you got to help me understand this one. You got ... Nathan, what are we doing here? And don't give me some bullshit about the greater good.
> *Muir*: That's exactly what it's about. Because what we do is unfortunately very, very necessary. And if you're not willing to sacrifice scum like Schmidt for those that want nothing more than their freedom, then you better take a long hard look at your chosen profession my friend. Because it doesn't get any easier.

Redford's jaded screen image complements his role – the Brad Pitt of his day now past his prime. His redemption within the film is a fantasy of what the CIA could be like if it stuck to its 'old-school' idealism. Schmidt, it should be added, is revealed to be a traitor to Bishop anyway.

Bishop and Muir are joined in their benevolent spirit by various other elements of the CIA's apparatus, namely the various workers in the field and the office with whom Muir has built up friendly relationships and who are willing to help him out. And anyway, why should CIA management provide favourable treatment to Bishop? He is an ex-agent who has broken the law, while trying to rescue a terrorist. Wilson and Harker are perhaps not as isolated in their seeing the world as shades of grey as are Bennett, Ritter and Cutter in *Clear and Present Danger*, but the films are similar in their attitude to US authorities.

Spy Game sets up a cinematically satisfying conclusion where US helicopters fly into Chinese territory, guns blazing, and rescue Bishop and his girl. The film's construction of victims, enemies and US power – albeit with a serious self-interested and cold-hearted strain in the CIA – sets up the audience to accept and applaud the application of US military force on Chinese sovereign territory without apparent regard to the consequences or legality of the action. All that matters is that America gets back its favourite son.

THIRTEEN DAYS

Thirteen Days is based on documented evidence from October 1962, during the Cuban Missile Crisis. The Pentagon gave a dismissive response to the film's script, complaining about the depiction of the downed U-2 reconnaissance plane and the characterisations of both General Curtis LeMay and General Maxwell Taylor (Chairmen of the Joint Chiefs) as 'unintelligent and bellicose'.[10] It is certainly true that the film is heavily critical of the military establishment of that time. However, it still manages to endorse the legitimacy and use of US power up to and including the right to use nuclear weapons. Not surprisingly, the credits reveal it did have some cooperation with the Kennedy family.

Most of the action in *Thirteen Days* is seen through the eyes of Kenny O'Donnell (Kevin Costner), special adviser to the President. American U-2 surveillance photos reveal that the Soviet Union is in the process of placing nuclear weapons in Cuba. Once operational, these weapons would give the USSR first-strike capacity against US territory. The Joint Chiefs of Staff under General Curtis LeMay (Kevin Conway) advise military strikes against Cuba, which could lead the way to another invasion of the island, but President John F. Kennedy (Bruce Greenwood) is reluctant to follow through because of the predictable retaliation from Moscow that could escalate to global nuclear war. Kennedy imposes 'quarantine' on Cuba, which eventually is effective in repelling most Soviet ships approaching Cuba, but he is ultimately forced to withdraw US nuclear weapons from Turkey and to guarantee not to invade Cuba in a secret deal that ends the stand-off.

The Joint Chiefs are portrayed as aggressive anti-Communists, who see warfare as a legitimate, effective and useful policy tool. O'Donnell says that they 'want a war' to 'make up for' the Bay of Pigs debacle and the film makes it clear that such a stance would likely have apocalyptic consequences. LeMay is depicted as a warmonger – excited by the idea of attacking the 'big red dog' that is 'digging' in the US's 'backyard' – and showing an arrogant carelessness about the consequences. At the same time though, we are invited to accept the theory, propagated by both military and civilian authorities, that 'appeasement only makes the aggressor more aggressive' and that, one way or another, the missiles must be removed from Cuba or else the world will be forced into war. Just as Hunter says to Ramsey in *Crimson Tide*, O'Donnell explains that ultimately the Pentagon desire to apply immediate force could 'well be right'.

The American civilian authorities in the film are portrayed in glowing terms. The presentation of the civilian administration is consistent with the popular image of 'Camelot', a description of Kennedy's thousand days in office which was initially propagated by Kennedy's speechwriters Arthur Schlesinger Jr[11] and Theodore Sorensen[12] and that still holds true in popular programming – including the TV series *R.F.K.* (1997), the made-for-TV movie *RFK* (2002), and the movie *Bobby* (2006). Even Soviet Ambassador Anatoly Dobrynin (Elya Baskin) in *Thirteen Days* says that John and Bobby are good men.

O'Donnell functions as the 'Everyman' character, who allows us, the audience, to get an insider's view of the Kennedy brothers' partnership. Rather than being a secretive association, then, the Kennedys are shown bringing us/O'Donnell into their lives and therefore enhancing the myth of open government in this period. They are prepared to put the world and their nation above narrower interests, Bobby exclaiming 'I don't care if this administration ends up in the freaking toilet!' When O'Donnell's wife tells him that he is smart, he responds wistfully – almost romantically – 'not like them', as though there is something intangibly wonderful about the leadership of these two brothers. More broadly, the Kennedys represent something about America as a nation: the 'free world' that repeatedly emphasises a 'sneak attack' is counter to US values. As we shall see, this is in stark contrast to the historical record.

Americans, specifically the US authorities themselves, are the principal victims in the film. The rest of the American population is largely ignored, not to mention the Russians, the Cubans, and the rest of the world. Every member of the executive is shown to be under tremendous strain. The President is taking painkillers, is unable to sleep, and repeatedly expresses a lack of enjoyment in holding Presidential office at this time. Bobby feels pressurised to be brilliant and ruthless, which he claims almost tearfully does not come naturally to him. The film closes with a respectful President paying tribute to the fallen airman over-laden with respectful images of his coffin draped in the Stars and Stripes.

Meanwhile, the Soviets are duplicitous and conniving. O'Donnell equates the missiles with the ship that bombed Pearl Harbor, thereby associating the Soviet Union with imperial Japan and acting as though an attack was already under way. The Russian spy who makes an overture to the US turns out to have been a decoy. The Soviet Embassy is framed in ominous terms – shrouded in darkness, the iconic hammer and sickle fluttering in the breeze, smoke billowing from its chimney as it burns documents in preparation for war.

Some historical perspective from leading historians on the 13 days in question reveals just how deferential the film's narrative is to the Kennedy administration. The film misleadingly presents the Cuban Missile Crisis as being unprovoked by the US and solved exclusively by the Kennedys.

In truth, following Fidel Castro's overthrow of the Cuban dictator General Fulgencio Batista in January 1959, in the winter of 1959–60, Morris Morley says 'there was a significant increase in CIA-supervised bombing and incendiary raids piloted by exiled Cubans' based in the US.[13] Robert Kennedy led the top-level interagency group that oversaw Operation Mongoose, a programme of paramilitary operations, economic warfare and sabotage launched in late 1961 to topple Castro,[14] a programme which was 'the centerpiece of American policy toward Cuba from late 1961 until the onset of the 1962 missile crisis', reports Mark White.[15] Robert Kennedy informed the CIA that the Cuban problem carries 'the top priority in the United States Government – all else is secondary – no time, no effort, or manpower is to be spared' in the effort to overthrow the Castro regime.[16] The chief of Operation Mongoose, Edward Lansdale, provided a timetable leading to 'open revolt and overthrow of the Communist regime' in October 1962. The 'final definition' of the programme recognised that 'success will require decisive US military intervention', after terrorism and subversion had laid the basis. The implication is that US military intervention would take place in October 1962 – when the missile crisis erupted.[17]

Raymond Garthoff is slightly more circumspect, arguing that there was 'no political decision or intention' to invade Cuba again before October 1962, but agrees that the Kennedy administration directed Mongoose and that it 'was not unreasonable for Castro and the Soviet government to be concerned over the possibility of intensified US hostile action against Cuba in 1962'.[18] Famously, Kennedy had aborted at the last minute an earlier CIA-sponsored invasion, leaving thousands of exiled Cubans to be killed by Castro's forces at the Bay of Pigs in April 1961. If the military had to 'make up for' the Bay of Pigs, as O'Donnell says, the civilian authorities were surely in the same boat.

US operations continued in Cuba during the most tense moments of the missile crisis. They were formally cancelled on 30 October, several days after the agreement between Kennedy and the Russian Premier Khrushchev, but went on none the less. Garthoff writes that on 8 November, 'a Cuban covert action sabotage team dispatched from the United States successfully blew up a Cuban industrial facility', and that 'the Soviets could only see' US actions as efforts 'to back-pedal on what was, for them, the key question remaining: American assurances not to attack Cuba'.[19] Even after the crisis ended, Kennedy renewed the terrorist campaign and ten days before his assassination, he approved a CIA plan for 'destruction operations' by US proxy forces 'against a large oil refinery and storage facilities, a large electric plant, sugar refineries, railroad bridges, harbour facilities, and underwater demolition of docks and ships'.[20]

The Political Film Society nominated *Thirteen Days* in its 2001 Expose category, but the film ignores and denies overwhelming evidence for repeated US and US-sponsored 'sneak attacks' on Cuba, known about by Kennedy, and thereby helping to provoke the 13 days of crisis. The film legitimises US civilian power in the Kennedy era and only criticises those military leaders still mired in the Second World War paradigm (the military behave honourably elsewhere). No wonder the Bush administration saw fit to screen *Thirteen Days* at the White House, even while the Air Force refused to show it.[21]

It is true that Kennedy handled the immediate 13 days of crisis with a cool head, in the sense that he did not follow the lunatic council of his Joint Chiefs. Still, who would ever know from Hollywood the part played by Vasili Arkhipov, the Russian submarine commander who prevailed on his fellow officers not to fire a nuclear torpedo, even though the first Soviet captain had given the order on 27 October? US destroyers under orders to enforce the Cuban blockade did not know that the Soviet submarines that Moscow had sent as protection for its ships were carrying nuclear weapons, so the Americans began firing depth charges to force them to the surface – a move the Soviets interpreted as the start of the Third World War. Arkhipov 'saved the world', according to Thomas Blanton, director of the National Security Archive,[22] but his story is forgotten – replaced instead by a similar but fictionalised tale with a US-friendly makeover in *Crimson Tide*.

Thirteen Days emphasises the difficulties of applying US force in a complex world but, in effect, as with *The Sum of All Fears*, it excuses the executive in what would have been world-wide genocide/suicide. It is the US elites themselves, not ordinary people or even American citizens, that are shown to endure the burden of power and it is only they – the heroic leaders of the free world – who are ultimately able to stave off disaster and pave the way for peace and stability. The film sidelines the real-world Kennedy administration's preoccupation with launching secret attacks, including an attempted invasion, against Cuba, which persisted into the crisis and beyond. Rather, it buys into and perpetuates a glorious vision of the Kennedy administration that elides key narratives based on a lesser-known documentary record.

A FEW GOOD MEN

Like *Thirteen Days*, *A Few Good Men* (1992) followed a similar ideological line to *Crimson Tide* and, like *Thirteen Days*, did not interrogate the notion of a 'threat' from Cuba. In the film, Jack Nicholson plays a hard-line colonel trying to cover up his ordering of an extra-judicial punishment of a Marine under his command, whom he considered to be a liability in the ongoing Cold War with Cuba. By having military lawyers Tom Cruise and Demi Moore successfully prosecute the colonel, the film appears to criticise the excesses of US power. However, *A Few Good Men* simultaneously indicates that the military is capable of regulating itself from within, and the very fact that the question is raised – that is, should the military be above the law when national security is at stake? – suggests that US power is of fundamental importance in controlling a dangerous world. This completely ignores the fact that Cuba provides no conceivable military threat to the US – particularly in the post-Cold War world – and that, on the contrary, it is the US that has inflicted economic and military punishment on the Communist island for decades.

THE FILMS OF OLIVER STONE

JFK and *Nixon*, Oliver Stone's 'Presidential films', alleged a high-level conspiracy to perpetuate and escalate US warmongering, notably in South East Asia and crucially by killing the 'peacemaker' President Kennedy. Mainstream commentators condemned both *JFK* and *Nixon* as conspiracy theory masquerading as truth.[23]

The two films challenged US foreign policy by showing it as the product of its constituent military and corporate interests, which it did explicitly, and to an extent that is unprecedented in mainstream Hollywood cinema. Nevertheless, both hearken back to a mythical age of enlightenment under Kennedy that legitimates US power retrospectively, ignoring the victims of the Kennedy administration.

In *JFK*, New Orleans District Attorney Jim Garrison (Kevin Costner) reopens the investigation into the assassination of President Kennedy. Soon, he and his family come under threat from shadowy government, anti-Castro Cuban, and Mafia forces. Garrison becomes increasingly convinced that the ostensible assassin, Lee Harvey Oswald (Gary Oldman), was not guilty and that elements of the civilian and military elite were responsible for the murder and subsequent cover-up, as well as further assassinations such as that of brother Bobby in 1968. Garrison is contacted by an anonymous man who claims to have insider information, Mr X (Donald Sutherland), who explains to Garrison that certain authorities killed Kennedy because he was going to withdraw US forces from Vietnam and that they wanted to maintain a war economy regardless of human cost. Armed with this knowledge, Garrison presses ahead with his doomed prosecution of Clay Shaw (Tommy Lee Jones), who appears to know more than he is admitting about the powers involved.

Nixon is a biopic of Richard M. Nixon, 37th president of the United States. The film begins with the Watergate burglary which precipitated his downfall. Nixon's actions are driven by nebulous personal insecurities and a key aspect of his obsession with cover-ups is to do with events surrounding the assassination of Kennedy, which was the result of blowback from operations in Cuba in the early 1960s. The film argues that Nixon, along with other establishment figures, was involved in these operations, knew some of the gangsters involved – gangsters that were also used to break into the Watergate Hotel – and suspects that they were part of the same team that murdered Kennedy.

In both films, US authorities are not shown to be operating for common values, but rather for powerful and maligned domestic interests. Garrison and his team face a cabal of fascists which hold powerful positions in, and characterise the culture of, the US civilian and military elites. Mr X outlines in detail how these forces hated the Kennedys for their progressive politics and arranged for his murder, cynically using Oswald as a patsy. The conspiracy included President Lyndon Johnson himself and utilized the Mafia and anti-Castro Cubans. These power systems are portrayed in frightening terms –

faces concealed, operating in the dark, and associated with weird sexual rituals. *Nixon* actually characterises the system as 'the beast', incarnated as Larry (previously *Dallas*'s 'J.R.') Hagman's oil tycoon and Bob Hoskin's predatory J. Edgar Hoover. In a pivotal scene set at the Lincoln Memorial, a young female peace protester tells the President he is unable to stop the war 'even if [he] wanted to'. because he is not in control, which a stunned Nixon recognises as a fundamental truth that had previously eluded him.

The principal victims of US power in *JFK* are the American people themselves. It is they who have been deceived, they who are suppressed and killed, they who lost their 'slain father' President. There is little discussion of the consequences of the war economy to people outside the United States under Kennedy and other administrations who were killed, injured and displaced in their millions. *Nixon* goes little further in addressing this issue – the principal victim of the film is Nixon himself, who comes across as a tragic figure who could have been great if only he had been loved in his childhood. There are some brief references and images of the US bombing of Cambodia and Laos, but their effects are not depicted. *Nixon* perpetuates the idea that Kennedy was innocent and unaware of CIA efforts to assassinate Castro, when independent evidence (see above) and even Stone's own script footnotes admit that this was not the case.[24] Such an approach to history suggests all will be 'like the old days' when the 'good guys' were in office, if only we can root out the villains.

Nixon depicts Kennedy as 'stealing' the 1960 election, which avoids Stone's earlier idolisation of Kennedy. *Nixon* also provides information about the nefarious activities of the Nixon administration more broadly, rather than fetishising the Kennedy assassination so absolutely as in *JFK*. Nevertheless, in *Nixon*, Kennedy remains the last best hope for the US – the man that people 'want to be'. Stone's focus also ignores arguably more fundamental abuses of power. As part of its psychological study, *Nixon* lauds Tricky Dickie's achievements in recognising China and signing arms agreements with Russia, but sidelines or neglects to mention other foreign policy incidents, such as Nixon's back-channel promises (subsequently broken) to the Vietcong, urging them not to sign a peace deal with the Democrats.[25]

Nevertheless, Stone's films *are* amongst the most radical attacks on US power to have been produced in mainstream cinema in the post-Cold War world. Though it made just $78 million at box office, *JFK* generated a colossal amount of political debate in the mainstream press – something that even giant films like *Avatar* cannot do. *JFK* was the decisive factor behind Washington's decision to release millions of pages of previously secret files about the Kennedy assassination. No wonder that the 1992 Assassination Materials Disclosure Act is commonly referred to as the 'Oliver Stone Act'.[26]

Furthermore, when we consider Stone's full gamut of work, we see a quite comprehensive interrogation of US exceptionalism. Of note, *Platoon* (1986) extensively depicted the horrific rape of a Vietnamese girl by US forces; *Heaven & Earth* (1993) was shot entirely from the perspective of Le Ly, a Vietnamese woman caught between the fighting factions in Vietnam and forced into prostitution and poverty after living an idyllic life in the countryside. Although Tommy Lee Jones's character – a Marine who tortured Vietcong for Special Operations – is also a pitiful figure, it is Le Ly (who eventually becomes the Marine's wife) who is the principal sympathetic victim. Ultimately, then, Stone's focus in the Presidential films is America-centric, but overall in the 1980s and '90s, he has produced work that is challenging to the usual Hollywood perspectives about US power.

And yet Oliver Stone did a political about-turn for his 2006 *World Trade Center*, which depicted a story of heroic firemen trapped in the World Trade Center on 9/11, in what syndicated columnist Cal Thomas called 'one of the greatest pro-American, pro-family, pro-faith, pro-male, flag-waving, god-bless America films you will ever see'.[27] L. Brent Bozell III, president of the conservative Media Research Center and founder of the Parents Television Council, called *World Trade Center* 'a masterpiece', and emailed 400,000 people saying 'go see this film.'[28] The marketing team behind *World Trade Center* was Creative Response Concepts, the same team which advised the group Swift Boat Veterans for Truth that had assaulted Democrat presidential candidate John Kerry's war record in the 2004 election. Strange that for all his fulminations about the New World Order – whatever that is – Stone seems happy to work with it.

Stone added some all-American machismo to his *World Trade Center* script: US Marine Dave Karnes sees the television news footage in his suburban Connecticut office, declares 'This country's at war!', and later predicts that some good men will be needed to 'revenge this' (*sic*). Karnes visits his pastor, tells him the Lord is calling him, gets a regulation haircut, dons his Marine uniform and drives straight to Ground Zero where he enters the disaster site. As the credits roll, we learn that Karnes re-enlisted for two more tours of duty and fought in Iraq.[29] In *Sight and Sound*, B. Ruby Rich calls

Stone's Karnes 'a biblical warrior out of the New Testament by way of Vietnam', and asks 'Did ex-military man Stone, like Karnes, snap back into some wartime persona and forget all the political positions and conspiracy investigations of his career?'[30] In light of this, it is laughable that Paramount followed the usual procedure for any movie that seems political, namely telling the press that this is 'not a political movie'.[31]

Strikingly, prior to *World Trade Center*, Stone had repeatedly denounced the film industry, hinted at believing the 'inside job' story of 9/11, and had expressed the desire to make a balanced film about terrorism. In a panel discussion in October 2001, he exclaimed, 'there's been conglomeration under six principal princes', referring to Hollywood corporations like Fox and Time Warner, 'they are kings, they are barons! – and these six companies have control of the world. Michael Eisner decides, "I can't make a movie about Martin Luther King, Jr – there will be rioting at the gates of Disneyland!" That's bullshit! But that's what the new world order is.'[32]

Stone was referring to his thwarted attempts to make *Memphis*, a film about the conspiracies surrounding the murder of Martin Luther King. In 1997, Stone was also reported to be considering scripts about the activist Randall Terry and the Israel–Palestinian conflict.[33] Stone also considered making *Mission Impossible II* with Tom Cruise, which he said would be 'a vehicle to say something about the state of corporate culture and technology and global politics in the 21st century'.[34] None of this happened, and Stone also turned down the offer to make *The Peacemaker*[35] (surely he would have made a more challenging picture out of it), in favour of making the apolitical *U-Turn* (1997), which his co-producer Dan Halfstad explained was about making a movie 'that wasn't going to be reviewed on the op-ed pages'.[36]

At the 2001 panel discussion, Stone called for a new film along the lines of *The Battle of Algiers* (1966), which had sympathised with Algerian terrorists resisting French occupation, and then elaborated:

> You show the Arab side and the American side in a chase film with a *French Connection* urgency, where you track people by satellite, like in *Enemy of the State*. My movie would have the CIA guys and the FBI guys, but they blow it. They are a bunch of drunks from World War II who haven't recovered from the disasters of the '60s – the Kennedy assassination and Vietnam. My movie would show the new heroes of security, people who really get the job done, who know where the secrets are.[37]

He hasn't made it yet. Instead, we were treated to *W.* (2008), which was, by Stone's former standards, also politically tame. The tone does darken towards the end, as Dick Cheney gives an audiovisual presentation in which he explains the necessity of deploying force in the Middle East to secure resources. Yet the focus of the film is on Bush as a recovering alcoholic, with personal insecurities to do with his father. As such, Bush comes off as a sympathetic character and we understand his journey. More important, there is little systematic critique in the narrative – the 'beast' of *JFK* and *Nixon* is virtually absent.

In 2003, Stone said:

> If I had the youthful energy I had when I did *JFK*, and I could take all the abuse I would take – which I was a little ignorant of then – to do [a movie] about terrorism would be a great contribution. But I don't know if it could get made or distributed because of the controversy it would arouse.[38]

Oliver Stone has continued to present challenging political ideas and 'secret histories' in his low-budget documentary films about figures such as Fidel Castro and Hugo Chavez. In terms of feature films though, he has seemed neither willing nor able to provide a critical perspective on US power for at least the 15-year period since the mid-1990s.

SYRIANA

Which Political Dramas offer interrogative viewpoints on the US's place in the world? Four in particular stand out: *Syriana* (2005), *Lord of War* (2005), *The Good Shepherd* (2006), and Steven Soderbergh's *Che* (2008) (omitted here for reasons of space).

Syriana (2005) perhaps most comprehensively questioned the nature of US elite business interests, victims and heroes, in a plotline that echoed real-life US Middle Eastern policy towards, say, Iran during the fluctuating fortunes of the Shah. In the film, the heir to an emirate in a fictional Arab state gives an oil contract to China, cutting out a US company that promptly fires its immigrant workers and merges with a small firm that has landed a Kazakh oil contract. Two of the laid-off migrant workers are manipulated by Islamist clerics into becoming suicide bombers. The CIA assassinates the Emir to ensure the succession of his more dictatorial, but US-friendly younger brother.

That *Syriana* was made in the first place was the result of various unusual occurrences. It was based on the 2003 book *See No Evil: The True Story of a Ground Soldier in the CIA's War Against Terrorism*, by ex-CIA case officer Bob Baer. In an interview with my colleague, Baer claimed:

> Warner Brothers didn't want to make *Syriana*; they were forced to. I mean you have Time Warner who asks 'who's gonna watch a movie about big oil?' They didn't think it was marketable because it didn't have a very pleasant message. But then Clooney gave up his salary and Matt Damon, and the guy from Ebay got involved in the film [the billionaire Jeff Skoll], and all of the sudden a $120 million movie got knocked down to 60 million, with Warner Brothers just paying a fraction of the movie.[39]

Its star, George Clooney, commented that *Syriana* 'make[s] *Three Kings* look like a Frank Capra film ... [it] is trouble ... It's hardcore, serious, and the next time you and me do an interview, it'll probably be from a bunker, or under a table.'[40] It should be added, though, it might have been more 'trouble' if, as Victoria Segal put it pithily in the *New Statesman*, it hadn't seemed 'as if somebody has knocked over a government filing cabinet, randomly gathered up a load of suspect dossiers, and decided to bundle the whole lot together as a script'.[41] There's no need for Clooney to hunker down just yet.

LORD OF WAR

Lord of War depicts an international arms trader, Yuri Orlov (Nicolas Cage) and his plunge into the depravity of his career. The film was supported wholeheartedly by Amnesty International and was based on the alleged gunrunning activities of the Russian, Viktor Bout. In the 1990s, Bout was wanted by Interpol and, in 2000, the British Foreign Office Minister responsible for Africa, Peter Hain, called him 'the chief sanctions buster and ... a merchant of death who owns air companies that ferry arms'.[42]

The key political message of *Lord of War* is articulated by Orlov to federal agent Jack Valentine (Ethan Hawke), shortly after his arrest. Orlov is convinced he will not be sentenced:

> The reason I'll be released is the same reason you think I'll be convicted. I do rub shoulders with some of the most vile, sadistic men calling themselves leaders today. But some of these men are

> the enemies of your enemies. And while the biggest arms dealer in the world is your boss – the President of the United States, who ships more merchandise in a day than I do in a year – sometimes it's embarrassing to have his fingerprints on the guns. Sometimes he needs a freelancer like me to supply forces he can't be seen supplying. So. You call me evil, but unfortunately for you, I'm a necessary evil.

Douglas Farah and Stephen Braun report: 'Despite revelations that his planes had secretly aided Islamic militants in Afghanistan, Bout's organization not only has survived but also flourished – astonishingly, by flying weapons and supplies for the US military and private contractors in Iraq, reaping millions from the nation that once pursued him.'[43]

The US media was beaten to this story by *Le Monde*, which reported on 14 May 2004 that Bout's planes, 'flying under the name of [the] airline company British Gulf, [which is] likely to disappear as fast as it was created, are assuring "transport of materiel" for the American army in Iraq'.[44]

Lord of War was remarkably prescient. Although Bout was not arrested prior to the release of the movie, in 2008 he was detained in Bangkok. On 11 August 2009, the court ruled in favour of Mr Bout. US officials were said to have been surprised by this decision, while a spokesman for Russia's foreign ministry stated that Russia was 'satisfied by the decision and we hope that Viktor Bout will return to his homeland in the near future'.[45]

THE GOOD SHEPHERD

The Good Shepherd also interrogated US power, presenting a vision of the CIA from its beginnings in the Second World War to the debacle at the Bay of Pigs in 1961. Bill Sullivan (Robert De Niro) says he wants his CIA to be the US's 'eyes and ears' rather than its 'heart and soul', but his hopes are dashed. The CIA is shown to be willing and able to intervene covertly in other countries to advance US corporate and political interests, including through the use of the Mafia to topple Castro in Cuba, and the use of cockroaches against Third World crops, an allusion to the God-like status CIA has acquired for itself. By 1961, the main protagonist, Edward Wilson, is told that he is 'the CIA's heart and soul', but he barely has a soul himself, having willingly sold out his own son.

In contrast, the film hints that the threat from the Soviet Union was mythical. Agents give LSD to a Russian defector as part of their secret and controversial MK-ULTRA programme. In a trance, the Russian tells them:

> Soviet power is a myth, a great joke. There are no spare parts; nothing is working – nothing. It's nothing but painted rust. But you, you need to keep the Russian myth alive to maintain your military-industrial complex. Your system depends on Russia being perceived as a mortal threat. It's not a threat. It was never a threat. It will never be a threat. It is a rotted, bloated cow.

When asked if he had been tempted to go further with his criticism of the US government, De Niro reportedly became 'visibly uncomfortable' and made the fair point that 'Being critical means taking a hard position on something and I prefer to see what something is all about and try to get behind it. Why people do things is more interesting to me. I want to try and understand where they are coming from.' He expressed the view that the CIA was a 'necessary evil'.[46] In other words, a critical stance was not of paramount importance to him, though one might be tempted to ask whether perhaps this also had anything to do with his various advisers, which included the CIA's Milt Bearden who was on set 'with De Niro from set decorating to editing'.[47]

For his part, Bearden clarified:

> There was never any intent to do anything except capture an era, in both the CIA and America. I certainly wouldn't have been involved with any movie that was blatantly anti CIA. The old hands criticising it want something that is either a recruiting film for the CIA or a documentary, which this is not.[48]

Bearden agreed that the CIA was a 'necessary evil', and added 'But I would say all intelligence services are necessary evils if you want to be philosophical about it. But, you know ... put the stress on "necessary".'[49]

General John Singlaub, chairman of the OSS Society, attacked the film as 'a collection of all the evil things imagined and fabricated by our enemies and those disaffected employees searching for a scapegoat'. CIA historians complained that the film wrongly suggested that the Bay of Pigs operation failed because someone leaked the name of the landing site and that the Allen Dulles character (dubbed 'Philip Allen' in the film) is wrongly shown to resign because he is caught embezzling money. The film also suggests that the CIA used armed soldiers to arrest people at the Presidential palace in Guatemala, which the historians point out never happened. They complained that the story of Russian defectors was conflated with a story about the MK-ULTRA experiments and that the main figures within CIA at the time were not members of the secretive Skull and Bones society.[50]

Other CIA statements revealed what really bugged them about the film: '*The Good Shepherd* is a *Godfather*-type tale told through the imagined lens of the Eastern Establishment', and 'One of the themes you see throughout the film is a proto-Marxist position that economic interests of the capitalist elite are primary.'[51] What the CIA had wanted was an equivalent of the Marines' *Flags of Our Fathers* as part of its desire for a 'culture of truth' that was 'undermined' by *The Good Shepherd*.[52] What they got was a somewhat sinister historical critique of their organisation.

MUNICH

Steven Spielberg's *Munich* (2005) feigned a critical stance on the issue of Western use of force. The film is based on the true-to-life book *Vengeance* by George Jonas and tells the story of Golda Meir's Israeli government ordering an operation whereby a secret team of soldiers are tasked with killing members of a Palestinian terrorist group, Black September, that had murdered 13 Israeli athletes at the 1972 Olympic Games.[53] The group is led by Avner (Eric Bana) who, following numerous assassinations and extensive collateral damage, goes through a breakdown and decides to quit. Although the film deals with Israel, the parallels with the broader 'War on Terror' are drawn explicitly, complete with a final lingering shot of the Twin Towers and Israeli characters played by actors from throughout the West.

Some Israeli and conservative groups thought that Spielberg had gone too far, with AIM complaining that the film 'is typical liberal Hollywood propaganda' and a 'direct assault on the Bush administration'.[54] The Zionist Organization of America (ZOA) called for a boycott of the film, saying that one of the screenwriters, Tony Kushner, was an 'Israel-hater'. Mainstream commentators widely saw it as an 'evenhanded cry for peace',[55] with Roger Ebert complaining that it was in fact too impartial.[56]

To be sure, *Munich* was politically exacting by Hollywood standards, and Spielberg presented rather less cartoonish Arab villains than his previous efforts such as *Raiders of the Lost Ark* (1981). There are even some special comments that criticise US foreign policy quite forcefully for fleeting moments: the most 'reluctant' Israeli assassin, Carl (Ciarán Hinds) makes the point: 'How do you think we got control of the land? By being nice?' Elsewhere, Mahmoud Hamshari, head of Black September in France, says:

> We are, for twenty-four years, the world's largest refugee population. Our homes taken from us. Living in camps, no future, no food. Nothing decent for our children ... For twenty four years our civilians have been attacked by the Israelis day after day ... You know Israel just bombed two refugee camps in Syria and Lebanon ... 200 people killed. Just after Munich they did this.

Aside from such sporadic nods towards a balanced argument, however, the film repeatedly reinforces underlying myths and assumptions about Western benevolence. Dennis Ross, former US Middle East Envoy, explains that the film 'creates a context that explains why the Israelis do what they do', and that although the movie doesn't create a caricature of Arabs, '[It] is told through the perspective of Israeli eyes' and 'the debate that goes on is an entirely internal Israeli one.'[57]

Spielberg (2005) himself comments on the DVD's introductory documentary:

> When we [the West] have to respond to terror today what's relevant is the need to go through a careful process – not to paralyse ourselves and not to prevent us from acting but to try and ensure the results that we produce are the ones that we really intend. I mean, it is the unintended results that are probably some of the worst and that are ultimately going to really bedevil us.[58]

Spielberg adds that *Munich* is not an attempt to answer 'should there be targeted killings or not?', but rather to highlight some of the related 'issues' and 'dilemmas'.[59] Though he implies that targeted killings by our side are basically OK, except when they have 'unintended consequences'. Amongst the unintended consequences, Spielberg articulates through Avner, are that every time we kill a terrorist six more take his place, which can become expensive ($1 million per head) and can provoke retaliatory assassinations against the security services. These 'unintended results' are, of course, all tactical and self-serving rather than being genuine expressions of remorse for the damage being done to others.

Spielberg spelled out his position more explicitly in an interview for the *Sunday Telegraph*:

> I am as truly pro-Israeli as you can possibly imagine. From the day I became morally and politically conscious of the importance of the state of Israel and its necessity to exist, I have believed that not just Israel but the rest of the world needs Israel to exist. ... What I believe is every act of terrorism requires a strong response, but we must also pay attention to the causes. ... Israel had to respond [to the Munich massacre], or it would have been perceived as weak: I agree with Golda Meir's response.'[60]

Munich does this by presenting the Israelis as constantly interrogating their moral stance. Apologist phrases like 'Whatever it takes ... we [the Jews] have a place [Israel] on Earth' and 'Every civilization finds it necessary to negotiate compromises with its own values' pepper the script. When Avner's team kill a teenager who is defending Salameh, they almost comically shout 'Oh no!', as though this was an utterly unthinkable action. By the end of the film, Avner is going through purgatory, presented with disturbing sexual imagery. In contrast, the Arabs are shown as without conscience – 'No qualms about rejoicing on their side, eh?', says the Israeli Steve (Daniel Craig), observing Arabs celebrating a terror attack against the West.

Despite all the Israeli characters' hand-wringing and in direct contradiction to Spielberg's assertion that 'I don't think he [Avner] will ever find peace', according to George Jonas, Avner still 'fully supports the decision that sent him and his partners on their mission, and has absolutely no qualms about anything they did'.[61]

Jonas emphasised his view after watching Spielberg's rendering, exclaiming that 'Moral posturing allows you to have it both ways – In Tinseltown terms, after the gunslinger blows everyone away, he has a proper crisis of conscience.' Asked whether Avner had a crisis of confidence, Jonas explained, 'My "Avner" may have questioned the utility of his mission toward the end – targeted assassinations barely slowed down terrorism, let alone stopped it – but he never questioned the morality of what his country had asked him to do – he had no pangs of guilt.'[62] Spielberg also claims to have met 'Avner' and was apparently given an impression to the contrary.[63]

The characters in *Munich* are designed as Spielberg's equivocal political mouthpieces. The film also omits the so-called 'Lillehammer affair', where Israeli assassins murdered a completely innocent Moroccan waiter in Norway – a case of mistaken identity for which Tel Aviv 23 provided compensation 23 years later, though offering no apology.[64] No mention, either, of the car bomb used to kill Salameh which killed eight other people – including an English student and a German nun[65] – even though it would have been easy enough to tack onto the closing caption that draws our attention to his subsequent assassination.

A scene between Avner and a Palestinian terrorist was touted as the film's strongest claim to fairness. Without this scene, Spielberg told the *Washington Post*, 'I would have been making a Charles Bronson movie – good guys vs. bad guys and Jews killing Arabs without any context. And I was never going to make that picture.' The *Post* editorialised, saying that 'the Palestinian talks powerfully and at length about home and about his people having lost their land; the land to which he refers isn't only Gaza or the West Bank, but what became, in 1948, Israel.'[66]

In truth, the scene in question is a two-and-a-half minute exchange, which at most points out that Palestinians are motivated by a desire for 'home' but, more saliently, suggests that their struggle is futile and immoral. The terrorist begins the discussion imagining a future war after which Israel will 'cease to exist'. Avner replies, 'You can't take back a country you never had.' Terrorist: 'You sound like a Jew.' Avner maintains his cover by saying 'Fuck you' and then observes, 'I'm the voice inside your head telling you what you already know. You people have nothing to bargain with. You'll never get the land back. You'll all die old men in refugee camps waiting for Palestine.'

The terrorist retorts with the threatening comment: ' … we can make the whole planet unsafe for Jews'. Avner points out 'You are Arabs. There are lots of places for Arabs', and points out that the land for which they fight is only arid old vineyards anyway – the not-so-subtle implication being that the Palestinians should just give up and move to another country which, without the audience bringing in knowledge from elsewhere, sounds like not such a bad idea.

Munich in essence asks the question 'should the Israeli Secret Service follow a secret and illegal policy of targeted assassinations throughout the globe without regard to the consequences?' We are invited to think that the answer might overall be 'No', because such killings are counter-productive and upsetting ... for the Israelis. As Michelle Goldberg puts it, the film's 'central concern [is] the effect of retaliatory Jewish violence on the Jewish soul, not on the Palestinian flesh'.[67] Or, as Golda Meir apocryphally phrased it: 'We can never forgive them [the Palestinians] for making us kill their children.'

The case of *Munich* would be a little less disturbing if Spielberg also made a film from the Palestinian point of view, perhaps about the 1948 exodus, as Robert Fisk challenged him to do.[68] Clint Eastwood looked at two sides of the Second World War in *Flags of Our Fathers* and *Letters From Iwo Jima*, so such a pairing has its precedent. There is no sign that such a film will ever be made in the US, let alone by Spielberg, and pro-Israeli government docudramas like *The Chosen* (1981), *A Woman Golda* (1982) and *Raid on Entebbe* (1977) and cinematic releases like *Exodus* (1960) and *The Point Men* (2001) have marked a Hollywood history that has systematically omitted the Palestinian perspective. One exception – Costa Gavras' low-budget *Hanna K* (1983) – showed Palestinians in a sympathetic light but was buried by its own distributor.[69]

CONCLUSION

The Pentagon in the modern era has rarely been willing to cooperate with Political Dramas, which have tended to champion liberal politics and have contained some negative images of military men. Indeed, as one might expect, this genre has been more liable than any other examined in the book to raise questions about US foreign policy, as in *Syriana*, *Lord of War* and *The Good Shepherd*, which presented US power in thoughtful terms drawing on mainstream critical literature. Oliver Stone's mid-career films, notably *JFK* and *Nixon*, were also strong – though 'conspiracy' themed – challenges to established power.

The re-edits on *Rules of Engagement* made it so jingoistic and self-contradictory that even its lead actor, Guy Pearce, went on the record to express his disappointment.[70] However, it is the liberal-leaning films in this category that are most disturbing. *Munich*, *Crimson Tide*, *Spy Game* and *Thirteen Days* all pay lip-service to the possibilities for non-violent solutions to political problems, but all demonstrate how conditions are such that the US use of force – even extensive force – is legitimate. After all, it is standard practice in Hollywood to assume that foreigners don't matter, US enemies are implacably villainous, and US power is by definition selfless and good.

8
The Low-Budget Battlefield

By now, you may well have in mind a few films that seem more politically judicious with regards to the US world role than most of those discussed so far. There are certainly some critical movies made by Hollywood but *Reel Power* has focused thus far on those with budgets over $30 million and which therefore tend to be distributed by the majors rather than their subsidiaries. From an industry that produces several hundred films a year with an average budget of $60 million, are there some lower-budget offerings that slip through the net and criticise US foreign policy?

This chapter examines some of the most disruptive film products from below that $30 million budget mark, across a range of genres, observing how several of them have faced difficult roads on the way to release, even when their political content has been – in the cold light of day – fairly tame. 'The Low-Budget Battlefield' goes on to examine lower-budget films that appear antagonistic or neutral, but on closer inspection are revealed to be more conservative. Finally, I will examine some of the great many low-budget productions that trot out standard lines about the benevolent US role in world affairs.

THE ONES THAT GOT AWAY

Rendition

In *Rendition* (2007), Jake Gyllenhaal's CIA analyst increasingly begins to doubt the wisdom of abducting and torturing a terrorist suspect, as ordered by the governments of the US and an unspecified North African country (synonymous with Morocco or Egypt). The foreign society is portrayed in human, sympathetic terms and the rendition itself is based on the true story of Khalid El-Masri, whom the CIA mistook for a terrorist and kidnapped.

The essential message of the film is articulated by Gyllenhaal when he questions an official about what is being done:

> In all the years you've been doing this, how often can you say that we've produced truly legitimate intelligence? Once? Twice?

> Ten times? Give me a statistic; give me a number. Give me a pi chart, I love pi charts. Anything, anything that outweighs the fact that if you torture one person you create ten, a hundred, a thousand new enemies.

There are also even more films with ultra-low budgets – just a thousand or a few hundred thousand dollars – receiving even less cinematic screening. Many of these are documentaries, such as *Deadly Deception: General Electric, Nuclear Weapons and Our Environment* (1991), *Manufacturing Consent: Noam Chomsky and the Media* (1992), *11 09 01 – September 11* (2002), *Iraq for Sale: The War Profiteers* (2006), *Fog of War* (2004), *Taxi to the Dark Side* (2007), *Standard Operating Procedure* (2008), *Why We Fight* (2005) and Oliver Stone's interviews with Latin American leaders Fidel Castro (*Commandante* (2003), *Looking for Fidel* (2004)) and Hugo Chavez (*South of the Border* (2009)). Similarly, Tim Robbin's *Embedded* (2003) assaulted the thinly fictionalised 'Office of Special Plans' whose members, as neoconservatives, preside over a world in which journalists line up as soldiers and shout 'Sir! I am a maggot journalist, sir!' The 'film', however, was in fact a stage play – later transposed onto DVD.

At this ultra-low budget, it is very difficult to make an attractive feature – but not impossible. *Infinite Justice* (2007), which was a challenging view of the war on terror, cost just a few hundred thousand dollars and received some cinema screening, albeit very limited. A British comedy, Armando Iannucci's *In The Loop* (2009) – in which an ineffectual British government minister is used by the US political system as a pawn during the wind-up to a new war in the Middle East – also gained some screentime in both the US and Europe, and was even nominated for an Oscar in 2010.

UNDER THE RADAR, STILL UNDER FIRE

Buffalo Soldiers

However, where there is stronger potential for success, the political system is more likely to close in. *Buffalo Soldiers* charts the life of Army Clerk Ray Elwood (Joaquin Phoenix) on the Theodore Roosevelt US Army base in Stuttgart, West Germany at the end of the Cold War. Elwood is making money illegally by selling giant plastic tankards of Army-issue Mop 'n' Glo on the black market, and by his involvement in the base's supply chain of heroin.

Although filming for *Buffalo Soldiers* was completed by January 2001, it was hit perhaps harder than any other production by 9/11 and then the Iraq War, meaning that it did not reach cinema screens until the summer of 2003. Although *Variety*'s critic Todd McCarthy (2001) claimed *Buffalo Soldiers* was 'the wrong film at the wrong time' because of 'public opinion',[1] its dreadful box-office showing (just a few hundred thousand dollars) was largely due to the fact that it was only actually released in New York and Los Angeles. In other words, *Buffalo Soldiers* was the 'wrong film' for a system closely wedded to elite power – how audiences would have responded under more normal conditions is unknown because it was pretty much scrapped by its own cinematic distributors.

The question is, why? Eric Weiss, one of the film's writers accurately pointed out: 'I don't see the movie as unpatriotic. It doesn't really comment on what we are doing now [in Iraq, Afghanistan, etc.]', and Miramax's chief operating officer, Rick Sands, said that they 'want to be sensitive to the current situation in the world'.[2] They could have added several other points to make their case. For example, Ellwood has no political beef with his civilian or military masters, there is no systemic critique of the US presence in Europe, and although top sergeant Lee (Scott Glenn) is a shocking sadist and the men are criminals, this is a regrettable consequence of peace: 'war is hell but peace is fucking boring', as Ellwood puts. Moreover, the portrayal of the gentle Commander Wallace Berman (Ed Harris) suggests that the Army is a broad church.

Director Gregor Jordan observed:

> I've got documents which show things like murder rates on US Army bases here were between 25 and 30 murders a year. And things like accidental deaths – there was between 2 and 3 a day. And suicide rates ... There's also statistics about how many weapons went missing during the course of the cold war. Billions of dollars worth of weapons just disappeared. And drug use – the army in the end had to introduce drug testing to try and stamp it out. If anything, what is depicted in the film is toned down from reality. What really happened was much, much worse.[3]

War, Inc.

Other Comedies hit similar distribution problems, though they were actually much more critical than *Buffalo Soldiers*. *War Inc.*'s (2008) narrative unfolds in the fictional Middle Eastern country of Turaqistan, which is controlled by a corporation, modelled on Halliburton, which is owned by the former US Vice President, modelled on Dick Cheney. The film was not even touched by Disney, which had produced the unofficial prequel *Grosse Pointe Blank*, and it was stifled by extremely limited distribution, screening in just 33 theatres nationwide and making $580,000.

Fahrenheit 9/11

Michael Moore's documentary *Fahrenheit 9/11* (2004) depicted the US as a corporate monolith, headed by an idiotic President – George W. Bush. The enemies of the film are not just Islamic terrorists but rather elites themselves, whom Moore portrayed as self-interested warmongers, whose willingness to use violence after 9/11 has disturbing consequences.

Disney tried to block its subsidiary Miramax from releasing the film, complaining that its distribution would be counterproductive to their interests.[4] Moore's agent Ari Emanuel alleged that Disney's CEO Michael Eisner had told him he wanted to back out of the deal due to concerns about political fall-out from conservative politicians, especially regarding tax breaks given to Disney properties in Florida like Walt Disney World (where the governor was the then US President's brother, Jeb Bush). Disney also had ties to the Saudi royal family, which was unfavourably represented in the film: a powerful member of the family, Al-Walid bin Talal, worked with the Carlyle Group to buy up a large share of Euro Disney after it had run into financial difficulties.[5] Disney denied any such high-stakes political ball game, explaining they were worried about being 'dragged into a highly charged partisan political battle', which it said would alienate customers.[6]

The right wing was really gunning for Moore. His anti-weapons lobby film *Bowling for Columbine* (2002) had been the highest grossing documentary of all time – despite it being slapped with an 'R' rating by the MPAA – and his stated aim for *Fahrenheit 9/11* was to remove Bush from office. The film provoked a wave of defamatory websites, fulminations from the usual pundits and, amazingly, even several counter-documentaries: *Michael Moore Hates America* (2004), *Celsius 41.11* (2004), *Michael & Me* (2004), *FahrenHYPE 9/11* (2004) and *Manufacturing Dissent* (2004). He is also satirised in the $20 million David Zucker comedy *An American Carol* aka *Big Fat Important Movie* (2008).

In truth, although *Fahrenheit 9/11* was a powerful anti-Bush polemic, it had some glaring political limitations if it was to be considered seriously as a critique of US foreign policy at a systemic level. It avoids any mention of the US's key Middle Eastern ally, Israel, which is surely a key component of even the briefest discussion of the region, given Israel's controversial position – perhaps any comment would have gone against the likes of Moore's agent, a signatory of the 2006 petition supporting Israel's war on Lebanon and brother to Obama's White House Chief of Staff. Moore also stymies his views in *Fahrenheit 9/11* with regard to the controversial history of 9/11 itself – he said elsewhere that 'official investigations haven't even told us half the truth', and he called for the release of Pentagon surveillance footage from the terror attack.[7]

Additionally, although in the real world it was certain Muslims and Islamic nations who were most severely punished by the US government, *Fahrenheit 9/11*'s victims are white Americans such as Lila Lipscomb (who questions the Iraq War following the death of her son in Iraq), the group of peace activists that were infiltrated by the police, and the American military. The film's fleeting depictions of the world outside the US are an Iraqi mother saying Americans are murderers, a brief shot of a wedding party, and some boys playing with a kite in Saddam-era Iraq. The film ends with Moore asking 'will they ever trust us again?', with reference to the government's betrayal of 'our' military, sending them to fight an unjust war in Iraq.

Thus, while *Fahrenheit 9/11* does draw on a mass of critical literature and the deep well of public hatred for George W. Bush, it remains in the same hermetically sealed American-centric universe that characterises the rest of mainstream Hollywood; the film functions as a morally dubious piece of agit-prop and pulls back from a more sweeping and legitimate critique of US power. This was arguably a major strength of the film, as it was able to draw on American patriotism and the Democrat base, but it also meant that it was a shallow, partial and transient commentary on US power.

The Quiet American

The Quiet American (2002) was also a victim of the post-9/11 self-censorship culture. The *New York Times* reported that test-audience reaction was 'OK' when Miramax acquired the film on 10 September 2001, according to co-chairman Harvey Weinstein. 'What freaked me out after the 10th was the 11th. I showed the film to some people and staff, and they said: "Are you out of your mind? You can't release this now, it's unpatriotic. America has to be cohesive, and band together." We were concerned that nobody had the stomach for a movie about bad Americans anymore,' explained Weinstein.[8] Miramax released the film in two cities for two weeks, reportedly because its star Michael Caine mobilised his star appeal to argue that the film could make Miramax a lot of money if he won the award for Best Actor, which requires a one-week commercial run in LA to qualify for the Academy Awards.[9]

The Quiet American revolves around the relationship between Thomas Fowler (Michael Caine), an ageing English reporter and Alden Pyle (Brendan Fraser), a young American CIA agent masquerading as a relief worker; they compete for the affections of Phuong (Do Thi Hai Yen). Fowler discovers that Pyle is providing support, including plastic explosives, to General Thé (Quang Hai), a military leader of what Pyle calls the 'Third Force', which is neither allied to the Communists nor the old colonialists. Although Fowler likes Pyle personally, he disagrees with his tactics and is ambivalent about his goals.

The film was certainly critical of US foreign policy, depicting Pyle as a wrong-headed and criminal ideologue, albeit affable. Still, as we might expect from the director of *Clear and Present Danger*, the film perpetuates the idea that the war was a regrettable tragedy, which resulted from the US blundering idealistically into a situation it did not fully understand and was unable to control. Director Phillip Noyce explained, 'I thought at the time, it's weird how his [Greene's] portrait of the American political evangelist of the early '50s contained the same zeal that has guided American foreign policy through to the present zeal born out of the best intentions.'[10]

The fact that this movie – which discussed US foreign policy from the 1950s in critical but hardly radical terms – was given restricted screening by its own distributor was an indication of the remarkably low level of criticism of US power that the film industry was willing to countenance screening, and believed its audiences could tolerate at the time.

Wag the Dog

There is also the case of *Wag the Dog* (1997), which did not have trouble being released but was made under fairly unusual circumstances. It was actually produced during an unscheduled break in the production of *Sphere* (1998), an $80 million, mainstream sci-fi flick also directed by Barry Levinson and starring Dustin Hoffman that was suspended due to 'budget concerns'. Levinson directed *Wag the Dog* in the intervening period for $15 million.[11]

In *Wag the Dog*, White House adviser Conrad Bream (Robert De Niro) and Hollywood producer Stanley Moss (Dustin Hoffman) fabricate a war with Albania to divert the country's attention from the President's sexual wrongdoings. US power is dictated by its constituent interests: the White House is campaigning for the President without questioning the morality of defending a child abuser; the CIA and NSA initially act as a check on the White House, arresting Bream, but he convinces them that it is in their interests to allow the 'war' to go ahead; Bream equates fighting for 'their way of life' – the textbook reason to go to war – with fighting for their own jobs. Without a credible enemy, 'What good are you?', he asks.

Again, the film is critical of US institutions and foreign policy. Again, it is perhaps tamer than first impressions suggest. So, for instance, *Wag the Dog* portrays Bream and Moss as fictitious mavericks that amuse the audience with their audacious and ridiculous spin in an absurd situation, but this ignores the more obvious and more challenging notion that real-world US foreign policy is routinely accompanied by a multimillion-dollar corporate propaganda machine. The 1990–91 US-led Persian Gulf War, for instance, was sold by a huge public relations exercise: nine days after Saddam's army marched into Kuwait, the Emir's government (with US support) funded a multi-million dollar PR front company called 'Citizens for a Free Kuwait', run by Hill and Knowlton – then the world's largest PR firm. The campaign included outright fabrications, such as a young woman, later identified as the daughter of the Kuwaiti Ambassador to the US, claiming to have seen Iraqi soldiers taking away baby incubators from Kuwaiti hospitals.[12]

Additionally, the war in *Wag the Dog* is victimless: no one is killed on either the American or Albanian side (although the final scene tantalisingly suggests that the 'war' is about to spin out of control). *Wag the Dog* is therefore something of an American 'in-joke', but one which might be rather less shocking or outrageously amusing if the wider context of US propaganda was better known to audiences.

OPERATION WHITEWASH

Hotel Rwanda

Other low-budget films gave the impression of neutrality or critical perspectives on US foreign policy, but they actually obfuscated reality in ways that are arguably more insidious than out-and-out fantasy. Consider United Artists' *Hotel Rwanda* (2004), which even *Salon* magazine – usually well-versed in challenging establishment narratives – compared favourably to 'the muckraking films that Warner Bros. turned out in the early '30s ... that aimed to shake up audiences' sense of justice and moral outrage'.[13] *Hotel Rwanda* in fact followed the state line on Rwanda and was based on a government-funded book written by Philip Gourevitch,[14] who worked closely with his brother-in-law, Secretary of State James Rubin.[15] It may be nothing more than coincidence, but military contractor United Technologies has major commercial interests in the region and one of its board members, Alexander '*Red Dawn*' Haig, also sat on the board of United Artists' senior partner MGM.

Hotel Rwanda is about the true story of hotelier Paul Rusesabagina (Don Cheadle) during the 1994 Rwandan genocide, who saves his family and more than a thousand other refugees by granting them shelter in the besieged Hôtel des Mille Collines.

The standard story about Rwanda, replicated in the film, is that the US turned a blind eye to the hundred-day frenzy of genocide pre-planned by the Hutu government against the Tutsi minority and some moderate Hutus. Supposedly, the US was concerned about putting its troops in harm's way, especially given the debacle in Somalia the previous year; thus it ignored what Gourevitch called 'the Jews of Africa' (the Tutsis) and became 'bystanders to genocide', as Samantha Power famously put it.[16] In short, the US is tortured by its own temporary soullessness; Africa suffers; the Rwandan Patriotic Front (RPF) are disciplined and heroic; America should deploy troops next time.

The problem is that consensus over the Rwandan tragedy is far from established, as the official narrative has come under sustained attack. Phil Taylor, former investigator for the International Criminal Tribunal for Rwanda (ICTR) claimed that 'for anyone who followed closely the 1994 crisis in Rwanda the highly touted film *Hotel Rwanda* is merely propaganda statements interrupted by bouts of acting'.[17]

Some critics argue that not only did the US fail to intervene to prevent 'genocide', it intervened both before and after the massacres to ensure its side – the RPF – won. So, for instance, according to a French judge, it was Paul Kagame and his Tutsi associates who shot down the Hutu president's plane, killing all on board including President Habyarimana himself and President Ntaryamira of Burundi – commonly accepted as the trigger for the genocide.[18] This act was part of the Kagame-Tutsi final assault to seize power after a four-year war, with the assistance of the US-sponsored Ugandan military. A third Hutu leader, Melchior Ndadaye, an earlier president of Burundi, had been assassinated by his Tutsi military in October 1993, which was followed by an anti-Hutu pogrom that killed tens of thousands and drove hundreds of thousands of Burundian-Hutu refugees into Rwanda.

The RPF gained power and their preferred status in the West cleared the ground for Kagame and Yoweri Museveni – Kagame's ally and fellow US client and dictator (of Uganda) – periodically to invade and occupy Eastern Congo without 'international community' opposition to clear out the *genocidaires*. This led to the killing of hundreds of thousands of civilian Hutu refugees in a series of mass slaughters, and also provided cover for a wider Kagame-Museveni assault in the Congo that has led to millions of deaths in what has been commonly described as 'Africa's World War'.[19] This was again compatible with narrow Western interests and policy, as it contributed to the replacement of Mobutu with the more amenable Kabila and opened up the Congo to a new surge of mineral exploitation by Western companies.[20]

The subject of the film, Paul Rusesabagina, wrote in his autobiography that 'Rwanda is today a nation governed by and for the benefit of a small group of elite Tutsis ... Those few Hutus who have been elevated to high-ranking posts are usually empty suits without any real authority of their own. They are known locally as Hutus de service or Hutus for hire.'[21] In December 2006, he wrote to the Queen of England to say that Kagame was a 'war criminal'.[22]

There is no doubt that Hutus were culpable in genocide and *Hotel Rwanda* remains, like *United 93* (discussed below), a sensitive, humane and powerful piece of film-making. Still, it is striking how the history of the bloodshed has been spun in line with Western interests. *Hotel Rwanda* certainly condemned elements of US policy towards Rwanda during the 1994 genocide, but it did so within ideological boundaries which ensured the film reflected the interests of US state and private power. *Salon* concluded, 'We know how little attention the West paid to the Rwandan genocide as it was occurring. The question is, How much attention will be paid to this movie?'[23] *Hotel Rwanda* generated a huge amount of news coverage and made $34 million on its $17 million investment. People are paying attention. The real question is: should they?

United 93

Paul Greengrass's *United 93* was generally received as a neutral piece of work with emphasis placed on its avoidance of a sensationalist style, through the use of unknown actors, its decentralisation of the famous 'Let's roll' line, and its use of hand-held cameras.[24] It is a literal depiction of what happened to Flight 93 on 11 September 2001, namely the terrorist take-over, the passengers rebelling and then crash-landing the plane in rural Pennsylvania. In other words, it was not a jingoistic piece of Hollywood trash, but rather a sensitively made piece of work that dealt respectfully with the human beings who all lost their lives on that day.

Still, a closer look at the film suggests it is not as neutral as it appeared. 9/11 had occurred whilst Paul Greengrass was making *Bloody Sunday* (2002), which recreated the 1972 massacre in Northern Ireland. Greengrass commented, '[9/11] made what I was doing seem a bit irrelevant. But then, as we carried on working, it became for me oddly relevant, because *Bloody Sunday* was really about how we overreacted, how we militarised the early stages of the conflict and made it much worse.'[25]

United 93 raised no such issues, so it is hard to see how Greengrass saw it as 'oddly relevant'. The film's 'Bible', as Greengrass put it (DVD commentary), was the Bush administration's official *9/11 Commission Report*, which simply presented the events as described on the day. Perhaps this is what Bush had in mind when he said 'See, in my line of work you got to keep repeating things over and over and over again for the truth to sink in, to kind of catapult the propaganda.'[26]

The film was embellished with a few artistic flourishes which further added to the film's Bush-friendly ethos: First, Greengrass characterises a German passenger, Christian Adams, as the only character counselling appeasement, which led to his real-life widow refusing to cooperate with the film[27] – in contradiction to the White House press release that 'Greengrass had the blessings of survivors of all 40 individuals killed aboard the plane.'[28] Secondly, as Dennis Lim pointed out, Greengrass made sure to 'dangle some red-state red meat', as in the blurry finale the passengers appear to kill two of the terrorists.[29]

The Pentagon received Greengrass's 'special thanks' on the credits. He explained that the military brass were 'incredibly creative in helping us', and they were apparently motivated by the idea that 'if we can do this [make the film] we can perhaps raise our game for the next time [there's an attack]' (a pretty strange reason to make a film, surely).

The Bush administration also welcomed the release of *United 93* with open arms. Soon after the film's nationwide release date, 'tears flowed' at a 'very emotional night'[30] when President Bush 'invited relatives of some of the 40 passengers and crew members' for a private screening at the White House.[31] Attendance figures were not offered; the families had already had a private screening,[32] and the White House cinema only has 44 seats anyway,[33] so we might surmise that providing a cathartic experience for 'some of' those affected was rather less important to the incumbents than continuing to associate themselves with what they called the 'heroes' of Flight 93, who had struck what Bush called 'the first counter-attack to World War III'.[34]

Reflecting on the *Bourne* films, Greengrass says, 'we have to search for our own answers', rather than rely on untrustworthy power systems. This is not an approach he applies to *United 93*. Greengrass didn't seem to care about the calls for a fresh enquiry into 9/11, or the concerns raised by serious commentators that Flight 93 might have been shot down by the military.[35] He seems to be as ignorant as Condoleezza Rice about the pre-9/11 warnings of just such an attack using aeroplanes, as he says more than once that 'this thing was literally unimagined and unimaginable' (DVD commentary). Instead, Greengrass felt that it was more important for him to 'create a believable truth' as a 'good place to start a discussion' (DVD commentary) (another strange reason to make a film).

He commented:

> A lot of people believe that Flight 93 was shot down by the military. I'm not knocking people who believe in conspiracy theories. What I'm pointing out is that conspiracy theories are comforting ... the truth is much more disturbing if you look at it for real and say, 'on that morning a small group of people hijacked a religion, hijacked four airplanes and had an entire civilian and military system break down inside an hour and if those passengers had not got up out of their seats the plane without a doubt would have hit the Capitol and flattened it.'[36]

It's hard to see what could be more 'comforting' in the dire circumstances of 9/11 than focusing on the day's one small victory, based on a government-approved history in which al-Qaeda terrorists are clubbed to death by Americans.

Discussing the decision to shut down US borders in the immediate aftermath of the Twin Towers attacks, Greengrass points out that 'in the aftermath of a terrorist attack civilian life begins to close down, military response becomes predominant, the delicate systems of a democracy become compromised … .' Greengrass is no fool. He recognises the dangerous trends within the US system. He just doesn't seem to appreciate that here he supported them.

Home of the Brave

Similarly, *Home of the Brave* (2006) was promoted as a thoughtful 'antiwar statement', turned down for assistance by the Pentagon and refused screening on Army bases.[37] In reality, it was a subtle endorsement of staying the course in Iraq, which the Pentagon wanted to sanitise still further by removing references to soldiers smoking cannabis.[38] Samuel L. Jackson plays Colonel LTC William Marsh, dealing with civilian life after returning from Iraq. Marsh argues with his teenage son:

> *Marsh*: So you're against the war? You don't know a damn thing about it.
> *Billy*: It's not a war, it's an occupation. They hate us.
> *Marsh*: We're trying to build a country. We did the same thing here a couple hundred years ago. It's not easy.
> *Billy*: Yeah, right, and we're doing a good job of it. Maybe if we flushed a couple more Korans down the toilet at Guantanamo to help speed things up.
> *Marsh*: So you think we should just leave, huh? Let them rip each other to pieces? It's not an easy decision, is it? There are some bad guys over there.
> *Billy*: Ha, what bad guys? What is this – a Schwarzenegger movie? Why don't you just admit it? We went over there for oil and the everything else is bullshit.
> *Shortly afterwards, Billy asks rhetorically*: Since when did our country decide it was our job to just piss everybody else off?
> *Marsh*: You don't know what the fuck you're talking about. You should read a history book.
> *Billy*: I will, when you go read a newspaper.
> *Marsh*: I don't have to. I was there.

The exchange is thus rendered a battle for truth between father and son, history books and newspapers, the mature and the adolescent, primary knowledge and second-hand opinions. There is some room for interpretation but ultimately for all these reasons Jackson's view is more convincing. A similar discussion occurs earlier in the film where a petulant female character is silenced and then brought to tears after her Army friend expresses his genuine belief in his mission in Iraq.

Home of the Brave ends with one soldier (Brian Presley) returning to Iraq, narrating a letter he has written to his parents, which deftly makes the case for ignoring the politics of the war:

> Maybe the leaders of our country didn't know what they were getting into. Maybe the [Iraqi] people don't want us there and maybe this whole thing is just making it worse. But even after all that I can't stay behind knowing there are soldiers over there getting attacked every day and dying every day. I don't feel like it's wrong for me to want to go back over there and help. It's a hard job being a soldier. Not just for me but for the people we leave behind. We all carry scars of war. But I know that if I do my part then maybe we'll all get out of there and get home to the ones who love us just a little bit quicker.

In other words, the experienced soldier – as a final thought in the movie – dismisses the anti-war stance, characterises the Bush administration as blunderers at worst, and suggests that applying further force is the solution to the Iraq crisis. 'Makes perfect sense to me', he concludes.

A similar political argument was promoted by *The Hurt Locker* (2009), endorsed by Obama's Defense Secretary Robert M. Gates,[39] but at least it did away with *Home of the Brave*'s handwringing and essentially conformist politics in favour of telling a story with an engaging lead character.

LET'S ROLL

Air Marshal

A considerable body of lower-budget products trot out standard political lines, often beefed up with some all-American machismo, particularly in the Action Adventure genre. In *Flight of the Intruder* (1991), a Navy pilot, frustrated with the pace of the war, takes an unsanctioned bombing mission to North Vietnam. In *Sniper* (1993), the US government sends Special Forces operative Tom Berenger to take out rebel Panamanians. In *The Point Men* (2001) – made in Israel – heroic Israeli Secret Service agents neutralise Palestinian bad guys trying to destroy the successful peace agreement. In *Stealth Fighter* (1999), the 'war on drugs' is explicitly discussed as being a fig-leaf to allow US pilots to destroy weapons factories in enemy territory (rather than the apparently pointless aim of stopping 'a couple of addicts from killing themselves'). There is even a lucrative industry in Christian fundamentalist films, such as the apocalyptic *Left Behind* series (2000–05), in which American Christians are whisked off to Heaven and the UN Secretary General is revealed to be the Antichrist.

In *Air Marshal* (2003), Islamic terrorists hijack a passenger plane and an air marshal saves the day. Unlike in *Executive Decision* – to which *Air Marshal* bears many similarities – even the US senator (Tim Thomerson) on board the plane is heroic. When trying to take control of the plane, the senator actually pilfers the 'Let's roll' line from the real-world 9/11 hero, Todd Beamer. A little 'all-American' boy helps fly the plane to safety at the end.

The film exudes a particular hatred for the bad guys. All of the Muslims are villains – young, old, male, female. It comments favourably on racial profiling and pointedly highlights that lots of passengers are called Mohammed. Jamal (Ammar Daraiseh) wants to smash the plane into a US aircraft carrier. He threatens the terrified passengers: 'You think we are playing by the old rules? Western rules? Human life on this Earth is sacred? No. But for Mohammed to die a martyr is the most Holy of acts. For you to die an infidel is our sacred duty.'

An exchange between Jamal and the senator exposes the heart of the movie:

Senator: The United States of America does not negotiate with terrorists.
Jamal: Terrorists? Who are the terrorists? The ones that bomb from 10 miles up killing women and children. The ones who have no remorse whatsoever.
Senator: Why do you hate us so? You obviously live in America. You know us.
Jamal: Exactly. I know your arrogance. Your contempt for the rest of the world. Your moral corruption. And your so-called freedom.
Senator: Yes, freedom that the rest of the world envies us for.

Jamal: Your freedom is a joke. The rich control everything. Control you, Senator.
Senator: You're fanatics. That's not religion.
Jamal: You Americans are fanatics about money. [*Shouts*] Money! Money!
Senator: I stand for family values, spiritual values. You people have no respect for human life. You treat women like cattle.

This 'debate' is interrupted by the older terrorist, Elijah (Eli Danker), who rubs his hands and discusses the 'bottom line', namely blackmailing the US government for $30 million. If the government doesn't pay up, he insists, he will start to 'deduct passengers'. In other words, it is not capitalist America which is obsessed with dollars, but rather other factions of the Islamist movement.

But we only need sit through a few seconds of *Air Marshal* to find a good indicator of its politics, since the film actually begins with US Special Forces assaulting 'Lybia' (*sic*). The fact that the country is spelt incorrectly is not so much an indication of the film-makers' level of literacy as it is of the casual contempt with which Hollywood feels it can depict countries that have already been thoroughly debased by the media.

In the Army Now

It is not just formulaic Action Adventures that endorse state violence, either. The comedy *Spymate* (2006) begins with Minkey the Chimp blowing up an Arab terrorist compound and beating up the Arabs just as they are about to detonate a missile at a 'peace summit' held by world leaders. A similarly convenient nut-case Arab dictator with a missile appears in *Ernest in the Army* (1998). In the Political Drama *Deterrence* (1999), the US president nukes Iraq when Saddam Hussein's son invades Kuwait and threatens to attack the world with black-market atomic bombs – though the narrative is rendered more sophisticated by the suggestion that the weaselly president might have gone too far.

Another case was *In the Army Now* (1994), which received a stunning but thoroughly deserved 0 per cent rating based on 15 reviews processed by rottentomatoes.com. A sequel has been announced.

In the Army Now tells the story of Bones Conway (Pauly Shore) and his friend Jack Kaufman (Andy Dick) who lose their jobs and join the US Army Reserves, believing that if they assign themselves to the Water Purifying Unit they will make enough money to set up their dream business without putting themselves in danger. However, the 'water boys' are called up to operate in desert conditions, as Libya threatens to invade Chad and, on a routine mission to resupply a forward base, their convoy is ambushed. In a Libyan POW camp they meet up with Sgt Stern (Esai Morales), who tells them his mission is to destroy mobile Scud missile launchers carrying missiles armed with chemical warheads aimed at American bases in the region.

The US military is depicted in reflexively idealised terms. For example, whereas films such as *Full Metal Jacket* (1987) have famously depicted military trainers as cruel, for all her gusto the attractive black female drill Sgt Ladd (Lynn Whitfield) tolerates Bones's subversive flirting and explains that she shouts so that 'everybody can hear and learn from mistakes'. Lower down the power scale, Bones's unit is a quaint little metaphorical family that explicitly invokes *The Waltons* (1972–81): Bones is the wisecracking father figure; Christine Jones (Lori Petty) is the wife (who offers herself sexually to Bones when he leads them well); Jack is the petulant but ultimately obedient older child, and Fred Ostroff is the scared and gullible little boy (literally playing a retarded black man).

In the Army Now gives every indication that the US is following an appropriately benign and diplomatic foreign policy – defending the UN, acquiring support of the regional people, including children, and 'deterring' a Libyan invasion of Chad. Furthermore, the film is careful to say that the US military and civilian authorities assume that the water boys are dead, or else the bombing campaign against Libya would be rather more controversial purely on the narrow grounds that the water boys would be put in danger.

Each member of Bones's terrified unit overcomes their fears, maintains and/or recovers their dignity, and becomes a hero through their contact with the US military. The water boys have to take the place of the incapacitated Special Forces and destroy the chemical weapons launch facility. Their experience also allows them to be better civilians when they leave: Christine fights in a war as she had always wanted; Bones becomes a real leader, who gets together with Christine, and who runs a shop with Jack – right next to the army recruitment store. The lame-brain black chap even conquers his fear of insects, which must have been nice for him.

Libyans have attacked UN forces, are preparing to launch chemical weapons at US installations and, of course, all look the same–- filthy, ugly Arabs. By the end, even their own animals turn against them: as an Arab sneaks up on Bones, the camel he had been petting earlier jumps on the Arab and pins him down. Sidesplitting family fun from Disney.

The Pentagon saw *In the Army Now* as an important propaganda and recruiting tool, especially for 13–18-year-olds;[40] its technical adviser Major Thomas McCollum explained that it 'shows the military has the capability of teaching an irresponsible individual [the Pauly Shore character] responsibility for his actions and the ability to help others'.[41] This 'responsibility' involves applying force – without any indication of future consequences – against aggressive Libyans who, implausibly, have the means and desire both to invade their neighbour and launch pre-emptive chemical weapons strikes against US bases.

CONCLUSION

There is great potential amongst lower-budget productions to push the ideological boundaries and challenge the common self-serving assumptions about US benevolence. Numerous films like *War, Inc.*, *The Quiet American* and *In the Loop* have done so, and particularly documentaries by the likes of Michael Moore, Mark Achbar and Oliver Stone.

Other films have had critical tones but a closer look suggests that they seriously pulled their punches, as in *Home of the Brave*, which dissented from the government position on such narrow grounds that it wound up supporting it in the key debate on maintaining troops in Iraq.

However, low-budget films are subject to similar pressures as their more expensive siblings. They typically still emerge ultimately from the majors, who have sometimes seemed all too willing to ditch any remotely critical product on their books – as occurred with *The Quiet American*, *Buffalo Soldiers* and *Fahrenheit 9/11*. They still need to be commercially viable, are still made in a society that perpetuates reflexive ideas about 'us' and 'them', and films like *In the Army Now* even have extensive production input from the Department of Defense.

Nor should we forget that despite the potential for broader minds within this range, the vast majority of products eschew this possibility entirely, in favour of churning out bargain-basement dross like *Air Marshal*. And perhaps most disturbing of all are pictures like *Hotel Rwanda* and *United 93*, since their apparent humanity obscures and shuts down the shocking historical debates from which they are drawn.

Part III

Reel Violence

'I play Terminator, but you guys are the true terminators.'
Arnold Schwarzenegger to US troops in Iraq, 4 July 2003

9
Conclusions

The liberal magazine *American Prospect* alleged in 2000 that 'Hollywood is manifestly leftist', and that it 'loves to warble the plaintive song of lefty idealism'.[1] Similarly, the *Washington Post* recently bought into the right-wing perspective that for thirty years Hollywood has been 'telling lies – loudly, constantly and almost always in support of a left-wing point of view'.[2] Calling for 'regime change' in Los Angeles, producer and screenwriter Andrew Klavan wrote in the celebrated newspaper that 'the Hollywood left-wing establishment' was responsible for 'grinding out' this 'propaganda' which, he explained elsewhere, should be replaced with 'gung-ho patriotic war movies that celebrate our fight'.[3]

Of course, there are prominent liberals in Hollywood, but is there a 'left-wing establishment'? Not unless we are to ignore numerous right-wing stars, censors and industry professionals, the presence of the national security services and – most importantly – the industry's business leaders working within a rigid corporate system. Nor can Hollywood output be described as 'left wing', unless we ignore the fact that mainstream productions repeatedly endorse US force and do not criticise the fundamental assumptions of US benevolence on the world stage.

Amongst the most extreme cases of regressive productions are *Stargate*, *Stealth*, *Transformers*, *Iron Man* (Science Fiction), *We Were Soldiers*, *Windtalkers*, *Black Hawk Down* (War Films), *True Lies*, *You Don't Mess With the Zohan* (Comedy), *Executive Decision*, *Air Force One*, *Collateral Damage*, *Rambo*, *The Peacemaker* (Action Adventure) and *Rules of Engagement* (Political Drama). But almost all films either ignore, marginalise, or denigrate critical viewpoints on US power, so the issue is more all-encompassing than a simple 'worst list' or what we might call a body of 'national security cinema'. Where films do seem to be more critical, as in *Thirteen Days* for example, they are only doing so on very narrow grounds, typically in support of another faction of the state and with force necessarily remaining high on the table of options.

Are audiences able to resist these messages? Certainly, not all of us join the armed forces or mug a foreigner as soon as we leave the movie theatre. But the cumulative effects on citizens are surely significant – and established power systems have assumed so since the early days of cinema, when two entrepreneurs made a one-shot film of a Spanish flag being replaced by the Stars and Stripes at the very start of the 1898 US–Spanish war.[4] Organisations and individuals, from the CIA to the FBI, from V.I. Lenin to Joseph Goebbels, have all expressed the view that cinema is the most important medium for transmitting political ideas.[5] 'If I could control the medium of the American motion picture', Soviet dictator Joseph Stalin said, 'I would need nothing else to convert the entire world to communism.'[6] Or, as Twentieth Century Fox founder Darryl Zanuck put it, 'If you have something worthwhile to say, dress it up in the glittering robes of entertainment and you will find a ready market ... without entertainment, no propaganda film is worth a dime.'[7]

Sometimes, such movies even have very direct, specific and disturbing effects. In the post-9/11 world, according to former US Army specialist Tony Lagouranis, the US military 'turned to television and movies [like *24*] to look for new ways of interrogating' suspects because they 'didn't have training in the more extreme tactics', such as mock executions, mock electrocutions, stress positions, isolation, hypothermia, and 'threatening to execute family members or rape detainees' wives'.[8] In the mid-1990s, the *New York Times* reported that Timothy McVeigh, the Oklahoma City bomber responsible for 168 deaths in 1995, watched the right-wing fantasy *Red Dawn* 'over and over', because it was the film he 'loved most'.[9] Following the release of *Top Gun*, according to retired Rear Admiral Alan 'Boot' Hill, young aviators at Miramar Naval Air Station began strutting around believing they actually were Tom Cruise, carloads of women began showing up and widespread allegations of sexual abuse ensued at the station's closely-related Tailhook convention in 1991. Previously, Tailhook had been 'an opportunity for junior officers to come and meet senior officers on an informal basis and talk about tactics, flying and tradition'.[10]

For a moment, let's consider a thought experiment. Based on what we know about the industry and its output, what would Hollywood be like as a news studio? Such a media organisation – let's call it 'Hollywood News, Inc.' – would relentlessly pump out stories ratcheting up the threats to the United States, particularly to its government, military and major cities. It would editorialise for the use of military force – unilateral and illegal where necessary – to solve these problems; force would be portrayed as a panacea which has been successful throughout history. In the dead of the night, barely watched – and with limited distribution – a ragtag body of actors would read a short dissenting bulletin, which would then be derided or more often ignored by the anchors for the rest of the day. Hollywood News, Inc. would, in short, be just as reactionary as Fox News. Bulletins would be announced on the hour to the theme from *The A-Team*.

There is a handful of exceptionally critical movies at the cinema. Among the low-budget productions, there is *Redacted*, as well as *War, Inc.* and *The Quiet American* – which typically had difficulties during the distribution phase. There are even some rare relatively critical films that emerge from the major studios with generous budgets, such as *Avatar*, *The Good Shepherd*, *Lord of War*, *Total Recall*, *Starship Troopers*, *Nixon* and *Syriana*. As Michael Medved observes, though, media messages are invariably more likely to have an impact on audiences when they are 'taken together and repeated with a mind numbing insistence year after year'.[11] The notions that the US is essentially good and that US force is an effective means of solving political problems have been hammered home as hard as any, so it seems unlikely that a few exceptional pictures are sufficient to offset that tradition.

Furthermore, only very rarely do films have some noticeable impact in terms of actually galvanising a movement for oppositional political change. Of the documentaries, *Deadly Deception* had some impact on GE's involvement in the arms trade and *Bowling for Columbine* prompted K-Mart to phase out selling ammunition for handguns ... but Michael Moore failed in his more ambitious attempt to oust Bush with *Fahrenheit 9/11*.[12] The category for fiction films that enact political change is even slimmer, though *JFK* at least forced the release of government files about the Kennedy assassination. Otherwise, Hollywood has helped ensure that the populace remain observers rather than participants in the political process.

In 1941, a Senate Investigation called the movie studios 'gigantic engines of propaganda'.[13] The world has thankfully been able to move on from the 'total war' philosophy that characterised the 1940s – and Hollywood has moved with it. Nor are we in an age, as predominated in the 1950s, when a government committee can ask industry figures the accusatory question 'Are you a member of the Communist Party and the Screen Actors Guild?', as though both were crimes – and comparable crimes at that.[14]

However, this is still an era of conformity in Hollywood over the essential elements of US power. In some ways, this is more serious than ever, as corporate and financial pressures on films to support the status quo and to cleanse critical content have increased. There are clear cases of scripts being toned down to take account of left-wing concerns and pressure groups, as in *Collateral Damage* and *Sum of All Fears*, but with few exceptions (*Bourne* being one) they remained fundamentally reactionary products none the less.

More frequent are the film products that began as intelligent or even progressive books, scripts, or concepts, but demonstrably became reactionary during the development/production phases, as with *The Peacemaker*, *Black Hawk Down*, *Jarhead*, *Behind Enemy Lines*, *Rules of Engagement*, *Charlie Wilson's War*, *Munich*, the *Terminator* franchise and arguably with *Tears of the Sun*. National security organisations, namely the CIA and the Defense Department, were rarely the clear and direct cause of extensive changes but their presence on the sets of roughly a third of contemporary films with foreign policy themes is a hefty counterweight to any film-maker trying to break the mould. The other pressures are harder to demonstrate on each and every film product, because decision-making processes on scripts are not usually subject to much scrutiny, but who can doubt that the desire to provide placement deals and commercial gimmicks did not contribute to the lightweight tone of films like *Transformers*? Mostly, though, films were designed to operate within predefined conventional lines right from their inception, since the culture in which they begin life is very hostile to challenging political narratives. As Jack Valenti put it, Hollywood and Washington are 'sprung from the same DNA'.[15]

It wouldn't take a gifted scriptwriter to make films more favourable to many commentators on the right. In the *New York Sun*, Michael Fumento asked, 'Just how many Hollywood movies ... [post 9/11] have been made in which the bad guys are Islamist terrorists ... ? If you have to guess, guess "none".'[16] To win the argument, which he made in 2005, Fumento excluded films about 9/11 itself (such as *DC 9/11: Time of Crisis* (2003)) and documentaries (such as *9/11* (2002) and *The Flight That Fought Back* (2005)). Our guess of 'none' would also neglect *Team America*, as well as made-for-TV or straight-to-DVD movies such as *Air Marshal* (2003) and – made in June 2001, but distributed in 2002 after the attacks – Chuck Norris's *The President's Man: A Line in the Sand* (2002). Fumento also sidelined several TV series such as *24* and *JAG*, which depicted Islamist terrorists, and the docudrama *Saving Jessica Lynch* (2003), which smeared specific Iraqis who had behaved impeccably in real life.[17] Still, in 2009, another conservative commentator, Andrew Breitbart, made the flimsy claim that 'You cannot get a film produced now that has Islamist terrorists',[18] ignoring recent cinematic releases like *United 93* (2006), *American Dreamz* (2006), *The Kingdom* (2007), *Vantage Point* (2008), *Iron Man* (2008) and *An American Carol* (2008), plus numerous films about Iraqi terrorists and insurgents.

'Hollywood can be vindicated' for such depictions of Islam because 'verisimilitude is the all important consideration', opined Daniel Mandel in the pages of *Middle East Quarterly*.[19] 'There are simply no Jewish versions of Osama Bin Laden or black versions of Sheik Omar Abdul Rahman,' he explained, so substituting Muslims for 'blacks or Jews' would be inappropriate. Mandel is right in the sense that some narratives do make more sense with Islamic villains. But should such villains be presented as identikit bad guys? Should Hollywood keep churning out so many pictures involving hijackings and insurgency against American targets? Wouldn't it be better for Hollywood to present Arabs and Muslims more frequently in other roles as well? And is it really true that no other groups – militias? Nazis? cults? – threaten the kind of terrorism Mandel is talking about?

The call for more depictions of Islamist terrorists also misses the fact that Hollywood has been awash with offensive images of Arabs and Muslims for a century, as Jack Shaheen observed from a lifetime of research. While Shaheen's *Reel Bad Arabs* only endorsed 65 of 950 films from 1914–2001,[20] his research indicates that there truly has been relative restraint on the demonisation of Islam post 9/11. In his 2008 book *Guilty*, which looked at the hundred or so relevant films made since the attacks, Shaheen actually recommended 23 and only placed 18 on his 'worst list'.[21] The likes of Fumento want to reverse and stamp out this trend, which is very much in its infancy, even while the portrayal of Arabs and Muslims remains extremely negative across all media right up to the present day. Would it really have been preferable for the film-makers behind *Sum of All Fears* to have stayed faithful to Tom Clancy's book and depicted an Iranian government-sponsored Palestinian nuclear attack on US soil?

Furthermore, is the West really so infested with dumb pacifists in positions of power that we 'need' to produce propaganda films to stiffen its resolve? Are Islamists the only real-world enemies the West has? Is the vilification of North Korea in just a handful of modern movies (*Tomorrow Never Dies* (1997), *Team America* (2004), *Behind Enemy Lines: Axis of Evil* (2005?)) sufficient for people like

Fumento, Klavan and Mark Steyn? The Chinese dictatorship has barely been used as a villain at all – should Hollywood have some productions in the pipeline to demonise the rival superpower, in case it decides to attack Taiwan? Should Hollywood knock off some abusive narratives indicting Venezuela, since Washington disagrees with the current elected government?

But the right should not be misconstrued as a monolithic bogeyman. 'There's certainly room for dark, disturbing, challenging material', explained the staunchly right-wing film critic Michael Medved, 'but ... [the] movie industry ... isn't responding to the public.'[22] Medved's point is well made – a mix of political ideas in cinema is most welcome. His proposed solution is for 'corporate responsibility',[23] which is also a great idea, although it will require active citizens to compel such an oxymoron to act conscientiously. Medved is concerned that the result of this unaccountable corporate power is that the pendulum has swung too far against traditional conservative and Christian values. This is a reasonable stance on issues such as the heavy use of swearwords on screen, but of much greater concern should be that US power remains routinely represented in hopelessly blinkered and self-congratulatory terms.

In response to the allegation that Americans are 'widely perceived to be selfish and self-indulgent', Geoff Zucker, director of NBC Entertainment said, 'Listen, we are not culpable for the images we portray on television. News informs the American public and keeps our politicians honest. Entertainment entertains the American public. The point is that we do this freely.'[24] This is quite a remarkable statement: Zucker is claiming he has no responsibility for his own work, and further rationalises this by saying that another system – which is owned by the same people – successfully holds the government to account.

Zucker's comment is also generally illuminating though, because it typifies how people working within power systems are unable to recognise the ideological boundaries set by state and corporate forces within which they work. This is hardly surprising – how can such people advance up the ladder if they are considered politically troublesome? And, if they do have challenging views about the dangers of unaccountable power, won't they have long since internalised them and/or learned to bite their tongues?

Although the focus of *Reel Power* has been on how the US is portrayed as almost universally benevolent, this is not to suggest that a lunge in the opposite direction would necessarily be more desirable. Is it 'progress' to present the US as a Christian demagogue in the Turkish *Valley of the Wolves: Iraq* (2006)? Or as killers and rapists as in the Egyptian farce *The Night That Baghdad Fell* (2005), in which a Condoleezza Rice look-alike belly-dancer performs a striptease? Or to suggest that the corporate classes of America and the rest of the world are so perverted that they bid huge sums of money to participate in grotesque torture-murders, as in the *Hostel* franchise?

A freer system would allow the production of more thoughtful, varied and imaginative narratives about US power, across all genres. With less merchandising and less concentrated ownership, film-makers would be less afraid to interrogate the corporate roots of US power. With less script interference by national security organisations, films would be less prone to the rampant militarism prevalent in current productions and less liable to make products that are in some cases little more than military recruitment films. If the media were to question state apparatchiks over their peddling of divisive and dubious theories like the 'clash of civilizations', the prevalent paradigm of 'US versus them' would hold less sway on screen. In short, a film industry less inured with political, economic and military elites would be better disposed to produce celebrated work like *Apocalypse Now*, *JFK*, *Planet of the Apes*, *Bourne*, *Dr Strangelove* and the Gulf War allegory *The Big Lebowski* (1998).

Such small but significant changes are hardly beyond the pale. In spite of the forces raging against it, Hollywood has made some inspiring and incendiary films. Until the 1970s, studios did not have such giant parent companies and film-making costs were much lower. Before the advent of sound in cinema, product placement was virtually absent.[25] Even the Pentagon has not been able to sustain its media campaign without hiccups, for example, when its Hollywood liaison office almost fell victim to budget cuts in the 1990s, or when Josh Rushing – the Pentagon's press officer who became famous in the documentary *Control Room* (2004) – had an attack of conscience and went to work for Al Jazeera.[26] Indeed, when a Republican congresswoman raised the fact that Homeland Security was spending $130,000 per year trying to burnish its on-screen image in Hollywood, the department's liaison was shut down entirely.[27]

The director of *The Kingdom* (2007), Peter Berg commented, 'I don't go to movies to be lectured about politics. There's been so few films that have been financially successful at pounding home messages. It's hard to make genocide fun.'[28] Is it? Should Steven Spielberg have not bothered to make the blockbusting *Schindler's*

List (1995)? What about the huge range of other Holocaust movies? Are they not 'fun' enough? Wasn't Berg's own film about a massacre of Americans? Berg's position becomes clearer when we hear his corollary: 'American audiences are much more interested in Paris Hilton and her drinking than they are about genocide in Sudan.'[29] In other words, he thinks cinema isn't 'fun' when we are led to sympathise with foreign people. It is better to treat audiences as shallow fools. Sympathetic portrayals must be reserved for Americans, especially the authorities, and foreign cultures are to be simplified as the sources of despicable villainy.

How can such a reductive, solipsistic attitude prevail in the modern motion picture industry? It isn't just that audiences are resistant to 'message' films. The decisive factor is that political and corporate forces drive a wedge through the relationship between artist and audience – being concerned with neither art, nor entertainment, nor democracy.

Endnotes

1 Hollywood Screened

1. Medved, Michael (1993), 'Hollywood vs America', *Harper's*, pp. 216–20.
2. Orwell, George (1995), 'The Freedom of the Press, Rediscovered Preface to "Animal Farm"', *New Statesman and Society* 8 (366), p. 11.
3. Gomery, Douglas (2005), 'Economic and Institutional Analysis: Hollywood as Monopoly Capitalism' in Wayne, Mike, *Understanding Film: Marxist Perspectives*, London: Pluto Press, p. 179.
4. Epstein, Edward Jay (2005), *The Big Picture: The New Logic of Money and Power in Hollywood*, Random House, p. 106.
5. Miller, Toby et al. (2005), *Global Hollywood* 2, London: British Film Institute, pp. 82–3.
6. Ibid., pp. 95–103.
7. Ibid., p. 187.
8. Chidley, Joe (2000), 'Hollywood's Welfare Bums', *Canadian Business*, 3 April, p. 11.
9. McChesney, Robert (2000), *Rich Media, Poor Democracy: Poor Communication In Dubious Times*, New Press, p. 33; Miller, Toby et al. (2001), *Global Hollywood*, p. 4.
10. Kaufman, Anthony (2006), 'Is Foreign Film the New Endangered Species?', *New York Times*, 22 January <http://www.nytimes.com/2006/01/22/movies/22kauf.html>.
11. *Variety* (1995), 'Earth to Hollywood: You Win', 13–19 February, p. 1.
12. DiOrio, Carl (2004), '15% rise from previous year; Valenti confirms exit', *Video Business*, 23 March. For full report, see *MPAA* (2007), 'Theatrical Market Statistics', esp. p. 6 <http://www.mpaa.org/2007-US-Theatrical-Market-Statistics-Report.pdf>.
13. Rich, Joshua (2005), 'Monster Budgets: Why blockbusters are breaking the bank – We look at why 'King Kong' isn't the only movie with a supersized budget', *Entertainment Weekly*, No. 853, 9 December. The description of *The Godfather* as a metaphor for American capitalism is attributed to the series' director Francis Ford Coppola. See *Vanity Fair* (2009), 'The Godfather Wars', Features, March, Vol. 51, No. 3, p. 270.
14. Ibid.
15. Kivijarv, L (2005), *Product Placement Spending in Media 2005: History, Analysis and Forecast 1975–2009*, Stamford, CT: PQ Media.
16. Goettler, Ronald L. and Leslie, Phillip (2005), 'Cofinancing to Manage Risk in the Motion Picture Industry', *Journal of Economics & Management Strategy*, Vol. 14, No. 2, June, pp. 231–61.
17. Lehu, Jean (2007), *Branded Entertainment: Product placement and Brand Strategy in the Entertainment Business*, London and Philadelphia, PA: Kogan Page, p. 38.

18. Segrave, Kerry (2004), *Product Placement in Hollywood Films: A History*, McFarland and Company, p. 180.
19. Nitins, Tanya (2005), *Australia Screen Education*, 22 September, No. 40, pp. 44.
20. Crispin Miller, Mark (1990), 'Hollywood: The Ad', *Atlantic Monthly*, April.
21. Mahar, Ted (1987), 'Connections, Not Craftsmanship, Key to Success in Hollywood', *The Oregonian*, p. B08.
22. Bart, Peter (2001), 'The Monster That Ate Hollywood', April, *PBS Frontline* <www.pbs.org/wgbh/pages/frontline/shows/hollywood/>.
23. Lancaster, David (2005), 'Product Placement in Hollywood Films: A History' (review), *Film and History: An Interdisciplinary Journal of Film and Television Studies*, Vol. 35, No. 2, pp. 95–6.
24. Elliott, Stuart (1997), 'Reebok's Suit Over *Jerry Maguire* Shows Risks of Product Placement', *New York Times*, 7 February.
25. Andrews, Marke (2005), 'How companies get their products onto the screen: North Shore firm negotiates with studios for placement in movies, TV shows', *Vancouver Sun*, 4 February, 'Business BC' section, p. G1.
26. *Entertainment Weekly* (1997), 'Sneaky Business', 24 January, No. 363 <http://www.ew.com/ew/article/0,,286552,00.html>.
27. Churnin, Nancy (2000), 'Tiny Titan A.E's opening shows merchandising makes kind movies', *Dallas Morning News*, 28 June.
28. Black, Lewis (2003), 'More McCanlies, Texas', *The Austin Chronicle*, 19 September <http://www.austinchronicle.com/gyrobase/Issue/story?oid=oid:178259>.
29. Puig, Claudia (1999), 'Family-friendly concept crashes as "Giant Falls to Earth"', *USA Today*, 30 August, 'Life' section, p. 4D.
30. York, Anthony (2001), 'The Product Placement Monster that E.T. spawned', *Salon.com*, 26 April <http://dir.salon.com/tech/feature/2001/04/26/product_placement/index.html>.
31. See Conlogue, Ray (2001), 'Why Can't Hollywood kick the habit?', *Globe and Mail* (Canada), 'Globe Review' section, 13 February, p. R1; Wetzstein, Cheryl (1990), 'Tobacco companies decide to stop smoking up the silver screen', *Washington Times*, 20 December, p. C1; Booth, Jenny (2003), '"Give smoking in films an X-certificate" say doctors', *Sunday Telegraph* (London), 27 July, p. 8.
32. Guns are lobbied for and provided without charge. Andrew Molchan, Director of the National Association of Federally Licensed Firearms dealers, America's largest association of firearms retailers, estimates that the gun industry gets 90 per cent of its advertising through TV and movies, all for free. Magnum Research, producers of the Desert Eagle pistol has placed guns in over a hundred movies. The poster for *Last Action Hero* was changed to include a Desert Eagle gun after flagging ticket sales, though Schwarzenegger comments 'I don't pick myself as a role model ... I don't run around every day with a gun in my hand.' See Granados, Oriana de (2003), 'Selling Guns at the Box Office', *Christian Science Monitor*, 6 October, 'Opinion' section, p. 9; Hornaday, Ann (1999), 'Guns and Movies: An Uneasy Relationship', *The Star Ledger*, 15 February, p. 29. Owner of Weapons Specialists Utd Rick Washburn explained of the Desert Eagle pistol, 'Here's a gun that has very little practical useage. It's too big and heavy. There's not much of a market for handgun hunting. So I would say the success of that particular weapon owes

almost everything to the movies.' See Hornaday, Ann (1999), 'Hollywood and the gun: Firearms companies get free publicity but it can blow up in their faces', *Hamilton Spectator*, 23 January, p. W9.

33. Benjamin A. Goldberger (2003), 'How the "Summer of the Spinoff" Came to be: The Branding of Characters in American Mass Media', *Entertainment Law Review*, Vol. 23, No. 2, p. 301.
34. Ibid.
35. Holson, Laura M. and Lyman, Rick (2002), 'In Warner Brothers' Strategy, A Movie Is Now a Product Line; Making Franchise Films That Build Brand Names', *New York Times*, 11 February, p. 56; Goldberger, 'How the "Summer of the Spinoff" Came to be', p. 391.
36. Media Education Foundation (2000), *Behind the Screens: Hollywood Goes Hypercommercial*, Northampton, MA: Media Education Foundation.
37. Donaldson-Evans, Catherine (2007), 'GI Joe to Become Global Task Force in Movie', *Fox News*, 7 September <http://www.foxnews.com/story/0,2933,296054,00.html>; see also Beck, Glenn (host) (2007), 'Why Does Tinseltown Shirk American Heroes?', *CNN*, 30 October, 7:00 p.m.
38. Rosenberg, Alyssa (2009), 'G.I Joe and Company', *Atlantic Monthly*, August <http://www.theatlantic.com/doc/200908/gi-joe-war-movies>. For details on the explicit propaganda intent of *The Green Berets*, that deliberately concealed a production credit for Pentagon and which began life in correspondence between John Wayne and President Lyndon Johnson, see Taylor, Philip M., 'The Green Berets', in Ellwood, David, W. (ed.) (2000), *The Movies as History: Visions of the Twentieth Century*, Stroud, UK: Sutton Publishing, pp. 36–43.
39. Sutherland, Clare (2000), 'Testing times – Time Out', *Cairns Post/Cairns Sun* (Australia), 17 November, p. 31.
40. Asch, Solomon Elliott (1956), '*Studies of independence and conformity: A minority of one against a unanimous majority*', *Psychological Monographs*, Volume 70, American Psychological Association.
41. Sutherland (2000), 'Testing times – Time Out'.
42. Willens, Michele (2000), 'Film: Putting Films to the Test Every Time', *New York Times*, 25 June, 'Arts and Leisure' section, p. 11.
43. Mansbridge, Chris (2006), 'Welcome to Rambo town, BC. Officially, Hope, BC is the chainsaw capital of Canada, but its unofficial claim to fame – as the location of the movie *First Blood* – is what makes it intriguing', *Calgary Herald*, 25 August, p. 26.
44. For details on military involvement in *Birth of a Nation* and *Wings*, see Suid, Lawrence H. (2002), *Guts and Glory: The Making of the American Military Image in Film*, Lexington-Fayette: University Press of Kentucky, pp. 15 and 32–9 respectively.
45. Independent Film Channel et al. (2006) *This Film is Not Yet Rated*.
46. Fleisher, Jeff (2004), 'Operation Hollywood', *Mother Jones*, 20 September.
47. Robb, David L. (2004), *Operation Hollywood: How the Pentagon Shapes and Censors the Movies*, Amherst, MA: Prometheus Books, p. 91.
48. Klady, Leonard (1994), 'Backlot: Robin's Wooed; Fox Follies; Uppity Secretaries', *Daily Variety*, 18 January.
49. Robb (2004), *Operation Hollywood*, p. 46. Robb discovered that the Pentagon had a decisive role in preventing the production of several other films: *Field of Fire*, *The Smouldering Sea* and a film about the controversial Admiral Hyman Rickover. See pp. 125–7, 356 and 363–5 respectively.

50. *Hollywood Reporter* (1998), 'On Location', 29 April
51. Robb (2004), *Operation Hollywood*, pp. 363–4.
52. More than 5,000 pages of internal FBI memos released under the FOIA reveal that Hoover controlled every aspect of *The FBI*, approving the cast and crew, the writers, the directors and every word of the script. Anyone suspected of being a 'pervert' or remotely connected to the 'worldwide Communist conspiracy' was banned from the show; Hoover also at times threatened to can the show to pressurise ABC News to bend to his will. Hoover dictated there were to be no depictions of the Mafia, violence, civil rights issues, and none of the onscreen agents were to be shown doing anything wrong such as wiretapping or having a girlfriend. See the four part series of articles, Robb, David (2008), 'Special Report: J. Edgar Hoover's Hollywood Obsessions Revealed', *Hollywood Today*, 27 February <http://www.hollywoodtoday.net/2008/02/27/special-report-j-edgar-hoover's-hollywood-obsessions-revealed/>.
53. *Reuters* (2007), 'FBI, Fox on the Case with Drama Series', 8 August.
54. Ibid., p. 156.
55. Daniel J. Leab (2007), *Orwell Subverted: The CIA and the Filming of* Animal Farm, University Park: Pennsylvania State University Press, p. 93.
56. Bushnell, William S. (2006), 'Paying for the Damage: *The Quiet American* Revisited', *Film and History*, Vol. 36, No. 2, pp. 38–44.
57. Ibid. See also Neve, Brian (2007), 'Adaptation and the Cold War: Mankiewicz's *The Quiet American*', in James Welsh and Peter Lev (eds), *The Literature/Film Reader: Issues of Adaptation*, Lanham, MD: Scarecrow Press, pp. 235–44.
58. Leab (2007), *Orwell Subverted*, p. xiv.
59. CIA (2009) Personal correspondence with the author, 8 June. The CIA's Freedom of Information response was at least supplied without a fee and they provided copies of already declassified documents. For a similar request, the Pentagon found nothing and billed me $100.
60. CIA Press Release (1999), 'CIA Hosts Screening of In the Company of Spies', 14 October <https://www.cia.gov/news-information/press-releases-statements/press-release-archive-1999/pr101499.html>.
61. Kelbaugh, Paul (2008), Email to author, 6 August.
62. Anon. (2008), Telephone interview with Robbie Graham, 28 July.
63. Welkis, Robert W. (2008), 'Without a Trace', *Los Angeles Times*, 28 July.
64. Devore, Gary (1997), 'The Big Steal', draft script, undated. This script was kindly provided by the man lined up to the produce the film, Barry Rosenbush.
65. Honeycutt, Kirk (1997), 'Devore Rolls "Spare", "Father"', *Hollywood Reporter*, 7 April, p. 1.
66. In the confusion, Gary Devore's wife, Wendy, paid for a second autopsy. The coroner, Dr David Posey, noted that the hand bones the police had supposedly discovered in the car were in fact 200 years old. Posey also noted that the body had not received physical trauma during the alleged accident. His verdict: homicide by undetermined means. For details, see my online articles.
67. See the 158-page Department of California Highway Patrol (1997), 'Gary Martin Devore Accident Investigation', Southern Division Multidisciplinary Accident Investigation Team, 28 June.
68. Mike Burridge, the public spokesman for the Sheriff's Department on the Devore case expressed his doubts to me in December 2009.

69. Most notably, Wendy does not believe the official story and thinks that the intelligence services were somehow involved. I interviewed her several times from December 2009 onwards.
70. Jenkins, Tricia (2009), 'Get Smart: A Look at the Current Relationship between Hollywood and the CIA', *Historical Journal of Radio, Film and Television*, Vol. 29, No. 2, p. 232.
71. Ibid.
72. Daniel Forbes (2000), 'Prime-time propaganda: How the White House secretly hooked network TV on its anti-drug message', *Salon*, 13 January <http://archive.salon.com/news/feature/2000/01/13/drugs/>.
73. See the Motion Picture Association of America website at <http://www.mpaa.org/aboutus.asp>.
74. CNN Live (2001), 'Valenti and Rove Hold News Conference', transcript, 11 November <http://transcripts.cnn.com/TRANSCRIPTS/0111/11/se.03.html>.
75. Waxman, Sharon (2001), 'White House Looking to Enlist Hollywood in Terrorism War', *Washington Post*, 20 October, p. C01.
76. Hayes, Dade and McClintock, Pamela (2001), 'War Chores for Hollywood: White House, Moguls agree to step up showbiz efforts', *Variety*, 11 November <http://www.variety.com/article/VR1117855616.html?categoryid=18&cs=1&query=karl+and+rove&display=karl+and+rove>.
77. Chambers, David (2002), 'Will Hollywood Go to War?', *TBS*, No. 8, Spring/Summer <http://www.tbsjournal.com/Archives/Spring02/chambers.html; also see USO Centers and Programs at http://www.uso.org/pubs/uploads/USO2.pdf>.
78. White House cooperation on *DC 9/11* is reported in Rich, Frank (2006), 'Too Soon? It's Too Late for United 93', *New York Times*, 7 May, Section 4, p. 12.
79. Salon.com (2006), 'Jack Bauer Wants You', 19 September <www.salon.com/news/feature/2006/09/19/cia_ads/index.html>; CIA Website (2004), 'New Recruitment Video on the Central Intelligence Agency Careers Web Site Features Jennifer Garner', 8 March <http://www.cia.gov/news-information/press-releases-statements/press-release-archive-2004/pr03082004.html>.
80. Robb (2004), *Operation Hollywood*, p. 56.
81. Hershberger, Mary (2004), 'Peace Work, War Myths: Jane Fonda and the antiwar movement', *Peace and Change*, Vol. 29, Nos 3 and 4, July, pp. 556–7.
82. Ibid., pp. 557–8.
83. Ibid., pp. 567.
84. Ibid., p. 554.
85. Robinson, S. (1991), 'The Schmaltz and Stripes of Hollywood Celebs', *Herald Sun*, 13 February.
86. *National Enquirer* (1991), 'Ted Turner tells Jane Fonda: Keep Your Mouth Shut about the War', 26 February.
87. Davis, James Kirkpatrick (1992), *Spying on America: The FBI's Domestic Counterintelligence Program*, New York: Praeger, pp. 120–21.
88. Davidson, Bill (1990), *Jane Fonda: An Intimate Biography*, New York: Dutton, pp. 2–5
89. *New York Post* (2003), 'Don't Aid These Saddam Lovers', 19 March, p. 12.
90. Gumbel, Andrew (2003), 'Outspoken Stars Battle the Home Front', *New Zealand Herald*, 22 April.

91. Rutenberg, Jim (2004), 'Disney Is Blocking Distribution of Film That Criticizes Bush', *New York Times*, 5 May.
92. Finke, Nikki (2004), 'When Might Turns Right – Golly GE, Why Big Media is Pro-Bush', *LA Weekly*, 1–7 October.
93. Bill O'Reilly (2007), 'Talking Points' <http://www.youtube.com/watch?v=YiybkZeBSak>.
94. Carter, Sara A. (2007), 'War Film's portrayal of soldiers draws fire from GOP lawmaker', *Washington Times*, 22 November, p. A3.
95. Taylor Jr, Stuart (1987), 'Court Backs "Propaganda" Label for 3 Canadian Films', *New York Times*, 29 April, p. A28.
96. Thomson, Randall (2003), 'Hollywood's Last Taboo', 21 February, *Santa Fe New Mexican*, p. 50.
97. Litwak, Mark (1986), *Reel Power: The Struggle for Influence and Success in the New Hollywood*, Los Angeles, CA: Silman-James Press, p. 122.
98. *Fade In* magazine (2008), 'Gods and Monsters: Rating the Regimes', Vol. X, No. 3, p. 11 <http://www.fadeinonline.com/10_03/articles/gods_n_monsters/>.
99. Ibid., p. 17.
100. Ibid.
101. *Fade In* magazine (2009), 'Minority Report', Vol. XI, No. 1 <http://fadeinonline.com/articles/minority-report/>.
102. The National Association for the Advancement of Colored People (2008) 'Out of Focus-Out of Sync Take 4 NAACP Report', December. See also Khalil, Ashraf (2007), 'More Work, One Role for Arab Actors', *LA Times*, 4 October <http://www.benton.org/outgoingframe/7464>.
103. Gabler, Neil (1990), 'Film View; Jews, Blacks and Trouble in Hollywood', *New York Times*, 2 September, Section 2, p. 7.
104. Shaheen, Jack G. (2008), *Guilty: Hollywood's Verdict on Arabs After 9/11*, Northampton, MA: Interlink Books, pp. 58–61.
105. McKee, Robert (1999), *Story: Substance, Structure, Style and the Principles of Screenwriting*, London: Methuen, p. 4.
106. Ibid.
107. Ghomeshi, Jian (1998), 'Well Meaning and Dangerous', *Toronto Star*, 15 November, 'Entertainment' section.
108. Ibid.
109. Kupcham, Charles A. (1998), 'After Pax America: Benign Power, Regional Integration and the Sources of a Stable Multipolarity', *International Security*, Vol. 23, No. 2, Autumn, p. 41.
110. Kagan, Robert (1998), 'The Benevolent Empire', *Foreign Policy*, Issue 111, Summer, p. 26.
111. Ibid., p. 28.
112. Huntington, Samuel P. (1993), 'Why International Primacy Matters', *International Security*, Vol. 17, No. 4, Spring, pp. 82–3.
113. McNamara, Robert S. (1996), *In Retrospect: The Tragedy and Lessons of Vietnam*, Vintage, reprint edition, p. 10.
114. Tocqueville, Alexis de (1988), *Democracy in America*, trans. George Lawrence, ed. J.P. Meyer, New York: Harper Perennial.
115. Greene, Jack P. (1997), *The Intellectual Construction of America: Exceptionalism and Identity from 1492 to 1800*, Chapel Hill: University of North Carolina Press.

116. McCrisken, Trevor B. (2003), *American Exceptionalism and the Legacy of Vietnam: US Foreign Policy Since 1974*, Houndmills: Palgrave, p. 2.
117. Bush, George W (2001), White House press release, White House Website, 11 October <http://www.whitehouse.gov/news/releases/2001/10/20011011-7.html>.

2 Hollywood Deactivated

1. *Forbes Magazine* (2006), 'Tom Cruise ranked 1 among The Top 100 Celebrities In 2006', 5 January <http://www.forbes.com/lists/2006/53/6YG2.html>.
2. Thompson, Anne (2006), 'How the players fared after the Cruise attack', *Hollywood Reporter*, 25 August <http://www.hollywoodreporter.com/hr/search/article_display.jsp?vnu_content_id=1003053055>; Grover, Ron (2006), 'Q&A with Sumner Redstone', *Business Week*, 5 September <http://www.businessweek.com/technology/content/sep2006/tc20060905_340632.htm>.
3. In *Entertainment Weekly*'s 1994 power list, Murdoch was top. Other notables included Hanks (16) and Cruise (22). See *PR Newswire* (1994), 'Rupert Murdoch Rises to Number 1 List of Entertainment's Most Powerful People', 20 October. In 2000, the *Hollywood Reporter* published its list of the most powerful living or dead players since it began publishing in 1930; the list included talent agent Lew Wasserman at number 1, with Murdoch (2), Spielberg (3), media baron Randolph Hearst (4), Twentieth Century Fox founder Darryl F. Zanuck (6), former Disney CEO Michael Eisner (8) and MGM founder Louis B Mayer (10). See *Coventry Evening Telegraph* (2000), 'Movie Agent Tops Power League', 23 November, p. 31. See also Smith, Sean (2009), 'The $4 billion man: Hanks, Cruise and Gibson used to be the top guns, but not anymore. Meet the new most powerful actor on the planet – Will Smith', *Newsweek*, 2 March <http://www.newsweek.com/id/35744>. Murdoch came top again for *Vanity Fair*'s list in 2006, with Hanks coming in at 25. See Tharp, Paul (200), 'New Face Atop VF's Power List', *New York Post*, 7 September, p. 45. Power lists are only rough indicators, that usually claim to determine the power to make movies, stop movies being made and control how they are made. Peter Bart expresses cynicism about the way such lists are compiled. See Bart, Peter (2002), 'Power Outtage Hits Hollywood Execs', *Variety*, 21 October, Vol. 388, Issue 10, p. 6.
4. BBC News (2005), 'Who Has the Power in Hollywood?', 30 September <http://news.bbc.co.uk/1/hi/entertainment/4297592.stm>. Tony Angelotti described Murdoch as 'the guy – the supreme leader'.
5. Litwak, Mark (1986) *Reel Power: The Struggle for Influence and Success in the New Hollywood*, Los Angeles, CA: Silman-James Press, p. 95.
6. BBC News (2005), 'Who Has the Power in Hollywood?'. For more on the historic power of the studio owners, see Kent, Nicolas (1991), *Naked Hollywood: Money and Power in the Movies Today* New York: St Martin's Press, pp. 40-45. For more on the weak position of the screenwriter, see ibid., pp. 115–46.
7. Litwak (1986), *Reel Power*, p. 174.
8. *Fade In* magazine (2008), 'Gods and Monsters: Rating the Regimes', Vol. X, No. 3, p. 11 <http://www.fadeinonline.com/10_03/articles/gods_n_monsters/>, p. 16.

9. *Asia Wall Street Journal* (2004), 'Guess Who's a GOP Booster? The CEO of CBS's parent company endorses President Bush', 24 September.
10. Gordon, N. (2004), 'Windfalls of War: General Electric Company', *The Center for Public Integrity*, 31 March <http://www.publicintegrity.org/wow/bio.aspx?act=pro&ddlC=23>.
11. Rose, Charlie (2001), 'Neutron Jack in his Own Words', 24 October, Transcript #3059 <http://makethemaccountable.com/coverup/NeutronJack.htm>.
12. Finke, Nikki (2004), 'When Might Turns Right – Golly GE, Why Big Media is Pro-Bush', *LA Weekly*, 1–7 October. Bob Wright worked closely with Universal. See Holson, Laura M. (2004), 'Six Sigma: A Hollywood Studio Learns the GE Way', *New York Times*, 26 September, p. C1.
13. O'Boyle, Thomas F. (1999), *At Any Cost: Jack Welch, General Electric, and the Pursuit of Profit*, Vintage Books, New York, p. 11. Neutron bombs famously kill living things but leave buildings intact. The moniker had an additional distasteful element – GE was the company that manufactured neutron bombs for the government (ibid., p. 155).
14. Bauder, David (2001), 'Congressman says GE's Welch spent two hours at NBC decision desk on election night', *Associated Press Worldstream*, 10 September. Also see Lappé, Anthony, Marshall, Stephen and Inaba, Ian (2004), *True Lies*, Plume Press, p. 2.
15. *The News Media & the Law* (2001), 'Congressman, NBC Clash Over Election Night Tapes', Fall, p. 33. Also see Cohen, Jeff (2001), 'The Case Against GE: Unfair Access: An Interview with Jeff Cohen', *Multinational Monitor*, July/August 2001, Vol. 22, Nos 7 and 8 <http://multinationalmonitor.org/mm2001/01july-august/julyaug01interviewcohen.html>.
16. Groom, Nichola (2008), 'GE's Immelt: still a Republican?', 13 March <http://blogs.reuters.com/environment/2008/03/13/ges-immelt-still-a-republican/>.
17. Finke (2004), 'When Might Turns Right'.
18. Anderson, Patrick (1968), *The Presidents' Men; White House assistants of Franklin D. Roosevelt, Harry S. Truman, Dwight D. Eisenhower, John F. Kennedy, and Lyndon B. Johnson*, New York: Doubleday, p. 312.
19. Kelly, David (1992), 'Valenti Calls *JFK* a "hoax"; Ex-LBJ aide says Stone's film like Nazi's *Triumph of the Will*', *Hollywood Reporter*, 3 April; Clancy, Luke (1994), 'Defender of Hollywood, Friend of President's Jack Valenti was in the Dallas Motorcade when JFK was Shot. He now represents the US Film Industry in GATT talks', *City Edition*, 6 December.
20. Ibid.
21. Valenti, Jack (2002), 'Hollywood and the War Against Terror (The West and Islam)' *New Perspectives Quarterly*, Spring, Vol. 19, Issue 2, p. 70.
22. Ibid., p. 71.
23. Ibid.
24. Valenti, Jack (2007), 'Up Close', *Politico.com*, 24 January.
25. *PR Newswire* (1994), 'Rupert Murdoch Rises to #1 on List of Entertainment's 101 Most Powerful People', 20 October; *Hobart Mercury* (Australia) (2000), 'Hollywood's Most Powerful', 22 November, p. 15.
26. Comments by Peter Chernin, chairman of Fox Filmed Entertainment. See Weinraub, Bernard (1996), 'In a Far-Flung Empire, Some Winners, Losers and Works in Progress; Independence Day for 20th Century Fox', *New York Times*, 29 July.

27. Wolff, Michael (2008), *The Man Who Owns the News: Inside the Secret World of Rupert Murdoch*, London: Bodley Head, p. 299.
28. Neil, Andrew (1997), *Full Disclosure*, Pan Books, p. 213.
29. Ibid., p. 204.
30. Ibid.
31. Ibid., p. 212.
32. Ibid., p. 208
33. Day, Julia (2003), 'Murdoch Backs "Courageous" Blair Over Iraq', *Guardian*, 11 February <http://www.guardian.co.uk/media/2003/feb/11/iraqandthemedia.news>.
34. During the US invasions of Afghanistan and Iraq, Boeing received $16.6 billion in Pentagon contracts. See Hartung, William D. (2004), 'Making Money on Terrorism', *The Nation*, 23 February <http://www.commondreams.org/views04/0206-09.htm>.
35. Gordon, N. (2004), *Windfalls of War: General Electric Company*, Washington, DC: The Center for Public Integrity, 31 March <http://www.publicintegrity.org/wow/bio.aspx?act=pro&ddlC=23>.
36. O'Boyle, Thomas F. (1999), *At Any Cost: Jack Welch, General Electric, and the Pursuit of Profit*, New York: Vintage Books. Until the early 1990s, GE was involved in more instances of Pentagon fraud than any other military contractor, with 15 criminal convictions and civil judgments between 1985 and 1992 (see p. 13). Details of the scandal involving the Israeli Air Force are available in O'Boyle's book (pp. 255–76). GE's involvement in nuclear arms was extensive and become scandalous. Declassified documents reveal that government and GE managers in 1949 deliberately released a cloud of radioactive iodine 131 and xenon to see how far downwind it could be traced. It drifted 400 miles, carrying at least several hundred times more radiation than was emitted at Three Mile Island. A congressional subcommittee discovered that GE had been involved in experiments that irradiated the scrotum and testes of 63 inmates, in the context of much wider human radiation experimentation in the United States during the 1960s (pp. 152–63). GE's contamination of the Hudson River is discussed throughout the book, for example, pp. 185–92.
37. Mosk, Matthew and Rich, Eric (2006), 'Prominent Ties Among Comcast Hires; Politicians' Relatives, Ex-Officials on Payroll', *Washington Post*, 7 May, p. A01.
38. Down, John (2001), 'The Song Machine', *Open Democracy*, 25 October <http://www.opendemocracy.net/arts-Film/article_369.jsp>.
39. O'Boyle (1999), *At Any Cost*, p. 157.
40. Ibid., pp. 154–5.
41. Ibid., pp. 181–2.
42. Bart, Peter (1997), 'Shooting it the McVeigh Way', *Daily Variety*, 16 June, 'Back Lot' section, p. 34; Bender, J.P and Duggan, Ed (2001), 'Haig's Global Reach Based in Palm Beach', *South Florida Business Journal*, Vol. 21, No. 31, p. 1A. Also see Kastor, Elizabeth (1984), 'The Night of *Red Dawn*; Alexander Haig Offers a Sneak Preview', *Washington Post*, 9 August, p. D1, for details about how Haig introduced a private screening of the film.
43. Independent Film Channel, (2006), *This Film Is Not (Yet) Rated.*
44. Ibid.

45. Webb, Teresa, et al. (2007), 'Violent Entertainment Pitched to Adolescents: An Analysis of PG-13 Films', *Pediatrics*, Vol. 119, No. 6, June, pp. e1219–e1229.
46. Independent Film Channel (2006), *This Film is Not (Yet) Rated.*
47. Rampell, Ed (2005), *Progressive Hollywood: A People's Film History of the United States*, London: Turnaround Publishers.
48. Dickenson, Ben (2006), *Hollywood's New Radicalism: War, Globalisation and Movies From Reagan to George W. Bush*, London: I.B Tauris, p. xiv.
49. Department of Defense, Office of the Assistant Secretary of Defense (Public Affairs) News Transcript (1999), Presenter: Secretary Cohen Awards Steven Spielberg August 11th Award Ceremony with Secretary Cohen and Steven Spielberg <http://www.defenselink.mil/transcripts/transcript.aspx?transcriptid=396>.
50. Rush, George; Malloy, Joanna; Rozdeba, Suzanne, and Louie, Rebecca (2002), 'Hollywood Goes to War Over Iraq Policy', *Daily News* (New York), 27 September, p. 24.
51. McCarthy, Philip (2002), 'Hollywood declares WAR on war', *The Age* (Melbourne, Australia), 12 October, p. 1.
52. Rush et al. (2002), 'Hollywood Goes to War Over Iraq Policy', p. 24.
53. Wonkette (2007), 'Scooter Libby Loves Tom Cruise!', 25 January <wonkette.com/231486/scooter-libby-loves-tom-cruise>.
54. *MX* (Melbourne, Australia) (2001), 'Tom Boosts CIA Image', 1 November, p. 4. I have corresponded with the media consultant and Defense Department contractor Michael Sands, who also mentioned Cruise's CIA links. Sands also claimed that Robert Towne, who wrote the first two instalments in the *Mission Impossible* series, was close to Chase Brandon.
55. Brooks, Xan (2002), 'That's Militainment', *Guardian*, 22 May.
56. Robinson, S. (1991), 'The Schmaltz and Stripes of Hollywood Celebs', *Herald Sun*, 13 February.
57. Ibid.
58. United Press (1991), 'Hollywood's Tribute to Gulf War Vets Rejects Peace Group', 27 April, 'Domestic news' section, *United Press International*, BC Cycle.
59. Cooper, Mark (1999), 'Postcards From the Left', *The Nation*, 5 April <www.thenation.com/doc/19990405/cooper (29.04.07)>.
60. Biskind, Peter (ed.) (1999), 'On Movies, Money and Politics: Beatty, Baldwin, Glover, Robbins, Stone and Lear', *The Nation*, 5 April, p. 14.
61. Ehrenreich, Ben (1999), 'The War at Home: Local Progressives Talk About Kosovo', *LA Weekly*, 5 May, www.laweekly.com/news/news/the-war-at-home/6638/>.
62. See IMDB, Biography for James Woods <http://www.imdb.com/name/nm0000249/bio>.
63. Bonin, Liane (2003), 'Fighting Words', *Entertainment Weekly*, 31 March <http://www.ew.com/ew/article/0,,439222,00.html>.
64. Available on YouTube at <http://www.youtube.com/watch?v=7h3GPc_yMCE>.
65. <http://www.brightlightsfilm.com/42/arnold.php#7end>; see also Rush, George and Molloy, Joanna et al. (2002), 'Talking Politics with the Squirminator', *Daily News* (New York), 14 November; Dickenson (2004), *Hollywood's New Radicalism*, p. 189.

66. BBC News, 'Sombre Celebrations for US Iraq Troops', 4 July <http://news.bbc.co.uk/1/hi/world/middle_east/3044878.stm>.
67. McEntee, Marni (2004), 'Schwarzenegger Visits Ramstein', 5 May <http://www.stripes.com/article.asp?section=104&article=22008>.
68. Rosellini, Lynn (1990), 'Pumping the Public Persona', *U.S. News & World Report*, 26 November, Vol. 109, No. 21, pp. 62, 64.
69. Broder, John M (2002), 'Threats and Responses: Hollywood; Celebrities Known for Political Outspokenness Have Little to Say About Iraq', *New York Times*, 6 October, p.A22.
70. Ibid.
71. Ibid.
72. Ibid.
73. Hall, Carla (1991), 'Quiet On the Wartime Set; Actors Slow to Speak Out on Gulf Conflict', *Washington Post*, 26 January, p. D2.
74. Lauerman, Kerry (2003), 'Should Celebrity Activists Shut Up For Now?', *Salon.com*, 21 March <http://dir.salon.com/story/ent/feature/2003/03/21/protest/index.html>.
75. Broder, John M. (2002), 'Threats and Responses', *New York Times*, 6 October.
76. Brooke, Tom (2003), 'Hollywood's March Against War', *BBC News*, 28 February <http://news.bbc.co.uk/1/hi/entertainment/2809125.stm>.
77. *Townsville Bulletin Townsville Sun* (Australia) (2003), 'Hollywood Slammed for Anti-war Stance', 3 March, p. 14.
78. See <http://winwithoutwarus.org/html/coalition.html>. As *Reel Power* went to press, the Win Without War site was updated and no longer mentions Hollywood at all, except by its specific involvement with film-maker Robert Greenwald.
79. Kalman, Matthew (2006), 'Landslide for Hamas – limbo in Mideast: Leaders say Israel won't be recognized', *Chronicle Foreign Service*, 27 January; *BBC News* (2006), 'Hamas sweeps to election victory', 26 January <http://news.bbc.co.uk/1/hi/world/middle_east/4650788.stm>.
80. The row over the exhibit was solved following a personal intervention by Saudi Prince Al Walid bin Talal to Disney CEO Michael Eisner. We are asked to believe that the same channel was not used to stifle distribution of the anti-Saudi documentary *Fahrenheit 9/11*. See *BBC News* (1999), 'Middle East Disney drops Jerusalem plan', 18 September. Also see Goldman, Julia (1999), 'Epcot exhibit calls Jerusalem the "heart" of Israel', *Jewish Telegraphic Agency*, 8 October; Fisher, Marc (1999), 'Disney Brokers a Mideast peace of sorts', *Washington Post*, 1 October, p. A2.
81. Biskind, Peter (2007), 'Free Willis', *Vanity Fair*, June, No. 562, p. 168.
82. Poole, Dave (2003), 'Star Cavalry's Comin' to Bush's Aid', *Columbus Dispatch* (Ohio), 3 March, p. E2.
83. Cooper (1999), 'Postcards From the Left'.
84. Ibid.
85. Corn, David (1999), 'Looking For Mr. Right: Who's Running the Conservative Club in Town? David Horowitz's Wednesday Morning Club Battles Liberalism in Hollywood', *The Nation*, 5 April, Vol. 268, No. 3, p. 52.
86. Stanley, Alessandra (1992), 'Hidden Hollywood', *New York Times*, 31 May, Section 9, p. 1.

87. *Center for Defense Information* (1997), 'The Military in the Movies'. Transcript available at <http://ics.leeds.ac.uk/papers/vp01.cfm?outfit=pmt&folder=932&paper=1103>.
88. Buckley, Kevin (1972), 'Pacification's Deadly Price', *Newsweek*, 19 June, pp. 42–3 <http://chss.montclair.edu/english/furr/vietnam/buckley.html>; See also Hitchens, Christopher (2002), *The Trial of Henry Kissinger*, London: Verso.

3 War

1. Cropley, Ed (2005), 'Thirty years on, U.S. bombs still killing in Laos', 1 December <http://www.redorbit.com/news/international/317941/thirty_years_on_us_bombs_still_killing_in_laos/ Redorbit.com>.
2. Suid, Lawrence H. (2002), *Guts and Glory: The Making of the American Military Image in Film*, Lexington-Fayette: University Press of Kentucky, pp. 653–4, 657–8.
3. Bernstein, Alison R. (1991), *American Indians and World War II*, Norman: Oklahoma University Press.
4. Robb, David (2002), 'To the Shores of Hollywood: Marine Corps Fights to Polish Image in "Windtalkers"', *Washington Post*, 15 June; p. C1 <www.washingtonpost.com/ac2/wp-dyn/A54632-2002Jun14?language=printer>.
5. Ibid.
6. Ibid.
7. Robb, David L. (2004), *Operation Hollywood: How the Pentagon Shapes and Censors the Movies*, Amherst, MA: Prometheus Books, p. 64.
8. Andrews, Nigel (2002), 'War Weapons to Blow Your Mind', *Financial Times*, 29 August, p. 16.
9. Suid (2002), *Guts and Glory*, p. 638.
10. McCrisken, Trevor and Pepper, Andrew (2005), *American History and Contemporary Hollywood Film*, Edinburgh: Edinburgh University Press, p. 101.
11. Ibid., p 123.
12. Ibid.
13. Ibid., p. 102.
14. Ibid., p. 123.
15. Ito, Robert (2006), 'Theatre of War: a Few Good Men – and One Woman – Help Hollywood Filmmakers Send in the Marines', *Los Angeles Magazine*, 1 November, Vol. 51, No. 11, p. 106.
16. *The Essence of Combat: Making Black Hawk Down* (2002) <http://www.imdb.com/title/tt0367710/>.
17. Suid (2002), *Guts and Glory*, p. 670.
18. Kozaryn, Linda D. (2002), 'Army Declares "Black Hawk Down" "Authentic"', *Department of Defense News* <http://www.defenselink.mil/news/newsarticle.aspx?id=43855>.
19. *United States* v. *John Stebbins* (2005), United States Court of Appeals for the Armed Forces, Argued January 26, 2005, Decided August 30 <www.armfor.uscourts.gov/opinions/2005Term/03-0678.htm>; Robb (2004), *Operation Hollywood*.
20. Waal, Alex de (1998), 'US War Crimes in Somalia', *New Left Review*, Issue 230, July–August <www.newleftreview.org.ezp2.bath.ac.uk/?view=1962>.

21. Lancaster, John (1992), 'For Marine Corps, Somalia Operation Offers New Esprit; Mission Could Generate "Good News" As Service Confronts Shrinking Budgets', *Washington Post*, 6 December, p. A34.
22. Nelan, Bruce W. (1992), 'Taking on the Thugs', *Time Magazine*, 14 December, p. 29; Lancaster (1992), 'For Marine Corps, Somalia Operation Offers New Esprit', p. A34.
23. Fineman, Mark (1993), 'The Oil Factor in Somalia', *LA Times*, 18 January <www.netnomad.com/fineman.html>.
24. Bowden, Mark (2002), *Black Hawk Down*, New York: Corgi Books, p. 110.
25. Nolan, Ken, Scott, Ridley, Bruckheimer, Jerry and Bowden, Mark (2002), *Black Hawk Down: The Shooting Script*, Newmarket Shooting Script Series, p. 2.
26. *BBC News Online* (2002), 'Warlord Thumbs Down for Somalia Film', 29 January <http://news.bbc.co.uk/1/hi/world/africa/1789170.stm>.
27. Schmitt, Eric (1993), 'Somali War Casualties May Be 10,000', *New York Times*, 8 December, p. A14.
28. Bowden (2002), *Black Hawk Down*, pp. 54–7.
29. Ibid., p. 42.
30. Ibid., pp. 49–50.
31. Ibid., p. 116.
32. Ibid., pp. 110–14; 143–4.
33. Ibid., pp. 72, 77.
34. Ibid., p. 115.
35. Ibid., p. 319.
36. Ibid., p. 228.
37. Robb (2004), *Operation Hollywood*, p. 93.
38. Bowden (2002), *Black Hawk Down*, p. 119.
39. Gray, Geoffrey (2002), 'Activists Protest No. 1 Movie: "Black Hawk" Damned', 6–12 February <http://www.banadir.com/damned.shtml>.
40. Ibid.
41. The DVD commentary reveals the film-makers considered adding a caption to this effect.
42. Ibid.
43. Ibid., p. 476.
44. Vancheri, Barbara (2003), 'Tears Director had two fold aim; Africa's agonies, Seal's heroism', *The Record* (Bergen County, NJ), 9 March.
45. Vancheri, Barbara (2003), 'Fuqua Hopes *Tears of the Sun* Isn't Lost in War Propaganda', *Pittsburgh Post-Gazette*, 9 March, p. G5.
46. Ibid.
47. Hebert, James (2003), 'k230 Hollywood, etc: A rose is a rose – for now', *Copley News Service*, 17 March.
48. Hansen, Liane (2003), 'Director Antoine Fuqua discusses his latest film, "Tears of the Sun"', National Public Radio, 9 March.
49. Arnold, Gary (2003), 'Director's Salute; Fuqua's film lauds US Special Forces', *Washington Times*, 8 March, p. D1.
50. Vancheri (2003), 'Fuqua Hopes *Tears of the Sun* Isn't Lost in War Propaganda', p. G5. Fuqua's book was Peress, Gilles (1995), *The Silence – Rwanda*, Zurich: Scalo.
51. Robb (2004), *Operation Hollywood*, p. 182.

52. For more, see Weber, Cynthia (2006), *Imagining America at War: Morality, Politics and Film*, London: Routledge, p. 14.
53. Mann, James (2009), 'At the White House, What's Old May Be New', *New York Times*, 25 January, 'Weekend Op-Ed' section, p. 12.
54. Kelly, Mary Pat (1996), *Good to Go: The Rescue of Capt Scott O'Grady, USAF, From Bosnia*, Annapolis, MD: Naval Institute Press, p. 31.
55. Ibid., p. 11.
56. Ibid., pp. 170–71.
57. Nason, Pat (2002), 'US pilot downed in Bosnia sues Hollywood', *United Press International*, 21 August.
58. Sylvester, Sherri (2001), 'Hackman, Wilson hit the (ship) deck for "Enemy Lines"', *CNN Showbiz Today*, 28 November.
59. Suid (2002), *Guts and Glory*, pp. 612–16.
60. Keller, Bill (2002), 'The Fighting Next Time', *New York Times*, 10 March, Section 6, p. 32.
61. *The Associated Press* (1994), 'Friendly Fire Accounted For One-Quarter Of Allied Gulf War Fatalities', 15 April.
62. Claiborne, William and Murphy, Caryle (1991), 'Retreat Down Highway of Doom; U.S. Warplanes Turned Iraqis' Escape Route Into Deathtrap', *Washington Post*, 2 March, p. A1.
63. Sloyan, Patrick J (2003), "What I saw was a bunch of filled-in trenches with people's arms and legs sticking out of them. For all I know, we could have killed thousands', *Guardian*, 14 February <www.guardian.co.uk/Iraq/Story/0,2763,895124,00.html>.
64. Smith, Adam (2006), 'Support War!', *Empire*, February, p. 86.
65. Ibid., pp. 86–7.
66. Graham, Jamie (2006), 'New Films: *Jarhead*: Dazed and Confused: One Man's stare at a blink-and-you'll-miss-it war ...', *Total Film*, February, Issue 111, p. 30.
67. Swofford, Anthony (2006) *Jarhead: A Soldier's Story of Modern War*, New York: Scribner, p. 21.
68. Graham (2006), 'New Films', p. 30.

4 Comedy

1. Gerrard, Nicci (1994), 'Truly Madly Jamie Lee', *Observer*, 31 July, p. 30.
2. Dole also denounced Quentin Tarantino's *True Romance* (1993) and *Natural Born Killers* (1994) as 'nightmares of depravity', whilst praising conservative features such as *Forrest Gump* (1994) and *The Lion King* (1994). He admitted he hadn't seen the films he was discussing. See Ebert, Roger (1995), 'Hollywood "Depravity" Under Fire; The Senator Plays Politics', *Chicago Sun-Times*, 4 June, 'Sunday News' section, p. 1. Also see *National Review* (2009), 'The Best Conservative Movies', 23 February, which lists the 50 best conservative films from the past quarter-century, including *Forrest Gump*, *We Were Soldiers*, *Team America*, *Air Force One*, *An American Carol*, *Three Kings*, *The Hunt for Red October*, *Tears of the Sun*, *Red Dawn* and *United 93*.
3. *MX* (Melbourne, Australia) (2003), 'Small Talk', 5 August, p. 22.
4. MacInnis, Craig (1991), 'Hot Shots! Stupefyingly Stupid', *Toronto Star*, 31 July, p. F1.
5. King, Geoff (2002), *Film Comedy*, London: Wallflower Press, p. 123.

6. Waller, Douglas and Barry, John (1992), 'The Day We Stopped the War', *Newsweek*, 20 January 20, US edn, Special Report, p. 16.
7. Semmerling, Tim Jon (2006), *Evil Arabs in American Popular Film: Orientalist Fear*, Austin: Texas University Press, p. 253.
8. Ibid., p. 254.
9. Singer, Leigh (2006), 'Super Marionette Brothers', *DVD Review*, Issue 77, p. 40.
10. *The Irish Times* (2005), 'Puppets of the State', 17 January, p. 12.
11. Scott, A.O. (2004), 'Moral Guidance From Class Clowns', *New York Times*, 15 October, p. E1.
12. Lehmann, Megan (2004), 'Puppet Masters – "Team America" Hits all the Right Strings', *New York Post*, 15 October, p. 43.
13. Gow, James (2006), '*Team America* – World Police: Down-Home Theories of Power and Peace', *Millennium: Journal of International Studies*, Vol. 34, Number 2, February, pp. 563.
14. Shriver, Maria (2008), 'The "R-word" is No joke', *Los Angeles Times*, 22 August.
15. Dawson, Angela (2008), 'System of a Downey', *VNU Entertainment News Wire* (Online), 6 August.
16. *Investors Business Daily* (2007), 'Reagan's War, Not Charlie Wilson's', 'Issues and Insights, Editorials', 26 December, p. A10. The editorial thought that the film should have congratulated Republicans for the Afghan campaign, namely Reagan, Under-Secretary of Defense Fred Ikle, CIA Director William Casey and Senator Gordon Humphrey.
17. Trisha Jenkins (2009), 'How the Central Intelligence Agency works with Hollywood', *Media Culture and Society*, p. 492.
18. Ressner, Jeffrey (2007), 'Political Movies Can Tweak the Truth', *Politico.com*, 19 December <www.politico.com/news/stories/1207/7477.html>.
19. Roddy, Melissa (2007), 'Tom Hanks Tells Hollywood Whopper in "Charlie Wilson's War"', *AlterNet*, 21 December <www.alternet.org/story/71286/>. Roddy and I corresponded in the winter of 2009–10 and her documentary about Afghanistan, *Conflict of Interest* (2010), is available at <http://afghan-info.blogspot.com/2009/05/conflict-of-interest-sample-clips.html>.
20. Email correspondence (2009), Edmund McWilliams, 11 December.
21. Sorkin, Aaron (2005), 'Charlie Wilson's War', 23 May, p. 107 (draft film script). The script was leaked to Juliarobertsforums.com. The reference to al-Qaeda in the original screenplay is slightly misleading, as the terrorist organisation was not formed until at least the late 1980s – still during Soviet occupation but several years after it is placed in the script.
22. Rozen, Laura (2007), 'Hollywood and the CIA: The Spook Stays in the Picture', *Mother Jones* <http://www.motherjones.com/politics/2007/12/hollywood-and-cia-spook-stays-picture>.
23. Sorkin (2005), 'Charlie Wilson's War', p 55.
24. Ibid., p. 56.
25. Ibid., p. 57.
26. Ibid., p 136.
27. Ibid., p 138.
28. Ibid., pp. 138–9.
29. Ibid., p 143.
30. Ressner (2007), 'Political Movies Can Tweak the Truth'.

31. *Le Nouvel Observateur* (1998), 'The CIA's Intervention in Afghanistan: Interview with Zbigniew Brezezinski', 15–21 January, transcript at <http://www.globalresearch.ca/articles/BRZ110A.html>.
32. Johnston, David (2003), '"Charlie Wilson's War": Arming the Mujahedeen', *New York Times*, 25 May <www.nytimes.com/2003/05/25/books/wilson-the-warrior.html>.
33. Iddings, Bill (2008), 'Hezbollah zaniness on Gaza Strip? Blame the Zohan', *Muskegon Chronicle* (Michigan), 6 June, p. B10.
34. Driscoll, Adam (2008), 'The Movies: "We can't be afraid to offend"', *Western Mail*, 15 August, 'Features' section, p. 2.
35. Portman, Jamie (2008), 'Zohan messes with the politics; Adam Sandler talks about making a feel-good comedy about the Israeli–Palestinian conflict', *Ottawa Citizen*, 7 June, 'Canwest News Service Arts and Life', p. F1.
36. Itzkoff, Dave (2008), 'Israelis and Arabs Walk Into a Film', *New York Times*, 25 May, 'Movies' section, p. 1, <http://www.nytimes.com/2008/05/25/movies/25itzk.html>.
37. Treiman, Daniel (2008), 'The Commentator; Film; Is Adam Sandler Our Greatest Jewish Mind?', *The Forward*, 27 June, 'Arts and Culture' section, p. 13.
38. The same narrative twist device is used elsewhere, for example, to tag black robbers in *Traffic* (2000) and Islamic terrorists in *24*.
39. Sandler, Adam, Smigel, Robert and Apatow, Judd (2007), *You Don't Mess With the Zohan* (draft), 5 February <http://www.mypdfscripts.com/screenplays/you-dont-mess-with-the-zohan>.
40. Portman (2008), 'Zohan messes with the politics'.
41. Ibid.
42. Treiman, Daniel (2008), 'The Commentator'.
43. Trento, J.J. (2005), *Prelude to Terror: The Rogue CIA and the Legacy of America's Private Intelligence Network*, New York: Carroll & Graf Publishers.
44. Maslin, Janet (1999), 'Film Review: Three Kings: Fighting the Battle Of Money and Greed', *New York Times*, 1 October <http://query.nytimes.com/gst/fullpage.html?res=9E04E6DD123EF932A35753C1A96F958260>.
45. McCrisken, Trevor and Pepper, Andrew (2005), *American History and Contemporary Hollywood Film*, Edinburgh: Edinburgh University Press, pp. 188–202.
46. Jack G. Shaheen (2001), *Reel Bad Arabs: How Hollywood Vilifies a People*, New York: Olive Branch Press, pp. 485–7.
47. Finnigan, David (1999), 'Arab-Americans Cheer 3 Kings', *Hollywood Reporter*, 1 October, p. 1.
48. Waxman, Sharon (2005), *Rebels on the Backlot: Six Maverick Filmmakers and How They Conquered the Hollywood Studio System*, New York: HarperCollins, p. 219.
49. Ibid., p. 248.
50. Hehir, Andrew (2004), 'Soldiers Pay', *Salon.com*, 21 October <http://www.salon.com/entertainment/feature/2004/10/21/soldiers_pay>; Mathieson, Craig (2005), 'Even a Documenetary Pays the Price of Involvement in Iraq', *The Age* (Melbourne, Australia), 22 January, Section A2, p. 2.
51. Hottelet, Richard C. (1992), 'Iraq's New Borders Create New Grudges', *Christian Science Monitor*, 29 May, 'Opinion' section, p. 19.

52. Friedman, Thomas L. (1990), 'Confrontation in The Gulf: Behind Bush's Hard Line: Washington Considers a Clear Iraqi Defeat To Be Necessary to Bolster Its Arab Allies', *New York Times*, 22 August 22, p. A1.
53. Larry Everest (2004), *Oil, Power, & Empire: Iraq and the U.S. Global Agenda*, Monroe, ME: Common Courage Press.
54. Gumble, Andrew (2004), 'Film: Back to the Future; in 1999, Three Kings – a Film on the Gulf War – Made Little Impact', *The Independent*, 28 May, 'Features' section, p. 10.
55. See, for example, Kaufman, Will (1997), *The Comedian as Confidence Man: Studies in Irony Fatigue*, Detroit, MI: Wayne State University Press, p. 143.
56. Fox News (2009), *Bill O'Reilly*, 5 May; see <http://www.youtube.com/watch?v=y7bqyOzZzfI>.

5 Action Adventure

1. Robb, David L. (2004), *Operation Hollywood: How the Pentagon Shapes and Censors the Movies*, Amherst, MA: Prometheus Books, pp. 29–30.
2. *DVD Review* (2005), 'Still Dangerous', Issue 76, pp. 50–54.
3. Smith, Adam (2002), 'Retro: The Making of ... *Top Gun*: The Jet Set: The Drugs. The Dogfights. The Musical?', *Empire*, August, p. 100.
4. Robb (2004), *Operation Hollywood*, p. 182.
5. Office of the Inspector General (2003), 'The Tailhook Report: The Official Inquiry into the Events of Tailhook '91', New York: St Martin's Griffin, p. 83.
6. Robb (2004), *Operation Hollywood*, p. 182. Plans for a sequel were reported elsewhere in the press but without details of the Pentagon's involvement. See Sheridan, Peter (1993), 'Cruise Guns for £10m in Movie Sequel', 24 August, *Daily Mail*, p. 23.
7. Robb (2004), *Operation Hollywood*, pp. 101–4.
8. See Huntington, Samuel P. (1993), 'The Clash of Civilizations?', *Foreign Affairs*, Vol. 72, No. 3, Summer, pp. 22–49; Huntington, *The Clash of Civilizations and the Remaking of World Order*, New York: Simon and Schuster, 1996.
9. Sandalow, Marc (2002), 'White House Defends Decision not to Publicize Hijack Warning', *San Francisco Chronicle*, 17 May, p. A1.
10. CNN US (2002), 'September 11 warnings: Who Knew What, and When?', 24 May <http://archives.cnn.com/2002/US/05/22/9.11.warnings.facts/index.html>.
11. Ibid.
12. Robb, (2004), *Operation Hollywood*, p. 35.
13. Ibid., p. 37.
14. Ballvé, Teo (2009), 'Mr. President: Don't Make Colombia Another Afghanistan', *The Progressive*, 9 August <http://www.progressive.org/mpballve080909.html>.
15. Amnesty International (1995), *Annual Report for Colombia* <http://www.amnestyusa.org/annualreport.php?id=A94484565573F40980256A0F005BB4CB&c=COL%20amnesty%201995>.
16. Santiago, Daniel (1993), *The Harvest of Justice: The Church of El Salvador Ten Years after Romero*, New York: Paulist Press, p. 12.
17. Bedard, Paul, Parker, Suzi, Kaplan, David E. and Fasulo, Linda (2002), 'CIA says Clancy spun it right in *Sum of All Fears*', *U.S. News & World Report*, 13

May, 'Washington Whispers' section, Vol. 132, No. 16, p. 4; Sciolino, Elaine (2001), 'CBS Infiltrates the CIA; Sort of; the Network is Filming a Series about the Agency, but Critics say it's just PR', *Contra Costa Times* (California), 6 May, p. A14.

18. CIA Website (2004), 'New Recruitment Video on the Central Intelligence Agency Careers Web Site Features Jennifer Garner', 8 March <https://www.cia.gov/news-information/press-releases-statements/press-release-archive-2004/pr03082004.html>.
19. Seelye, Katharine Q. (2002), 'When Hollywood Big Guns Come Right From the Source', 10 June, *New York Times*, A1.
20. Clancy, Tom (1993), *The Sum of all Fears*, New York: HarperCollins, pp. 108–11.
21. Clancy, Tom (1996), *Executive Orders*, New York: HarperCollins.
22. Holden, Stephen (2002), 'Film Review; Terrorism That's All Too Real', *New York Times*, 31 May <http://movies.nytimes.com/movie/review?res=9D05E6DF163AF932A05756C0A9649C8B63>.
23. Hunter, Stephen (2002), '"Collateral Damage" Overshoots Its Mark', *Washington Post*, 8 February, p. C01.
24. Amnesty International (2002), *Annual Report for Colombia* <http://www.amnestyusa.org/annualreport.php?id=0157D5560A0DBA0C80256A16004BE817&c=COLamnesty2001report>.
25. O'Herir, Andrew (2002), 'Entertaining Arnold' <http://dir.salon.com/ent/movies/int/2002/02/08/schwarzenegger/print.html>.
26. Ibid.
27. Ibid.
28. Cockburn, Andrew and Cockburn, Leslie (1992), *Dangerous Liaison: The Inside Story of the US–Israeli Covert Relationship*, New York: Harper Perennial; Cockburn, Leslie (1987), *Out of Control: The Story of the Reagan Administration's Secret War in Nicaragua, the Illegal Arms Pipeline, and the Contra Drug Connection*, New York: Atlantic Monthly Press; Cockburn, Andrew (2007), *Rumsfeld: An American Disaster*, London: Verso.
29. *Hollywood Reporter* (1997), 'George Clooney/The Peacemaker', 24 September. On a more edifying note, Clooney, Leder and Kidman also rejected studio pressure to have Celine Dion do a song for the soundtrack. See Portman, Jamie (1997), 'Peacemaker: Clooney feels Pressure from Dreamworks', *The Record* (Kitchener-Waterloo, Ontario), 25 September, 'Entertainment' section.
30. Film Scouts (1997), 'The Peacekeeper: About the Production' <http://www.filmscouts.com/scripts/matinee.cfm?Film=peacema&File=productn>.
31. Ibid., p. 223.
32. Weller, Robert (2001), 'Airforce Space Command Plan Warfare', *Washington Post*, 21 June <http://nucnews.net/nucnews/2001nn/0106nn/010621nn.htm#430>.
33. US Space Command (1996), *Vision for 2020* <http://www.fas.org/spp/military/docops/usspac/visbook.pdf>.
34. Kristensen, Hans (1997), 'Targets of Opportunity: How Nuclear Planners Found New Targets for Old Weapons', *Bulletin of Atomic Scientists*, Vol. 55, No. 5, September/October, 1997, pp. 22–8, quoting US Strategic Command, *Essentials of Post-Cold War Deterrence* [n.d., probably April 1995], pp. 3, 4 (partially declassified and released under the Freedom of Information Act) <http://www.nautilus.org/archives/nukestrat/bas97.pdf/>.

35. *Hollywood Reporter* (1997), 'George Clooney/The Peacemaker'.
36. Pilisuk, Marc and Rountree, Jennifer Achord (2007), 'Behind the Repression in Burma', *Z-Magazine*, December <www.zmag.org/zmag/viewArticle/15925>.
37. Fox News (2008), 'Myanmar Magazine: Sylvester Stallone's Rambo Looks Like a Fat Lunatic', 22 February <http://www.foxnews.com/story/0,2933,331864,00.html>.
38. Miller, Martin (2007), '24 Gets a Lesson in Torture from the Experts', *Los Angeles Times*, 13 February < http://articles.latimes.com/2007/feb/13/entertainment/et-torture13>; Mayer, Jane (2007), 'Letters from Hollywood: Whatever it Takes: The Politics of the Man Behind "24"', *The New Yorker*, 19 February < http://www.newyorker.com/reporting/2007/02/19/070219fa_fact_mayer>.
39. Cummings, Bruce (2003), 'American Airpower and Nuclear Strategy in North East Asia', in Mark Selden and Alvin Y. So (eds), *War and State Terrorism: The United States, Japan, and the Asia Pacific in the Long Twentieth Century*, Lanham, MD: Rowman & Littlefield, pp. 63–90.
40. Draper, Allison Stark (2002), *Ebola*, New York: The Rosen Publishing Group.
41. Ibid.
42. Cited in Brodesser, Claude (2005), 'Brad and Angelina: A Honeymoon for Regency', *Variety*, 30 May–5 June, p. 1 <http://www.variety.com/article/VR1117923595.html?categoryid=13&cs=1>.
43. Fishman, Steve (2008), 'The Liman Identity', *New York Magazine*, 13 January.
44. O'Reilly, Bill (2007), 'The Bourne Buffoonery', 9 August <http://www.billoreilly.com/newslettercolumn?pid=21662>.
45. Brandon, Chase (2002), *Cloak and Dagger: Covert Ops*.
46. Robarge, David, McCollim, Gary, Dujmovic, Nicholas, and Coffey, Thomas G. (2007), 'The Good Shepherd: Intelligence in Recent Public Media', CIA website, 25 May <https://www.cia.gov/library/center-for-the-study-of-intelligence/csi-publications/csi-studies/studies/vol51no1/the-good-shepherd.html>.

6 Science Fiction

1. James, Caryn (1996), 'Independence Day (1996) "Giant Flying Saucers! Better Run and Hide"', *New York Times*, 21 July, p. 9 <http://movies.nytimes.com/movie/review?res=9500E0D61F39F932A15754C0A960958260>.
2. Robb, David L. (2004), *Operation Hollywood: How the Pentagon Shapes and Censors the Movies*, Amherst, MA: Prometheus Books, p. 69.
3. Suid, Lawrence H. (2002), *Guts and Glory: The Making of the American Military Image in Film*, Lexington-Fayette: University Press of Kentucky, pp. 590–91.
4. Ibid.
5. Weber, Cynthia (2001), *International Relations Theory: A Critical Introduction*, London: Routledge, p. 53.
6. Jay, Gregory (1997), *American Literature and the Culture Wars*, Ithaca, NY: Cornell University Press, p. 63.
7. Rogin, Michael (1998), *Independence Day: Or How I Learned to Stop Worrying and Love the Enola Gay*, London: BFI Modern Classics, p. 44.
8. Howell, Peter (2001), 'Survival of the Dumbest', *Toronto Star*, 8 June, p. F1; Meyer, George (2001), 'Slime Funny? Not Very', *Sarasota Herald-Tribune*,

8 June, 'Ticket' section, p. 21; Kempley, Rita (2001), 'Evolution: A Giant Step for Blobkind', *Washington Post*, 8 June, p. C5.
9. *Newsline* (1996), 'Dole: Independence Day OK', 30 July, p. 4; Lewis, Michael (1996), 'California, Here They Come', *The New Republic*, 19–26 August, p. 26.
10. Saksena, Ritu (2006), 'Mapping Terrorism: Amorphous Nations, Transient Loyalties', PhD Thesis, University of Maryland, p. 212.
11. Cheung, Floyd D. (1998), 'Imagining Danger, Imagining Nation: Postcolonial Discourse in Rising Sun and Stargate', *JOUVERT: A Journal of Postcolonial Studies*, Vol. 2, Issue 2, Winter <http://english.chass.ncsu.edu/jouvert/v2i2/CHEUNG.HTM>.
12. Malamud, Margaret (2000), 'Pyramids in Las Vegas and in Outer Space: Ancient Egypt in Twentieth-Century American Architecture and Film', *Journal of Popular Culture*, Vol. 34, No. 1, Summer, p. 44.
13. Ibid., p. 43.
14. Debruge, Peter (2009) 'Tanks a Lot, Uncle Sam', *Variety*, 22–28 June, p. 1.
15. Cohen, Sandy (2009), 'Jive-talking Twin Transformers Raise Race Issues', *Associated Press State & Local Wire*, 24 June.
16. Schiller, G. (2007), 'Firing on all Cylinders', *Hollywood Reporter*, 27 June.
17. Donna Miles, 'Edwards Team Stars in "Iron Man" Superhero Movie', *Air Force Link* <www.af.mil/news/story.asp?id=123051647>.
18. Respectively, Franklin, Garth (2008), 'Iron Man', 2 May <http://www.darkhorizons.com/reviews/423/Iron-Man>; *Chicago Sun Times* (2008), 'Downey steels the show as irrepressible "Iron Man"; Comic fans won't be only satisfied customers', 1 May, p. 33; Rickey, Carrie (2008), 'Superhero Genre Welded into a New Form', *Philadelphia Inquirer*, 2 May, p. W8; Bradshaw, Peter (2008), 'Scrap metal: Robert Downey Jr's Iron Man is a cheerfully unpretentious addition to the superhero pantheon. Unfortunately, it's also rather disposable', *Guardian*, 2 May, 'Film and Music' section, p. 7; Partridge, Des (2008), 'Hardcore hero', *Daily Telegraph* (Australia), 1 May, p. 43.
19. James, Caryn (1991), 'A Warmer, Fuzzier Arnold', *New York Times*, 14 July, p. H9.
20. French, Sean (1996), *The Terminator*, London: BFI Modern Classics and University of California Press, pp. 37–9.
21. The Pentagon (2001), 'Nuclear Posture Review [Excerpts]', Submitted to Congress on 31 December 2001, 8 January 2002 <http://www.globalsecurity.org/wmd/library/policy/dod/npr.htm>.
22. Staff Sgt. Matthew Bates (2009), 'US Air Force, Kirtland provides Airmen, location for "Terminator Salvation"', 6 April, US Air Force website <http://www.af.mil/news/story.asp?id=123139441>.
23. Hoscik, Martin (2009), 'Terminator Salvation: Crew interview', Seenit.co.uk, 3 June <http://www.seenit.co.uk/terminator-salvation-crew-interview/063517/>.
24. Sarantakes, Nicholas Evan (2005), 'Cold War Pop Culture and the Image of US Foreign Policy: The Perspective of the Original Star Trek Series', *Journal of Cold War Studies*, Vol. 7, No. 4, Fall, pp. 74–103.
25. Ibid., p. 77.
26. Ibid., p. 99.

27. Worland, Rick (1988), 'Captain Kirk: Cold Warrior' *Journal of Popular Film and Television*, Vol. 16, No. 3, Fall, pp. 109–17.
28. Bernardi, Daniel Leonard (1998), *Star Trek and History: Race-ing Toward a White Future*, New Brunswick, NJ and London: Rutgers University Press, pp. 101–102.
29. Vidal, Jon and Adam, David (2007), 'China overtakes US as world's biggest CO2 emitter', *Guardian*, 19 June <www.guardian.co.uk/environment/2007/jun/19/china.usnews>.
30. Summy, Ralph and Salla, Michael E. (eds) (1995), *Why the Cold War Ended: A Range of Interpretations*, Westport, CT and London: Greenwood Press.
31. Bernardi (1998), *Star Trek and History*, p. 101.
32. Segrave, Kerry (2004), *Product Placement in Hollywood Films: A History*, Jefferson, NC: McFarland and Company.
33. Kempley, Rita (1997), '"Starship Troopers": A Slew of Beauties Bash Big Bugs', *Washington Post*, 7 November, p. G1.
34. Hunter, Stephen (1997), 'Goosestepping at the Movies: "Starship Troopers" and the Nazi Aesthetic', *Washington Post*, 11 November, p. D1.
35. Ibid.
36. Devine, Miranda (2010), 'Hit by the Leftie Sledgehammer', *Sydney Morning Herald*, 2 January, p. 7.
37. Atzmon, Gilad (2009), 'Avatar and Humanism in Hollywood', *Pacific Free Press*, 30 December <www.pacificfreepress.com/.../5286-avatar-and-humanism-in-hollywood.html>.
38. See, for example, Medved, Michael (2009), '*Avatar* Offers Stunning Style, Inane Substance', 23 December <http://townhall.com/blog/g/6e844544-e105-4cc2-89ce-0e90a341d1a0>.
39. Leader, Michael (2009), 'Avatar: producer Jon Landau interview', *Den of Geek*, 17 December <http://www.denofgeek.com/movies/383132/avatar_producer_jon_landau_interview.html>.
40. Murphy, Mekado (2009), 'A Few Questions for James Cameron', 21 December <http://carpetbagger.blogs.nytimes.com/2009/12/21/a-few-questions-for-james-cameron/>.
41. Ibid.
42. Thottam, Jyoti (2010), 'Echoes of *Avatar*: Is a Tribe in India the Real-Life Na'vi?', *Time*, 13 February 13 <http://www.time.com/time/world/article/0,8599,1964063,00.html#ixzz0ij205PqG>. Also Survival International, email correspondence with author, 18 March 2010.
43. Baar, Aaron (2009) 'McDonald's Ties Avatar To Big Mac Promo', *Marketing Daily*, 10 December <http://www.mediapost.com/publications/?fa=Articles.showArticle&art_aid=118900>.
44. *Fox Business* (2009), 'James Cameron the Impact of *Avatar*', 18 December <http://video.foxbusiness.com/v/3953732/james-cameron-the-impact-of-avatar/?playlist_id=87066>.
45. Devine (2010), 'Hit by the Leftie Sledgehammer'.
46. Goodyear, Dana (2009), 'Man of Extremes: The Return of James Cameron', *The New Yorker*, 26 October, Vol. 85, No. 34, p. 55.
47. Sontag, Susan (1974), 'The Imagination of Disaster', *Hal in the Classroom: Science Fiction Films*, Dayton, OH: Pflaum Publishers, p. 31.
48. Ibid., p. 28.

7 Political Drama

1. Bright, Martin (2001), 'Heartbroken of Kandahar', *The Observer*, 4 November <www.guardian.co.uk/film/2001/nov/04/features.martinbright>.
2. Studio Briefing (2000), 'Yemen Calls for Boycott of *Rules of Engagement*', 21 April <http://imdb.com/news/sb/2000-04-21#film4>.
3. CAIR Media Release (2000), 'Rules of Engagement Stereotypes Muslims', 11 April.
4. Klawans, Stuart (2000). 'Semper Fi, But Why?', *The Nation*, 1 May <http://www.thenation.com/docprint.mhtml?i=20000501&s=klawans>.
5. Fisk, Robert (2005), *The Great War for Civilisation – The Conquest of the Middle East*, London: Fourth Estate, pp. 318–29.
6. Kristensen, Hans (1997), 'Targets of Opportunity: How Nuclear Planners Found New Targets for Old Weapons', *Bulletin of Atomic Scientists*, Vol. 55, No. 5, September/October, quoting US Strategic Command, *Essentials of Post–Cold War Deterrence* [n.d probably April 1995], pp. 3, 4 (partially declassified and released under the Freedom of Information Act) <www.bullatomsci.org/issues/1997/so97/so97kristensen.html>.
7. The Pentagon (2001), 'Nuclear Posture Review [Excerpts]', Submitted to Congress on 31 December, 8 January 2002 <http://www.globalsecurity.org/wmd/library/policy/dod/npr.htm>.
8. Haverstick, Delores A. and Suid, Lawrence H. (2005), *Stars and Stripes on Screen: A Comprehensive Guide to Portrayals of American Military on Film*, Lanham, MD and Oxford: Scarecrow Press, Inc., p. 52.
9. Patterson, John (2001), 'The Caring, Sharing CIA: Central Intelligence Gets a Makeover', *The Guardian*, 5 October.
10. Robb, David L. (2004), *Operation Hollywood: How the Pentagon Shapes and Censors the Movies*, Amherst, MA: Prometheus Books, pp. 18–19.
11. Schlesinger Jr, Arthur (1965), *A Thousand Days: John F. Kennedy in the White House*, New York: Black Dog & Leventhal Publishers Inc.
12. Sorensen, Theodore C. (1965), *Kennedy*, New York: Harper & Row.
13. Morley, Morris (1987) *Imperial State and Revolution*, Cambridge, UK and New York: Cambridge University Press.
14. CIA Memorandum of 12 November 1962, cited by Piero Gleijeses (2002), *Conflicting Missions: Havana, Washington, and Africa, 1959–76*, Chapel Hill: North Carolina University Press, p. 16.
15. White, Mark J. (2001), *The Kennedys and Cuba: The Declassified Documentary History*, revised edn, Chicago, IL: Ivan R. Dee Publishers.
16. Ibid., p. 71.
17. Ibid.
18. Garthoff, Raymond L. (1987), *Reflections on the Cuban Missile Crisis*, Washington, DC: Brookings Institution, p. 5.
19. Ibid., pp. 77–9, 108–109.
20. Gleijeses (2002), *Conflicting Missions*, p. 25.
21. Robb (2004), *Operation Hollywood*, p. 56.
22. Lloyd, Marion (2002), 'Soviets Close to Using A-Bomb in 1962, Forum is Told', *Boston Globe*, 13 October.
23. Stone, Oliver and Sklar, Zachary (2000), *JFK: The Documented Screenplay*, New York: Applause Theatre Book Publishers.

24. Hamburg, Eric (ed.) (1995), *Nixon: An Oliver Stone Film*, London: Bloomsbury, p. 90.
25. Summers, Anthony (2000), *The Arrogance of Power: Secret World of Richard Nixon: The Secret World of Richard Nixon*, New York: Viking Adult, pp. 298–305.
26. Federal News Service (1992), 'Hearing of the Legislation and National Security Subcommittee of the House Government Operations Committee Subject: H.J Res 454, Assassination Materials Disclosure Act of 1992 Chaired by Representative John Conyers (D-MI)', Capitol Hill Hearing, 15 May.
27. Thomas, Cal (2006), '"World Trade Center' is a world class movie', 20 July <http://townhall.com/columnists/CalThomas/2006/07/20/world_trade_center_is_a_world_class_movie>.
28. Halbfinger, David M. (2006), 'Odd bedfellows align to market film about 9/11', *New York Times*, 27 July, p. A1
29. The film does not mention Afghanistan or al-Qaeda, which leaves it open to the interpretation that Iraq was responsible for 9/11.
30. Rich, Ruby B. (2007), 'Out of the Rubble', *Sight and Sound*, 27 June <www.bfi.org.uk/sightandsound/feature/49320>.
31. Triplett, William (2006), 'World Trade Center – Paramount said "not a political movie"', *Variety*, 31 July–6 August.
32. Friend, Tad (2001), 'Oliver Stone's Chaos Theory', *The New Yorker*, 22 October, p. 25.
33. Wolf, Jaime (1997), 'Stoning Oliver; Director a target whatever he films', *Plain Dealer* (Cleveland, OH), 5 October, p. 1l.
34. Wolf, Jaime (1997), 'Oliver Stone Doesn't Want to Start an Argument', *New York Times*, 21 September, p. F54.
35. Ibid.
36. Ibid.
37. Friend (2001), 'Oliver Stone's Chaos Theory'.
38. Said, S.F. (2003), 'Shooting Castro', *Daily Telegraph*, 23 September <http://www.telegraph.co.uk/culture/film/3603193/Shooting-Castro.html>.
39. Baer, Bob (2008), Telephone interview with Robbie Graham, April. This is taken from a rush transcript provided by Tricia Jenkins.
40. Lawrence, Will (2006), 'Into the Shadows', *Empire*, March, p. 112.
41. Segal, Victoria (2006), 'Mad, Bad World', *New Statesman*, 6 March, p. 47.
42. Farah, Douglas and Braun, Stephen (2008), *Merchant of Death: Money, Guns, Planes, and the Man who Makes War Possible*, Hoboken, NJ: John Wiley and Sons, p. 177.
43. Ibid., p. 7.
44. Rémy, Jean-Philippe (2004), 'The Trafficker Viktor Bout Lands', *Le Monde*, 18 May <http://www.globalpolicy.org/component/content/article/168/35929.html>.
45. Johnston, Tim and Belton, Catherine (2009), 'Ex-Soviet officer escapes US extradition', *Financial Times*, 11 August <http://www.ft.com/cms/s/0/441aa16c-8655-11de-9e8e-00144feabdc0.html?catid=22&SID=google>.
46. Goodridge, Mike (2007), 'The Day De Niro Joined the CIA', *Evening Standard*, 4 January.
47. Martin, Karen (2007), 'Filmmakers, ex-CIA agents talk about Spies in cinema', *Arkansas Democrat-Gazette*, 6 May; Garvin, Glenn (2009), 'Matt Damon Likes to mix his art with politics', *Miami Herald*, 30 January.

48. Dalton, Stephen (2007), 'Secrets of the Spying Game', *The Times* (London), 24 February, 'Features - The Knowledge' section, p. 16.
49. Ibid.
50. Robarge, David, McCollim, Gary, Dujmovic, Nicholas and Coffey, Thomas G. (2007) 'The Good Shepherd: Intelligence in Recent Public Media', CIA website, 25 May https://www.cia.gov/library/center-for-the-study-of-intelligence/csi-publications/csi-studies/studies/vol51no1/the-good-shepherd.html>.
51. Ibid.
52. Dujmovic, Nicholas (2008), 'Hollywood, Don't You Go Disrespectin' My Culture: The Good Shepherd Versus Real CIA History', *Intelligence and National Security*, Vol. 23, No. 1, February, pp. 25–41, especially pp. 26, 40.
53. Jonas, George (2006), *Vengeance*, New York: Harper Perennial.
54. Kincaid, Cliff and Aronoff, Roger (2006), 'Hollywood Surrenders to Terrorists', *AIM Report*, 20 January.
55. Turan, Kenneth (2005), '"Munich," about the hunt for the murderers of Israeli Olympians, is a call for peace', *Los Angeles Times*, 23 December <www.calendarlive.com/.../turan/cl-et-munich23dec23,0,4815169.story - United States>.
56. Ebert, Roger (2005), 'Munich', 23 December <http://rogerebert.suntimes.com/apps/pbcs.dll/article?AID=/20051222/REVIEWS/51214004>.
57. Naím, Moisés (interviewer) (2005), 'The Lessons of Munich', *Foreign Policy*, December <http://www.foreignpolicy.com/story/cms.php?story_id=3319>.
58. Spielberg, Steven (2005), 'Introduction', *Munich* DVD.
59. Ibid.
60. Ebert, Roger (2006), 'I Knew I Would Lose Friends Over This Film', *Sunday Telegraph*, 1 January, 'News Review and Comment' section, pp. 14–15.
61. Jonas (2006), *Vengeance*, p. 335.
62. Jonas, George (2006), 'The Spielberg Massacre', *Maclean's*, 9 January, p. 44.
63. Goodwin, Christopher (2006), 'Disagree With Me – That's What I Want', *Sunday Times* (London), 22 January, 'Weekend Review' section, p. 3.
64. *New York Times* (1996), 'Israelis to Compensate Families of Slain Waiter', 28 January <http://www.nytimes.com/1996/01/28/world/world-news-briefs-israelis-to-compensate-family-of-slain-waiter.html>.
65. *Time Magazine* (1979), 'Middle East: Death of a Terrorist', 5 February <http://www.time.com/time/magazine/article/0,9171,946209,00.html?internalid=ACA>.
66. Reich, Walter (2006), 'Something's Missing in Spielberg's *Munich*', *Washington Post*, 1 January.
67. Goldberg, Michelle (2005), 'The War on *Munich*', *Salon.com*, 20 December <http://dir.salon.com/story/ent/feature/2005/12/20/munich/index.html>.
68. Fisk, Robert (2006), 'My Challenge for Steven Spielberg', *The Independent*, 21 January.
69. The director's wife claimed that a Universal tour which was to have encompassed New York, Boston, Washington, Chicago and San Francisco was dropped at the last moment and a two-week run in New York substituted. Costa Gavras personally advertised the film in the *New York Times* at a cost of $50,000 after Universal refused to publicise the film; the studio even forbade him to use advertisements that had been prepared for the film. See Rubenberg, Cheryl A. (1989), *Israel and the American National Interest: A*

Critical Examination, Champaign: University of Illinois Press, p. 341. This cites Hanna Asadi's interview with Michelle Ray-Gavras and her article in *Al Fajr*, 8 February 1984.

70. Molitorisz, Sacha (2001), 'Guy Forks', *Sydney Morning Herald*, 7 April, 'Metropolitan' section, p. 3; Sutherland, Clare (2000), 'Pearce Just a Regular Guy', *The Advertiser*, 17 August, 'Features' section, p. 42; Pearce, Garth (2000), 'Keep Watching This Face', *The Times* (London), 19 October, 'Features' section.

8 The Low-Budget Battlefield

1. McCarthy, Todd (2001), 'Film Review: Buffalo Soldiers', *Variety*, 24–30 September, p. 25.
2. Horn, John (2003), 'Miramax's Dark Comedy is Soldier of Bad Fortune', *Los Angeles Times*, 26 April, p. D14.
3. Pierce, Nev (2003), 'Movies: Gregor Jordan: Buffalo Soldiers', 17 July <www.bbc.co.uk/.../2003/.../17/gregor_jordan_buffalo_soldiers_interview.shtml>.
4. Rutenberg, Jim (2004), 'Disney Is Blocking Distribution of Film That Criticizes Bush', *New York Times*, 5 May <www.nytimes.com/2004/.../disney-is-blocking-distribution-of-film-that-criticizes-bush.html?...>.
5. Rossant, John, Harbrecht, Douglas and Grover, Ronald (1994), 'How Disney Snared a Princely Sum Behind the $ 400 million bailout of EuroDisney: Carlyle Group', *Business Week*, 20 June, p. 61.
6. Rutenberg (2004), 'Disney Is Blocking Distribution of Film That Criticizes Bush'.
7. See <http://www.opednews.com/maxwrite/linkframe.php?linkid=37228>.
8. Thompson, Anne (2002), 'Films With War Themes Are Victims of Bad Timing', *New York Times*, 17 October, p. E1.
9. Wiener, Jon (2002), 'Quiet in Hollywood', *The Nation*, 16 December <www.thenation.com/docprint.mhtml?i=20021216&s=wiener>.
10. Blackwelder, Rob (2002), 'Noyce Delights in Double Duty', *SPLICEDwire*, 7 October <http://www.splicedonline.com/02features/pnoyce.html>.
11. *Daily News* (Los Angeles, CA) (1998), 'Levinson's Double Irony; Wag the Dog, Sphere, Two Wildly Different Filmmaking Experiences', 13 February <http://www.highbeam.com/doc/1G1-83810954.html>.
12. Roschwalb, Susanna A. (1994), 'Public Relations Review, September 22, The Hill & Knowlton cases: a brief on the controversy; ethical consideration in client selection by public relations firm', *Public Relations Ethics*, Special Issue, Vol. 20, No. 3, p. 267.
13. Taylor, Charles (2004), 'Eyes Wide Shut', *Salon.com*, 22 December <http://www.salon.com/entertainment/movies/review/2004/12/22/hotel_rwanda>.
14. Gourevitch, Philip G. (1999), *We Wish to Inform You that Tomorrow we will be Killed with our Families*, London: Picador. The book was funded by the United States Institute for Peace, which was established by Congress. See <http://www.usip.org/resources/we-wish-inform-you-tomorrow-we-will-be-killed-our-families-stories-rwanda>.
15. French, Howard (2004), *A Continent for the Taking*, New York: Knopf, p. 243.
16. Power, Samantha (2001), 'Bystanders to Genocide', *The Atlantic*, September <www.theatlantic.com/doc/200109/power-genocide>.

17. Taylor, Phil (2005), 'Hotel Rwanda: No room for the truth', *Taylor Report*, 17 January <http://www.taylor-report.com/articles/index.php?id=11>.
18. McGreal, Chris (2006), 'French judge accuses Rwandan president of assassination', *The Guardian*, 22 November < http://www.guardian.co.uk/world/2006/nov/22/france.rwanda>; Fergal Keane (2006), 'Will we ever learn the truth about this genocide?', *The Independent*, 22 November <http://www.independent.co.uk/opinion/commentators/fergal-keane-will-we-ever-learn-the-truth-about-this-genocide-425257.html>.
19. Simon Robinson and Vivienne Walt (2006), 'The Deadliest War in the World', *Time*, 28 May <http://www.time.com/time/magazine/article/0,9171,1198921,00.html>; International Rescue Committee (2006), '*The Lancet* Publishes IRC Mortality Study from DR Congo; 3.9 Million Have Died: 38,000 Die per Month', January <http://www.theirc.org/news/page-27819067.html>.
20. Da Silva, Steven (2007), 'Revisiting the "Rwanda Genocide"', *Center for Research on Globalization*, 1 June <http://www.globalresearch.ca/index.php?context=va&aid=5848>; Chossudovsky, Michel (2006), 'The Geopolitics Behind the Rwanda Genocide', *Center for Research on Globalization*, 23 November <http://www.globalresearch.ca/index.php?context=viewArticle&code=20061123&articleId=3958>.
21. Rusesabagina, Paul and Zoellner, Tom (2006), *An Ordinary Man: An Autobiography*, New York: Viking Adult, p. 199.
22. *Taylor Report*, 'Letter protests Kagame visit to England', 2 December <http://www.taylor-report.com/articles/index.php?id=28>.
23. Taylor (2004), 'Eyes Wide Shut'.
24. Hewitt, Chris (2006), 'Is it too soon for a film about 9/11? we ask', *Empire*, July, p. 100.
25. Ibid., p. 98.
26. Federal News Service (2005), 'Remarks by George W. Bush in a Conversation on Social Security (as released by the White House, Athena Performing Arts Center, Greece Athena Middle and High School, Rochester, New York', 24 May.
27. Youngs, Ian (2006), 'United 93 Actor Defends Portrayal', 5 June <http://news.bbc.co.uk/1/hi/entertainment/5042616.stm>.
28. Associated Press Worldstream (2006), 'Bush invites "United 93" families for White House screening of the Oliver Stone film', 30 May. It appears that the reference here to Oliver Stone is accidental.
29. Lim, Dennis (2006), 'Bloody Tuesday', *Village Voice*, 25 April, p.32.
30. Associated Press Worldstream (2006), 'Bush watches "United 93" movie with relatives of those killed in hijacking'.
31. Associated Press Worldstream (2006), 'Bush invites "United 93" families for White House screening of the Oliver Stone film'.
32. *United 93: The Families and the Film* (2006) < http://www.imdb.com/title/tt0899176/>.
33. Borger, Julian (2004), 'The Best Perk in the White House', *Guardian*, 4 June <http://www.guardian.co.uk/film/2004/jun/04/1>.
34. ABC News Online (2006), 'Bush likens "War on Terror" to WWIII', 5 June <http://www.abc.net.au/news/newsitems/200605/s1632213.html>.

35. Chossudovsky, Michel (2007), 'Slip of the tongue? Rumsfeld admits that "Flight 93" was shot down', video footage and transcripts, *Global Research*, 12 May <http://www.globalresearch.ca/index.php?context=va&aid=5626>.
36. *Film Review* (2006), 'Is it too Soon?', No. 671, Summer, p. 59.
37. Alvarez, Antoinette (2006), 'Interview: Irwin Winkler talks Home of the Brave', *Taylor Report*, 11 December <http://www.taylor-report.com/articles/index.php?id=11>.
38. Ibid.
39. Barnes, Julian E., Parker, Ned and Horn, John (2010), '*The Hurt Locker* sets off conflict', *LA Times*, 25 February. *The Hurt Locker* lost the official cooperation of the Pentagon during production because the DOD didn't trust the filmmakers to stick to the approved script.
40. Robb, David L. (2004), *Operation Hollywood: How the Pentagon Shapes and Censors the Movies*, Amherst, MA: Prometheus Books, pp. 184–5.
41. Suid, Lawrence H. (2002), *Guts and Glory: The Making of the American Military Image in Film*, Lexington-Fayette: University Press of Kentucky, p. 584.

9 Conclusions

1. Atkinson, Michael (2000), 'Hollywood Keeps Left', *American Prospect*, 17 January, p. 54.
2. Klavan, Andrew (2008), '5 Myths about those Tinseltown Liberals', *Washington Post*, 12 October, p. B3.
3. Klavan, Andrew (2006), 'The Nation Needs More Gung-ho, Patriotic War Movies That Celebrate Our Fight Against Islam-Fascists', *Los Angeles Times*, 7 May.
4. The film was called *Tearing Down the Spanish Flag* (1898) <http://www.imdb.com/title/tt0000214/>.
5. In the 1940s, the FBI was concerned about Communist infiltration of Hollywood, and as a result, operated on the assumption that 'the motion picture industry is beginning to be recognised as one of the greatest, if not the very greatest, influence upon the minds and culture, not only of the people of the United States, but of the entire world': see Sbardellati, John (2008), 'Brassbound G-Men and Celluloid reds: The FBI's search for communist propaganda in wartime Hollywood', *Film History: An International Journal*, Vol. 20, No. 4, pp. 412–36. Lenin was purported to have said 'the most important of all arts is the cinema.' See Kenez, Peter (1992), *Cinema and Soviet Society, 1917–1953*, Cambridge: Cambridge University Press, p. 27. Goebbels commented, 'We must give film a task and a mission in order that we may use it to conquer the world': see Rentschler, Eric (1996), *The Ministry of Illusion: Nazi Cinema and its Afterlife*, Cambridge, MA: Harvard University Press, p. 215.
6. See Nye, Joseph S. and Donahue, John D. (2000), *Governance in a Globalizing World*, Washington, DC: Brookings Institution, p. 133.
7. Shaw, Tony (2007) *Hollywood's Cold War*, Edinburgh: Edinburgh University Press, p. 9.
8. Turvey, Brent, E. (2008), *Criminal Profiling: An Introduction to Behavioural Evidence Analysis*, London: Academic Press, pp. xxiii–xxxv.

9. See Kifner, John (1995), 'McVeigh's Mind: A Special Report', *New York Times*, 31 December, p. A1.
10. Churchill, Marlowe (1998), 'Tailhook Tries to Gain Respectability', *Press Enterprise* (Riverside, CA), 20 September, p. A10.
11. National Public Radio (1992), '"America" Criticises Hollywood', *Morning Edition* with Bob Edwards, 12 November.
12. Fowler, Bree (2001), 'Kmart to Phase Out Ammunition Sale', *San Diego Union-Tribune*, 28 June, p. A10.
13. Moser, John E. (2001) '"Gigantic Engines of Propaganda": The 1941 Senate Investigation of Hollywood', *The Historian*, Vol. 63, Issue 4, June, pp. 715–905.
14. Independent Film Channel et al., *This Film is Not Yet Rated* (2006).
15. Valenti, Jack (1998), 'Hollywood and Washington: Sprung from the Same DNA', speech before the Los Angeles World Affairs Council, 1 October.
16. Fumento, Michael (2007), 'Hollywood Goes to War', *New York Sun*, 25 October, p. 9.
17. Kampfner, John (2003), 'Saving Private Lynch story "flawed"', 15 May <http://news.bbc.co.uk/1/hi/programmes/correspondent/3028585.stm>; MacAskill, Ewen (2007), 'Rambo Image Was Based on Lie, says US War Hero Jessica Lynch', *Guardian*, 25 April, p. 16.
18. Breitbart, Andrew and Robertson, Peter (host) (2009), 'The Politics of Hollywood', Hoover Institution: Stanford University, <http://www.youtube.com/watch?v=0mTxpFIw-3g>.
19. Mandel, Daniel (2001), 'Muslims on the Silver Screen', *Middle East Quarterly*, Vol. VIII, No. 2, 1 March.
20. Shaheen, Jack G. (2001), *Reel Bad Arabs: How Hollywood Vilifies a People*, New York: Olive Branch Press.
21. Ibid.
22. National Public Radio (1992), '"America" Criticises Hollywood'.
23. Ibid.
24. Chambers, David (2002), 'Will Hollywood Go to War?', *Times Book Supplement*, No. 8, Spring/Summer <http://www.tbsjournal.com/Archives/Spring02/chambers.html>.
25. Segrave, Kerry (2005), *Product Placement in Hollywood Films: A History*, Jefferson, NC: McFarland, p. 209.
26. Lamb, Scott (2004), 'Muzzling a Marine', *Salon.com*, 4 June <http://dir.salon.com/story/ent/feature/2004/06/04/control_room/index.html>.
27. Koppelman, Alex (2005), 'Dealing with insecurity at Homeland Security', *Salon.com*, 18 May <http://www.salon.com/politics/war_room/2005/05/18/insecurity/>.
28. Wright, Gerald (2007), 'Winning Hearts and Minds', *Sydney Morning Herald*, 8 September, p. 28.
29. Ibid.

Filmography

MAIN US THEATRICAL DISTRIBUTORS

Time Warner

WARNER BROTHERS
Body of Lies (2008)
Collateral Damage (2002)
Executive Decision (1996)
Heaven and Earth (1993)
Iron Giant (1999)
JFK (1991)
Letters from Iwo Jima (2006)
Outbreak (1995)
Police Academy: Mission to Moscow (1994)
Swordfish (2001)
Syriana (2005)
Terminator 3: Rise of the Machines (2003)
Terminator Salvation (2009)
Three Kings (1999)

NEWLINE CINEMA
Rendition (2007)
Thirteen Days (2000)
Wag the Dog (1997)

News Corporation

20TH CENTURY FOX
Avatar (2009)
Behind Enemy Lines (2001)
Bulworth (1998)
Courage Under Fire (1996)
Hot Shots! (1991)
Hot Shots! Part Deux (1993)
Independence Day (1996)
Man on Fire (2004)
Mr. & Mrs. Smith (2005)
Planet of the Apes (2001, orig. 1968)
The Siege (1998)
Speed (1994)
Taken (2008)
The Thin Red Line (1998)
True Lies (1994)
The X-Men (2000)

General Electric/Vivendi

UNIVERSAL
American Dreamz (2006)
The Bourne Identity (2002)
The Bourne Supremacy (2004)
The Bourne Ultimatum (2007)
Charlie Wilson's War (2007)
The Good Shepherd (2006)
Jarhead (2005)
The Kingdom (2007)
Munich (2005)
Schindler's List (1993)
Spy Game (2001)
Thunderbirds (2004)
United 93 (2006)

VIVENDI ENTERTAINMENT
An American Carol aka Big Fat Important Movie (2008)

The Walt Disney Company

TOUCHSTONE
Armageddon (1998)
Bad Company (2002)
Enemy of the State (1998)
Pearl Harbor (2001)
The Recruit (2003)
Reign of Fire (2002)

HOLLYWOOD PICTURES
Crimson Tide (1995)
In the Army Now (1994)
Nixon (1995)

MIRAMAX
Buffalo Soldiers (2001)
The Great Raid (2005)
The Quiet American (2002, orig. 1958)

Sony

COLUMBIA
Air Force One (1997)
Black Hawk Down (2001)
A Few Good Men (1992)
Point Men (2001)
Quantum of Solace (2008)
Stealth (2005)
Tears of the Sun (2003)
Vantage Point (2008)
You Don't Mess with the Zohan (2008)
TRISTAR

Air America (1990)
Godzilla (1998, orig. 1954)
Sniper (1993)
Total Recall (1990)

Viacom

Paramount
Clear and Present Danger (1994)
Flags of Our Fathers (2006)
The Flight of the Intruder (1991)
G.I. Joe: The Rise of the Cobra (2009)
The Hunt for Red October (1990)
Iron Man (2008)
Iron Man 2 (2010)
Rules of Engagement (1995)
South Park: Bigger, Longer and Uncut (1999)
Star Trek: The Undiscovered Country (1991)
The Sum of All Fears (2002)
Team America: World Police (2004)
Transformers (2007)
Transformers: Revenge of the Fallen (2009)
Tropic Thunder (2008)
War of the Worlds (2005, orig. 1953)
We Were Soldiers (2002)
World Trade Center (2006)

MGM

Bowling for Columbine (2002)
Die Another Day (2002)
Goldeneye (1995)
Home of the Brave (2006)
Hotel Rwanda (2004)
Lions for Lambs (2007)
Not Without My Daughter (1991)
Rescue Dawn (2006)
Stargate (1994)
Tomorrow Never Dies (1997)
Windtalkers (2002)

Dreamworks SKG

Eagle Eye (2008)
The Peacemaker (1997)
Saving Private Ryan (1998)

Independents and Overseas

Air Marshal (2003)
Canadian Bacon (1995)
Che: Part One (2008)

Che: Part Two (2008)
Chavez: Inside the Coup (2003)
Control Room (2004)
The Crazies (2010)
Deadly Deception: General Electric, Nuclear Weapons and Our Environment (1991)
District 9 (2009)
11 09 01 – September 11 (2002)
Embedded (2005)
Ernest in the Army (1998)
Fahrenheit 9/11 (2004)
The Fog of War: Eleven Lessons from the Life of Robert S. McNamara (2003)
Infinite Justice (2006)
Inglourious Basterds (2009)
In the Loop (2009)
Iraq for Sale: The War Profiteers (2006)
Left Behind: The Movie (2000)
Looking for Fidel (2006)
Lord of War (2005)
Manufacturing Consent: Noam Chomsky and the Media (1992)
Rambo IV (2008)
Redacted (2007)
South of the Border (2009)
Spymate (2006)
Standard Operating Procedure (2008)
Stealth Fighter (1999)
Taxi to the Dark Side (2007)
War, Inc. (2008)
Why We Fight (2005)

Other Cited Films

Airplane! (1980)
Aladdin (1992)
Aliens (1986)
Animal Farm (1954)
Apocalypse Now (1979)
Arrowhead (1953)
Battle of Algiers (1966)
Behind Enemy Lines: Columbia (2009)
Behind Enemy Lines II: Axis of Evil (2006)
Birth of a Nation (1915)
Bobby (2006)
Borat: Cultural Learnings of America for Make Benefit Glorious Nation of Kazakhstan (2006)
Bull Durham (1988)
The Caddy (1953)
Casualties of War
The Chosen (1984)
Commando (1985)
Confessions of a Nazi Spy (1939)

Cry Freetown (1987)
The Crying Game (1992)
Dr. Strangelove or: How I Learned to Stop Worrying and Love the Bomb (1964)
Eraser (1996)
First Blood (1982)
Full Metal Jacket (1987
The Godfather (1972)
Good Intentions, Deadly Results (2001)
The Great Escape (1963)
In the Bedroom (2001)
Invaders from Mars (1953)
Invasion USA (1952)
Last Action Hero (1993)
Mac and Me (1988)
*M*A*S*H* (1970)
The Night that Baghdad Fell (2005)
Nineteen Eighty-Four (1984)
Platoon (1986)
The Player (1992)
Raid on Entebbe (1976)
Rambo: First Blood Part II (1985)
Rambo III (1988)
Red Dawn (1984)
The Red Menace (1949)
Salt of the Earth (1954)
Salvador (1986)
Sangaree (1953)
Space Jam (1996)
Sphere (1996)
The Terminator (1984)
Terminator 2: Judgment Day (1991)
Three Days of the Condor (1975)
Top Gun (1986)
Top Secret (1984)
Toy Story (1995)
Trainspotting (1996)
Turner and Hooch (1989)
Valley of the Wolves – Iraq (2006)
A Woman Called Golda (1982)
Wings (1927)

Television Series/Movies

The Agency (2001)
Chicago Hope (1994–2000)
DC 9/11: Time of Crisis (2003)
ER (1994–2009)
The FBI (1965–74)
The Flight That Fought Back (2005)
The Practice (1997–2004)

The President's Man: A Line in the Sand (2002)
RFK (made-for-TV movie) (2002)
R.F.K. (TV series) (1997)
Sabrina the Teenage Witch (1996–2003)
Saving Jessica Lynch (2003)
She Spies (2002)
Strike Force (1981)
Threat Matrix (2003)
Today's FBI (1981–82)
24 (2001–)
Walking Tall (1981)

All box-office figures and production costs given in the text are taken from <www.imdb.com>, <www.the-numbers.com> and <www.boxofficemojo.com>.

Film Index

General Index

See Film Index for complete list of films discussed in the book